HAYNES MAX POWER Vauxhall

corsa

The definitive guide to **modifying**
by **Bob Jex**

HAYNES MAX POWER Vauxhall

corsa

The definitive guide to **modifying**

by **Bob Jex**

Haynes Publishing

© Haynes Publishing 2005

First published 2002
Reprinted 2003 and 2005
Updated and reprinted 2005

ISBN 1 84425 374 0

Printed by **J H Haynes & Co Ltd,**
Sparkford, Yeovil, Somerset BA22 7JJ, England.

Tel: 01963 442030 Fax: 01963 440001
Int. tel: +44 1963 442030 Fax: +44 1963 440001
E-mail: sales@haynes.co.uk
Web site: www.haynes.co.uk

Haynes North America, Inc
861 Lawrence Drive, Newbury Park, California 91320, USA

Editions Haynes
4, Rue de l'Abreuvoir
92415 COURBEVOIE CEDEX, France

Haynes Publishing Nordiska AB
Box 1504, 751 45 UPPSALA, Sweden

(3910–10AJ4-232)

It
wasn't my idea
guv'nor!

1 Advice on safety procedures and precautions is contained throughout this manual, and more specifically on page 226. You are strongly recommended to note these comments, and to pay close attention to any instructions that may be given by the parts supplier.

2 J H Haynes recommends that vehicle customisation should only be undertaken by individuals with experience of vehicle mechanics; if you are unsure as to how to go about the customisation, advice should be sought from a competent and experienced individual. Any queries regarding customisation should be addressed to the product manufacturer concerned, and not to J H Haynes, nor the vehicle manufacturer.

3 The instructions in this manual are followed at the risk of the reader who remains fully and solely responsible for the safety, roadworthiness and legality of his/her vehicle. Thus J H Haynes are giving only non-specific advice in this respect.

4 When modifying a car it is important to bear in mind the legal responsibilities placed on the owners, driver and modifiers of cars, including, but not limited to, the Road Traffic Act 1988. IN PARTICULAR, IT IS AN OFFENCE TO DRIVE ON A PUBLIC ROAD A VEHICLE WHICH IS NOT INSURED OR WHICH DOES NOT COMPLY WITH THE CONSTRUCTION AND USE REGULATIONS, OR WHICH IS DANGEROUS AND MAY CAUSE INJURY TO ANY PERSON, OR WHICH DOES NOT HOLD A CURRENT MOT CERTIFICATE OR DISPLAY A VALID TAX DISC.

5 The safety of any alteration and its compliance with construction and use regulations should be checked before a modified vehicle is sold as it may be an offence to sell a vehicle which is not roadworthy.

6 Any advice provided is correct to the best of our knowledge at the time of publication, but the reader should pay particular attention to any changes of specification to the vehicles, or parts, which can occur without notice.

7 Alterations to vehicles should be disclosed to insurers and licensing authorities, and legal advice taken from the police, vehicle testing centres, or appropriate regulatory bodies.

8 The vehicle has been chosen for this project as it is one of those most widely customised by its owners, and readers should not assume that the vehicle manufacturers have given their approval to the modifications.

9 Neither J H Haynes nor the manufacturers give any warranty as to the safety of a vehicle after alterations, such as those contained in this book, have been made. J H Haynes will not accept liability for any economic loss, damage to property or death and personal injury arising from use of this manual other than in respect of injury or death resulting directly from J H Haynes' negligence.

Contents

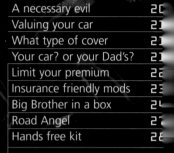

01

02

03

08

09

10

Security

04

Body styling

05

Lights & bulbs

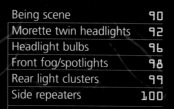

06

Wheels & tyres

07

11

ICE

12

Engines

13

Exhausts

14

Reference

Haynes Max Power

What's that then?

Haynes Publishing have, for the last forty years, been helping people keep their cars on the roads in countries all over the world by publishing maintenance manuals. Chances are you've either got one of them yourself or you know somebody who has.

"Lights & bulbs" includes fitting high-power blue headlight bulbs, coloured rear light clusters, etc.

Before

After

Remember what it feels like on your birthday, or at Christmas, when you're faced by a pile of pressies? So do we, that gnawing feeling in your gut, what's in them? What did I get? Take that feeling and multiply it by twelve, that's how we felt when we started this project. When we decided that it was time to try something new, we couldn't wait. Because the same theories apply to modifying your car as servicing it, we reckoned we'd better get on and do it ourselves. We don't pay other people to do it for us, and we get the same dodgy instructions with kit as everybody else.

So if you've ever wondered how to fit a universal door mirror properly, smooth a tailgate or just bolt a seat in, this book is for you.

We've picked up a skip full of tips along the way, and they're all here for you to use. We haven't tried to set any trends, but we've covered every possible process we think you'll need. So where we've tinted a front door window, the same rules apply to a rear one, job done.

If you look in the magazines and want some of that, join us, 'cos so do we, and we'll show you how to get it.

Keeping it real

Modifying a car is not without its problems in the 'real world', as opposed to the seemingly fantasy world of the glossy mags. For instance, it's pretty silly to spend hours fitting illegal window tints or smoked lights if you get pulled the first time you're out

afterwards. Of course, you can get pulled for all sorts of reasons (and just driving a modified car is reason enough sometimes), but keeping the car actually legal is one of the 'hidden' challenges with modifying. Throughout the book, our tips should give all the help you need to at least appear to be on the right side of the law. The annual MOT test is another favourite time for your mods to get panned, and again, we aim to give you all the help necessary to ensure at least that what you've changed doesn't lead to a fail.

Security is another major issue with a tweaked motor, and the perils of insurance cannot be taken lightly, either. We aim to give down-to-earth advice to help you keep the car in the first place, and to help you in not upsetting your insurers too much if the worst happens.

A word about fashion

In producing this book, we're aware that fashions change. What we show being fitted to our car might well be hideously out of date in 6 months time, or might not be your thing in the first place! Also, some of the stuff we've acquired from our various suppliers may no longer be available by the time you read this. We hope that, despite this, our approach of showing you step-by-step how to fit the various parts will mean that, even if the parts change slightly, the procedures we show for fitting will still be valid.

Our main project car was a 1.6 16v Sport, 1997 R reg, with some additional work being carried out on other Corsas.

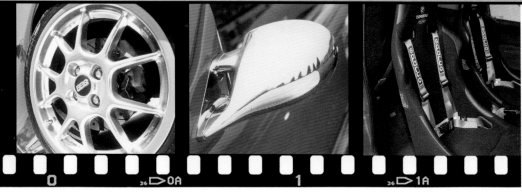

"Wheels & tyres" takes a detailed look at all the options.

"Body styling" shows you how to fit universal mirrors to full body kits.

"Interiors" includes seats, painting trim, gear knobs and loads more.

Super Nova

the lad's favourite

Like Fords, Vauxhalls have always been a big hit with young British drivers - plenty to choose from, easy on the wallet, and loads of spares and modding parts available. With the Nova, though, Vauxhall scored an absolute bullseye with the modifying world, and even though the car's been out of production for eight years and more, it's still got a huge following.

Why was the Nova such a hit? First of all, it's affordable. Cheap to buy and run, and even the GTE/GSi models aren't stupid money to insure, the Nova was always going to be popular with young drivers, but what turned it into such a lad's favourite?

Vauxhall have always been clever at playing a market, and realised early on there was a huge potential for a hot hatch version of the Nova. The insurance-friendly 1.3 SR model was an instant success when it came out way back in 1983, and since that time it grew into the 1.4 SR and SRi, and finally into the 1.6 GTE and GSi. In a similar way to the Golf, the Nova in standard trim was a plain-looking car, very under-stated and simple - crying out to be modified, in other words! By adding bodykit, some smart alloys, and a decent interior, the humble shopping trolley was transformed into a very sharp-looking machine with ease. This meant that the youngest of drivers could take a base-model Nova, and make it look cool while keeping the insurance half-sensible.

All the tuning and bodystyling companies love the Nova, too, so creating a personal look isn't difficult. And, since the car's mechanicals are similar to those of an Astra or Cavalier, uprating the engines isn't too big a challenge either - nothing like a 2.0 litre conversion for showing the way at the lights! All in all, the Nova makes a great first-time modder's motor - affordable and easy to work on.

Curvy Corsa

a new beginning

So - did Vauxhall really start with a clean sheet of paper when they designed the Corsa? Well, no - but it sure looked like it! The new curves certainly were fresh, but what else was new at its 1993 launch? Not too much, actually - the Nova's major mechanicals were carried over largely untouched. In the world of modifying, where style is all-important, what would the lads make of the new model?

It's taken a while, but the Corsa is now well-established as the successor to the Nova (at least for most people). A key factor in this has been the gradual drop-off in used Corsa prices, and now that the "Phase 2" model's out, prices for the original Corsa are only going one way. This has brought the Corsa within reach of younger drivers, who also enjoy lower premiums, model-for-model, than the old Nova! The Corsa's a pretty tasty looking little hatch, even in pre-modded form, and some of the more radical bodykits turn it into a real head-turning beast. Still retaining the same essential qualities which made the Nova such a big hit, the success of the Corsa with the modifying community was assured.

As far as Vauxhall are concerned, the Corsa has always been an economy model, and from a modifier's viewpoint, you could say the company's gone too far towards leaning-off the engines to ensure good fuel economy and low emissions, at the expense of power output. The clue to this was even stamped on the top of the engines in big letters - "ECOTEC". Many of the later engines were 16-valve designs, which usually results in free breathing, high revving, and useful power gains - but this hasn't always been the case with the Corsa units (when the 1.6 engine became an Ecotec unit, it lost power!). Fortunately, all this emissions-related strangling can be quite painlessly "undone", and like most Vauxhall engines, the Corsa units are in fact very tune-able for little money.

While the Nova's devoted following is unlikely to disappear overnight, it looks certain that the Corsa is set to succeed it as the first-time modifier's first-choice motor.

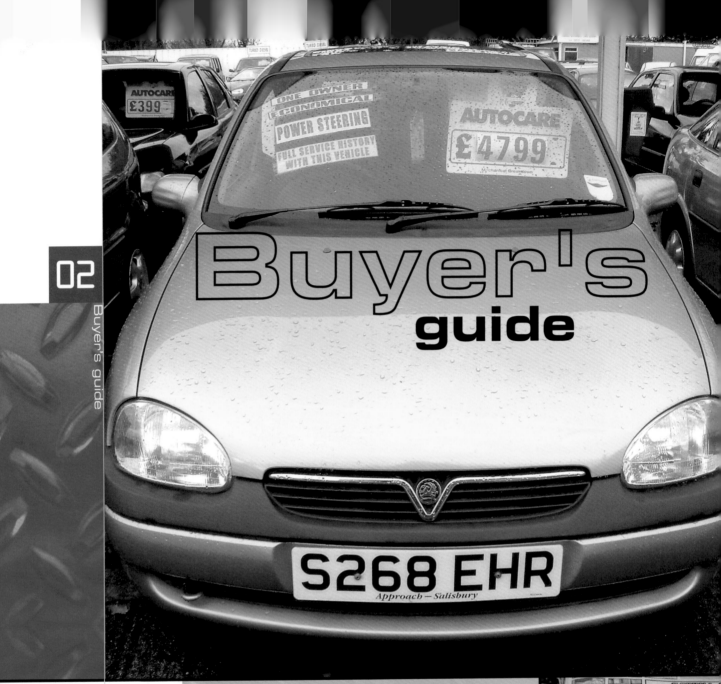

Buyer's
guide

What to look for

It's taken a long time, but now Corsa secondhand prices are beginning to get more sensible. For a long time the Corsa attracted premium prices, but the arrival of the "new-generation" Corsa's has helped to push prices of the original model down.

In general, the Corsa is a solid used buy, with very few problems worth noting. Early cars suffered problems with door hinges and the occasional glitch with instruments. The dreaded rust wasn't much of a factor on the Nova, so don't expect to see any on a Corsa - the only reason you might would be down to badly-repaired crash damage, so walk away. Many lesser Corsas you'll see would've been bought by women, who generally at least drive sensibly and have their cars dealer-serviced (though there are exceptions!).

While the trim on a Corsa is reasonably durable, it should still be obvious whether the car's been abused over a long period, or whether the mileage showing is genuine or not - Vauxhall trim usually hangs on well enough, but it gets floppy with age (sunroof and window winder handles are a good place to start checking if you're suspicious). Okay, so you may be planning to junk most of the interior at some point, but why should you pay over the odds for a tat car which the owner hasn't given a stuff about? If a scruffy interior doesn't actually put you off, then at least make out that you're not happy about it, and haggle the price down! If you find a really sad example, with dents and faded paint, and a smoky, noisy engine - walk away, unless it's very cheap. There's no point spending most of your budget just to get the car half-tidy before you start the real work on it, surely?

Unless you're planning on spending big money on a fairly new Corsa, it's far better to buy privately, as long as you know what you're doing. Dealers still think they can charge over the odds for small cars, but all you'll get for the extra money is a full valet and some degree of comeback if the car's a dog. Buying privately, you get to meet the owner, and this can tell you plenty about how the car's been treated. Everyone's nervous when buying a car, but don't ignore your "gut feelings" when you first see the car, or meet its owner. Also, don't make the common mistake of deciding to buy the car before you've even seen it - too many people make up their minds before setting out, and blindly ignore all the warning signs - remember, there are other cars, and you can walk away!

One sign of a genuine car is a good batch of old MOTs (assuming it's that old), and as many receipts as possible - even if they're for fairly irrelevant things like tyres (you can see if it's had new tyres, can't you?).

Full service history (fsh)

Is there any service history? If so, this is good, but study the service book carefully:

a *Which garage has done the servcing? Is it a proper dealer, or a backstreet bodger? Do you know the garage, and if so, would you use it?*

b *Do the mileages show a nice even progression, or are there huge gaps? Check the dates too.*

c *Does it look as if the stamps are authentic? Do the oldest ones look old, or could this 'service history' have been created last week, to make the car look good?*

d *When was the last service, and what exactly was carried out? When was the cambelt last changed? Has the owner got receipts for any of this servicing work?*

Don't buy a duffer

Check that the mileages and dates shown on the receipts and MOTs follow a pattern indicating normal use, with no gaps in the dates, and no sudden drop in the mileage between MOTs (which might suggest the mileage has been 'clocked'). If you are presented with a sheaf of paperwork, it's worth going through it - maybe the car's had a history of problems, or maybe it's just had some nice expensive new parts fitted (like a clutch, starter motor or alternator, for instance).

Check the chassis number (VIN number) and engine number on the registration document and on the car. Any sign of welding near one of these numbers should be treated with suspicion - to disguise the real number, a thief will run a line of weld over the old number, grind it flat, then stamp in a new number. Other scams include cutting the section of bodywork with the numbers on from another car, then cutting and welding this section into place. The VIN number appears on a plate at the front of the engine compartment; if there is any sign that this plate has been tampered with, walk away - the car could be stolen. The chassis number on this plate should match the one stamped into the floor next to the driver's seat (lift the flap for access) - again, if the numbers don't match, or if they're not in a straight line, leave the car well alone - it could be a "ringer" (a stolen car with a fake I.D.). Models from 1994 should also have the same VIN etched into the front and rear screens - a windscreen could've been legitimately replaced by now, but a rear window?

The engine number is stamped onto a flat machined surface at the front of the engine, not far from the dipstick tube. This number can be difficult to spot, but keep looking until you find it - if the number's been ground off, or if there's anything suspicious about it, you could be buying trouble.

Check the registration document very carefully - all the details should match the car. If buying privately, make sure that it's definitely the owner's name and address printed on it - if not, be very careful! If buying from a dealer, note the name and address, and try to contact the previous owner to confirm mileage, etc,

Tricks 'n' tips
Tyres can be a giveaway to a car maintained on a shoestring - four different makes of tyre, especially cheap brands, can indicate a penny-pinching attitude which won't have done the rest of the car any favours.

Check the VIN numbers etched into the glass. They should all match!

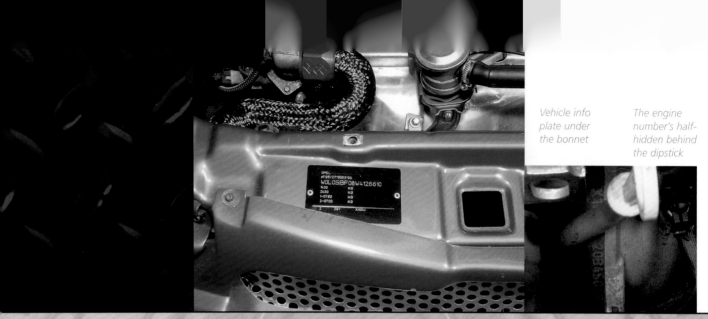

before handing over more than a deposit. Unless the car's very old, it should not have had too many previous owners - if it's into double figures, it may mean that the car is trouble, so checking its owner history is more important.

Corsas resist rust pretty well, but don't assume they don't rust at all. An old Vauxhall favourite spot is round the rear wheelarches, otherwise check the vulnerable bits like sills, and the front floor where it joins the wheelarches. Any other body damage should be cheap enough to repair (doors, bonnets and tailgates, etc, are all available from scrapyards by now) so don't panic, just haggle.

All models have engines fitted with hydraulic tappets - on these, the engines may rattle slightly when they're first started from cold. Any noise should die down after a few seconds; if not, this might indicate a problem - low oil level, lack of servicing, or the use of poor-quality oil might all be responsible. Older Vauxhalls were notorious for wearing out camshafts, and the familiar death-rattle sound is hard to mistake - hopefully, however, Vauxhall have got the problem licked on the Corsa (should only be a consideration at very high mileages, or if servicing has been neglected).

High-mileage cars may suffer from hardened/perished valve stem oil seals, giving rise to a trail of blue oil smoke in the exhaust. At start-up from cold, check the exhaust for blue smoke - on the test-drive, try lifting off the throttle for a few seconds (over-run), then accelerate again while watching in the mirror for smoke.

An oil leak at the front of the engine, near the oil filter, might be due to the oil pump gasket having failed - not serious, just get haggling.

The 16-valve Ecotec motors have the most to look out for. The cambelt idler pulleys were made of plastic, and had a nasty habit of breaking up, which then snaps the cambelt and wrecks the engine. Revised, stronger parts were made available when this problem came to light - any car with a full Vauxhall service history should have had these parts fitted by now, but if there's any doubt on this, it will have to be done ASAP. If you're buying from a dealer, it's always worth demanding a cambelt change as part of the deal - in this case, it's also vital that the idler pulleys are checked.

Another Ecotec problem is sticking valves, which can manifest itself in many different ways. Usually, sticking valves will give rise to very poor running and misfiring (the engine will be "down" on at least one cylinder). Any hint of misfiring or stalling on the test drive, and it's best to walk away - you'll be looking at a very fat bill to fix this. Don't let anyone tell you "it's just the plugs, mate".

Although you may feel a bit stupid doing it, check simple things too, like making sure the windows and sunroof open and shut, and that all the doors and tailgate can be locked. Check all the basic electrical equipment too, as far as possible - lights, front and rear wipers, heated rear window, heater fan; it's amazing how often these things are taken for granted by buyers! If your chosen Corsa already has alloys fitted, does it have locking wheel bolts? Where's the key?

Sealing the deal

Everything as expected and the car's just what you want? It's time to start haggling. Never just agree to hand over the full advertised price for the car, but don't be too ambitious, either (it's best to stay friendly at this point - winding-up the owner is the last thing you need). If the ad says "o.n.o.", expect at least 10% off - if not, why bother putting it on the ad? Try a low offer to test the owner's reaction (they can only say no!) then reluctantly increase the offer until you're both happy. Haggling can also include other considerations besides cash - will the owner chuck in the nice stereo and wheels, leave the tax on, or put a new MOT ("ticket") on it?

Tricks 'n' tips

If your understanding of the mechanical workings of the modern automobile is a bit vague and you want a second opinion, it may also be worth considering having the vehicle inspected. The AA and RAC offer this service, but there may be other people in your area too - check in the Yellow Pages. This is a bit pricier than the vehicle check, but will give you peace of mind and some comeback should things not be as expected. If you've got a friendly garage, maybe they could be persuaded to check the car over for a small fee.

Bagged a bargain? Great! Offer to leave a deposit (this shows you're serious), but before parting with any more cash, it may be worth considering the following.

Ask for time to get in touch with the previous owner shown on the "logbook" (registration document). If you can speak to them, it's a useful exercise in confirming the car's history and mileage.

A wise thing to do is to run a vehicle check with an organisation such as HPI or the AA. It'll cost you (usually around the 30-quid mark) but could save a lot of hassle in future. They'll need the details of all the identification numbers on the vehicle and documents, as well as the mileage, etc. For your money, they'll run the details of the car through their computer database. This database contains the records of all vehicles reported stolen, which have been total losses (ie. have been totalled after a serious accident) or have outstanding finance against them. They can then confirm over the phone the vehicle is straight, and in theory you can proceed with the deal, safe in the knowledge you're not about to purchase a ringer. Not only will you receive a nice certificate through the post with your vehicle details on it, but running the check also gives you financial insurance. The information given is guaranteed (usually to the tune of about ten grand) so if Plod turns up on your doorstep a month later, demanding you return your new vehicle to its rightful owner, you should be able to claim your cash back. No worries.

Model guide

Basic models

First of all, don't buy a 5-door. The reason? Nobody buys 5-doors. If the ad doesn't say which it is, ask. The 5-door just doesn't cut it. Many lesser Corsas were bought as second cars, and they can be the best buys of all, provided they've been looked after. Why pay extra for an SRi or Sport, if you're going to change everything anyway?

The base models are fairly sad inside, with a dull dash and no toys - smartening up with a full interior makeover would be a priority.

The 1.2 "E-Drive" models (1993 to 1995) and the 1.0 litre 3-cylinder babies (1997-on) are gutless, and there ain't much scope for easy improvement. If fuel economy is a must, but you'd still like your Corsa to have a bit of life, consider a 1.5 turbo-diesel (Group 5 insurance) - unlike the other Corsa diesels, these are quick.

The models you'll see most of will be 1.2 litre 8-valves (Merit, LS and various special editions), with modest performance reflected in Group 3 insurance. If you can afford it, the much later 1.2 16-valvers have 65 bhp, virtually match the 1.4s for performance, and are still in Group 3.

The best bargains in the base models have to be the 1.4 8-valve models (the Merit and LS). These are often in the same insurance group as the 1.2s (or usually only one higher), but with 60 bhp rather than 45, they're a good bit livelier. The 1.4 GLS always had the more pokey (81 bhp) version of the 1.4 engine, with multi-point rather than single-point fuel injection, and was placed in Group 6/7. In August 1994, the GLS got the even livelier (89 bhp) 1.4 16-valve engine, but the insurance grouping stayed the same - reasonable for the extra performance.

As with any car, go for the latest model you can afford. Some of the special editions had some useful extra kit, like sunroofs, tints and body-colour bumpers, as well as the obligatory ghastly interior! If you're going to fit fat tyres, try getting a car with power steering (top-spec or latest models).

One thing to check on all Corsas is that the catalytic converter ("cat") is working - this is a very expensive part to replace, but the best way to ensure at least one year's grace is to only buy a car with a full MOT (the cat is checked during the emissions test). All Corsas have an orange "engine management" warning light on the dash (next to the fuel gauge) - this should come on, then go out as the engine's started. If the light stays on, this could indicate many problems - don't be baffled by any bull on this point, and make sure the fault is really sorted before you buy.

Many Corsas have a driver's airbag fitted - if the airbag warning light stays on, this counts as an MOT fail. Curing the fault could be expensive (might also mean the airbag's gone off in a crash!).

Models from 1998 onwards had seat belt pre-tensioners fitted, which go off with the airbag system in a crash (to keep you pinned in your seat, and hopefully, safe). If the tensioners have gone off, there'll be a little yellow tag visible on the belt stalk between the front seats. If so, walk away.

Sporty models

Has it been treated well, or thrashed to death? Don't pay top dollar for any sporty Corsa without seeing evidence of careful maintenance, because any car will stand a good ranting much better if it's been properly serviced. Even a fully-stamped service book only tells half the story, though. Does the owner look bright enough to even know what a dipstick is, never mind how to check the oil level between services?

Remember that there's even more to look out for than on a lesser model. If the car's temptingly cheap (and even if it's not), never take anything just at face value - check everything you can about the car yourself. Getting your hands on a really good sporty Corsa is not a simple task - dodgy dealers (and owners!) know there's a market for repaired write-offs and stolen cars ("ringers"), and gullible private punters get ripped every day.

More so than any other model, check for signs of accident damage, especially at the front end. Ask if it's ever been in a shunt - if the seller says no, but there's paint overspray under the bonnet, what's going on? Also check for paint overspray on the window rubbers, light units and bumpers/trim. With the bonnet open, check that the headlight rear shells are the same colour - mis-matched or new-looking ones merit an explanation from the seller. Check the glass (and even the head and tail lights) for etched-in registration numbers - are they all the same, and does it match the car's actual registration? A windscreen could've been replaced for any number

of innocent reasons, but new side glass indicates a break-in at least - is the car a 'stolen/recovered' (joyridden) example? Find the chassis and engine numbers, as described earlier in this section, and satisfy yourself that they are genuine - check them against the "logbook" (registration document). An HPI check (or similar) is worthwhile, but won't tell you everything. If you're suspicious, or if the answers to your questions don't ring true, walk away.

The sporty models tend to get driven hard, and while they're better able to take this than some cars, hard driving will take its toll somewhere. The suspension should feel quite stiff and taut - any sogginess is usually caused by worn shock absorbers (not a problem, if you're fitting a full lowering kit, but use it to haggle the price down). Any vibration or juddering through the steering when braking indicates serious brake wear (warped brake discs), or possibly, play in the suspension/steering joints (fitting a lowering kit will not cure this kind of play, which also eats front tyres!).

It's a plus point if an approved (Thatcham Cat 1 or 2) alarm or immobiliser is fitted. Make sure that any aftermarket kit actually works, that it looks properly installed, with no stray wires hanging out, and that you get the Thatcham certificate or other paperwork to go with it. If possible, it's worth finding out exactly how it's been wired in - if it goes wrong later, you could be stranded with no chance of disabling the system to get you home. Many later models have immobilisers and alarms as standard - make sure you understand exactly how to work them.

1.4 litre SRi and Sport models

The 1.4 SRi and Sport are very good buys. Decent performance, GSi suspension and most of the desirable interior/exterior GSi features, without 1.6/GSi insurance premiums - in group 6/7, it's four groups lower. At the time of writing, the 1.4 models also benefit from cheaper road tax, too. The early SRis had an 81 bhp 8-valve engine; the 89 bhp 16-valve "Ecotec" engine arrived in August 1994, before the SRi finally became the Sport in September 1995.

A decent equipment level makes it a better starting point for a modified car than a base model, and it'll be more fun to drive around in while you're saving up for all the changes you want to make. Prices can be on the high side, though - owners (and especially dealers) know they've got a 'best-of-both-worlds' model, and you don't see many bargains…

1.6 litre Sport and GSi models

The daddies of the range, and the dearest to insure, but you still won't see any bargains, even though the insurance rules them out entirely for the youngest drivers. Ignore over-priced early models on the assumption that the owner isn't living in the real world! That said, the GSi is actually quite a rare car - it only stayed in production until June 1995, and was succeeded by the 1.6 Sport in April 1997. The only reason to hold out for a GSi over a Sport would be that the GSi had a full bodykit (with wheelarch and sill extensions), and a better interior.

The performance advantage of the 1.6s over the 1.4 SRi/Sport isn't great. The early 1.6 motor was good for 107 bhp, but this was reduced to 104 bhp in August 1994 when the engine became an emissions-friendly "Ecotec" unit. The only other benefit in choosing a 1.6 model is that the GSi and (some) Sport models had ABS as standard.

Model
history

Like many small-car ranges in recent years, the number of "special edition" models offered in the Corsa's history has been enormous. The models listed are a representative selection - to have listed them all would've taken half the book! Don't pay over the odds for a special edition, unless it's genuinely got some extra kit you're interested in having - most are just the 1.2 Merit with stickers and er... interesting seat trim!

March 1993 (K reg)

Corsa range introduced. 1.2 and 1.4 litre 8-valve engines, and GSi with 1.6 16-valve engine, ABS, alloys and bodykit. 1.4 SRi model has close-ratio gearbox and rear spoiler, and 81 bhp multi-point injection engine (shared with GLS models). 1.2 litre E-Drive "super-economy" models with high gearing and additional emissions kit. Three-door and five-door models, unusually, have totally different body styles - five-door has higher rear roofline, to maximise rear headroom.

April 1994 (L reg)

1.2 Swing special edition launched.

June 1994

All models now have "visible VIN" - etched into front and rear screens.

August 1994 (M reg)

Gas shock absorbers fitted across the range. 1.2 LS, GLS models gain close-ratio gearbox. 1.4 GLS, SRi now have 16-valve 89 bhp Ecotec

unit, and standard driver's airbag. 1.6 GSi 16-valve engine also re-designated Ecotec, with lower emissions; driver's airbag standard.

November 1994

SRi and GSi now have transponder (chip-in-key) immobiliser. 1.2 Breeze special edition launched.

April/June 1995

1.2 Arizona and Twist special editions launched.
1.6 GSi discontinued.

September 1995 (N reg)

1.4 SRi re-designated 1.4 16v Sport, with extra equipment. All 1.2 models and 1.4 Merit now have 5-speed gearbox. 1.2 Spin and 1.2/1.4 Montana special editions launched.

March/April 1996

1.2 Premier and Trip special editions launched.

October 1996 (P reg)

1.2/1.4 Vegas special editions launched.

April 1997

Revised range with V-grille launched. Mild restyling front and rear, trim improvements. Suspension uprated following work by Lotus. New 1.0 litre 3-cylinder 12-valve models introduced, initially as Sting special edition. New 1.6 16v Sport - spec as 1.4 Sport, with ABS.

October 1997 (R reg)

Air conditioning now available as an option (also in lieu of sunroof) on GLS, Sport and CDX models.

January 1998

1.0 Trip and Breeze special editions launched.

May 1998

1.4 Cabrio model launched. Very rare.

September 1998 (S reg)

1.2 engine now 16-valve, 1.4 8-valve engine dropped. All models have improved equipment levels, side impact bars, seat belt tensioners. Most models now have standard driver's airbag. 1.2 SXi special edition launched, with alloys, tinted glass, spoiler, sports seats.

October 1999 (V reg)

1.2 .com special edition launched, for "internet sale" only. 8-spoke alloys, metallic body-colour bumpers, sunroof.

October 2000 (X reg)

New Corsa range introduced.

Performance figures

	0-60 (sec)	Top speed (mph)
1.0	19.9	93
1.2 E-Drive	19.6	83
1.2 8-valve Merit/LS	18.5	90
1.2 16-valve	13.1	101
1.4 8-valve Merit/LS	13.3	95
1.4 8-valve SRi/GLS	11.5	106
1.4 16-valve	11.1	111
1.5 TD	13.1	104
1.6 GSi (pre-Ecotec)	8.7	118
1.6 GSi/Sport (Ecotec)	10.2	115

Insurance
A necessary evil

The way the insurance companies work out premiums and assess risks is a mystery to most of us. In general, the smaller the engine you have in your Corsa, the less you'll pay for insurance, so hopefully, a Corsa 1.2 Merit will be lots less to insure than a 1.6 GSi. However, different companies can give wildly different quotes so it's vital to shop around. Always ring as many brokers and get as many quotes as you possibly can. A few extra minutes spent on the phone once a year may result in an extra few hundred quid in your back pocket.

With modified cars, insurance becomes even more of a problem. By modifying a car, you're making it more of a target for thieves (yes, ok, I know you know this). The point is, the insurance companies know this too, and they don't want to be paying out for the car, plus all the money you've spent on it, should it go missing. There is a temptation 'not to tell the insurance' about the mods you've made. Let's deal with this right now. Our experience has been that, while it can be painful, honesty is best. If they find out (and if you have a claim, they may well come and inspect the car) they won't pay out a penny. And if you do make a claim, very few insurers pay out for the modifications, so you get paid out, but based on a standard car. There are many specialist insurers who are more friendly towards fully-loaded cars, but even they won't actually cover the cost of replacement goodies.

Valuing your car

When your insurance pays out in the event of a total loss or write-off, they base their offer on the current market value of an identical standard model to yours. The only way you'll get more than the average amount is to prove your Corsa is in above-average nick (with photos) or that the mileage was especially low for the year.

With this in mind, don't bother over-valuing your Corsa in the hope you'll get more in the event of a claim - you won't! The only way to do this is to seek out an "agreed-value" deal, which you can usually only get on classic-car policies (with these, the car's value is agreed in advance between you, not worked out later by the company with you having no say in it). By over-valuing your Corsa, you could be increasing your premium without gaining any benefit.

Equally though, don't under-value, in the hope you'll get a reduction in premium. You won't, and if there's a total loss claim, you won't get any more than your under-valued amount, no matter how loudly you complain.

Work on what you paid for the car, backed up with the sort of prices you see for similar cars in the ads (or use a secondhand car price guide). Add no more than 10% for the sake of optimism, and that's it.

What type of cover?

For most of us, cost means there's only one option - TPF&T (third party, fire and theft). Fully-comp insurance is an unattainable dream for most people until they reach the "magic" age of 25, but what's the real story?

Third Party only

The most basic cover you can get. Basically covers you for damage to other people's cars or property, and for personal injury claims. Virtually no cover for your own stuff, beyond what you get if you take the optional "legal protection" cover.

Third Party, Fire and Theft

As above, with cover for fire and theft, of course! Better, but not much better. This is really only cover in the event of a "total loss", if your car goes missing or goes up in smoke. Still no cover for your car if you stack it into a tree, or if someone breaks in and pinches your stereo.

Fully-comprehensive

In theory, covers you for any loss or damage. Will cover the cost of repairing or replacing your car regardless of whether it was your fault or not. With a fully-comp policy, you can "protect" your no-claims bonus for a small fee so you don't automatically lose those hard-earned years' worth of discount if you prang it All this extra cover costs more, but is often a better bet in the long run.

Your car, or your Dad's?

Don't pretend your Corsa belongs to your Dad, and get him to insure it, with you as a named driver. Insurance companies are not stupid. They know that your Dad isn't likely to be running around in a modified car, and they treat any "named driver" application with great suspicion in these cases. This dubious practice also does you no favours in future years. All the time you're living the lie, you're not building up any no-claims bonus of your own.

Not telling the insurance the whole truth gets a little tricky when you have to make a claim. You may think your insurance company is there for your benefit, but they're a business like any other, and their main aim in life is to make money. If the insurance assessor comes around to check your bent/burnt/stolen-and-recovered "standard" Corsa, and finds he's looking at a vehicle fitted with alloys/bodykit/modified interior, he's not going to turn a blind eye.

Limit your premium

When you phone for a quote your fate is pretty much sealed, but there are a few things you can do to help lower the premium

Golden Rule Number One

If in doubt, declare everything. Insurance companies are legally entitled to dispute any claim if the car is found to be non-standard in any way.

Golden Rule Number Two

Before modifying the car, ring your insurance, and ask them how it will affect things.

Fit an approved alarm or immobiliser

In general, any alarm or immobiliser with a Thatcham rating should be recognised by any insurance company, but it pays to check before fitting. In some cases, the discounts offered are not that great any more - but an alarm is still a nice way to get peace of mind.

Avoid speed cameras and The Law

Yes, okay, easier said than done! One SP30 isn't usually too bad, but much more and you'll pay for it, so go easy.

Make yourself the only driver

Pretty self-explanatory. The more people who drive your car, the greater the risk to the company. If you've built up 2 years' worth of no-claims, but your girlfriend/wife hasn't, putting her on your insurance will bump it up, due to her relative inexperience.

Build up your no-claims bonus

You'll only do this by owning and insuring a car in your own name, and then not making any claims. Simple really. Each claim free year you have will aid lowering how much you pay out.

Hang onto your no-claims bonus

Obviously, the less you claim, the less your insurance will cost. If something happens to your car, don't be in too big a hurry to make a claim before you've thought it all through. How much will it cost to fix? How much is your excess? If you can afford not to claim, then don't do it.

Limit your mileage

Most companies offer a discount if you only cover a small annual mileage. To get any meaningful reduction, the mileage has to be less than 10,000 per year. Don't try and pretend you only do 3000 if it's nearer 20,000. Few companies ever ask what the car's current mileage is - so how are they gonna know if you've gone over your self-imposed limit? But if they do find out you could be in trouble.

Get a garage

If you have access to a garage use it, insurers love a car to be locked away safe and sound at night.

Insurance-friendly mods?

So - what do insurance companies like and dislike, as far as mods go? No two companies will have the same outlook, and your own circumstances will play a big part too.

Engine mods

"Mild" mods, such as induction kits and exhausts don't often change premiums, but just the merest mention of "chipping" can make many companies load the premium, or even completely refuse to offer cover. With complete engine transplants, you may be required to give an engineer's report on the mods before they'll grant cover.

Interior mods

As with bodykits, unless you go absolutely mental it really shouldn't make a difference, but make sure you tell your insurers all the same.

Body mods

Even a tiny rear spoiler can be classed as a "bodykit" (yes, it's daft, but that's how it is). Anything which alters the exterior appearance should be declared. As long as the mods aren't too radical, the jump in premium should be fairly small. If anything at all.

Lights

As they're safety-related, you'll probably get asked for lots of details, but as long as you've kept it sensible (and legal, as far as possible) you'll be fine.

Security

Make sure you mention all security stuff - alarms, immobilisers (including mechanical devices), and locking wheel nuts. Don't tell them you've got a Cat 1 if your alarm really came from Argos, and don't tell them you garage the car at night if it's stuck out in the road, if they find out, you're on your own.

Suspension

Average suspension drops of 30-40mm are fine, go much lower and they may charge you more.

Wheels

The specialist insurers won't mind you having a nice set of alloys, but just about every other insurer will load the premium sadly. Make sure you fit locking wheel bolts.

Brakes

Uprating standard sized discs, maybe with grooved or drilled discs seldom affects the insurance, but some get a bit twitchy when you start fitting bigger discs and replacement calipers.

Big Brother in a Box

Speed cameras have to be one of the most unpopular things ever. We're talking worse than exams, dentists, alcohol-free beer, and the Budget. Does anyone actually like them? Well, the makers do - they should all be living it up on a beach in the Bahamas. The people making speed camera signs are obviously lovin' it. And the Chancellor? Nuff said.

Speed, of course, is fun. The sensation of speed is the main reason we enjoy driving, and it's one of the best ways to show off your motor. There's nothing like giving your ride a good caning, being pushed back in the seat, exhaust snarling, engine singing. Sounds like fun to me - so these things are really fun cameras, then?

Like it or not, we live in a world obsessed with limiting speed. Excess speed, we're told, causes accidents and costs lives. As most of us have realised by now, excess speed really means more money for the Government. What causes accidents is driving like a tw*t. But they don't have cameras for that.

Before we get ourselves in too much trouble, we have to admit the cameras might save lives in built-up areas with lots of peds, kids and old folk about. Driving like a hooligan in those situations probably should get you a slap on the wrist for 'endangering lives'. But at night, on a dead-straight road with no traffic? We think not.

Pay attention

The best you can say about cameras is that they're a necessary evil which we all have to live with. So what's the best way of avoiding the 'bad news' letter in the post?

There is one 100% foolproof method, which is totally legal, and it's dead simple - don't ever speed. That should do the trick. Yeah, right. Back in the real world, everyone speeds some time, even if it's only by a few mph. Add a few more miles-per because you weren't really watching your speed, and then do it somewhere there's a camera (or a sneaky mobile trap you'd never spotted before), and you're nicked. Is it any wonder that clean licences are getting as rare as rocking-horse leftovers?

Even on roads you know well, the do-gooders are forever lowering the limits, so if you don't watch it, you'll be sailing through more than 10 mph over today's new limit. And that's definitely worth a few points! You've gotta concentrate, to stay clean.

Know your enemy

First of all, you've got to know what you're up against. It's the only way (short of the fantasy world of never, ever speeding) that you stand a chance. And the first thing to know is - not all cameras are the same. Some can even be beaten.

Gatso (and PEEK)

The first, the best-known, the most common, and probably the most-hated. Invented by the winner of the 1953 Monte Carlo Rally, Gatsos are the familiar large, square box in stealth grey or high-viz yellow, with a square lens and flash unit (the later, less-common PEEK cameras have two round items, set one above the other). These are radar-operated (type 24) and can only 'get' you from behind, because they use a flash to take the photo, and this would blind you if it went off with you coming towards it. These cameras, therefore, cannot in theory catch you speeding towards them (don't quote us on that). As a result of this limitation, some authorities will turn the cameras round from time to time, to catch you out.

Gatsos have 35 mm film inside, with about 400 shots possible before the film runs out. It's obviously vital that the film is recovered from the camera, or a prosecution can't be made - these cameras get vandalised for all sorts of reasons. Some cameras are rumoured not to contain any film, so they flash without recording any evidence (that bloke down the pub could be wrong, though).

If the radar detects excess speed, the flash is triggered twice as you pass over the measured line markings on the road. From the distance you travel between the set flashes, your speed can be proved. It's anyone's guess where the trigger speed for a camera will be set, but it's almost bound to be quite a few mph over the posted limit - if it wasn't, the camera would quickly catch dozens of speeders, and run out of film. Be more wary of inner-city Gatsos, as they're probably 'emptied' more often, allowing a lower speed tolerance.

tricks 'n' tips
In a thirty limit, you're less likely to speed if you hook a lower gear than normal. Most cars will comfortably cruise through a thirty in 4th gear, but it's too easy to add speed in 4th. Try using 3rd, and the natural engine braking (and extra engine/exhaust noise) will help you keep a lid on your speed. It's not foolproof, but give it a try anyway.

RLCs are also Gatso-based, but they work through sensors in the road, which are active when the lights are on red. If your car passes over them in this condition, it's gotcha. Some RLCs use radar too, so if you speed through on red, you'll also get a speeding fine. Gee, thanks.

Truvelo

Oooh, nasty. The forward-facing 'gatso' is particularly unpleasant, but luckily for us, it's also more expensive than the rear-facing Gatso, so not as common. Yet. The Truvelo camera can be recognised by two round lenses side by side in the centre of its box, and one of these is a pinky-red colour (hence the 'pinkeye' nickname). The unusual pink 'lens' is actually a flash unit, fitted with a red filter to avoid blinding the driver. Because the photo's taken from the front, it's hard for the driver to claim someone else was driving, or that they 'don't know'

who was driving (a common ploy to try and 'get off' Gatso offences). The less-visible flash gives less warning to following motorists, too. Not that we're suggesting they're out to get us. Oh no.

These babies are triggered by the car passing over piezo sensors set into the road, not radar. If you see three stripes across your path, slow the heck down.

Red Light Cameras

Intended to catch people who go through traffic lights on red. Which, you have to say, is pretty dodgy. And have you ever risked it on a single amber? If you remember your Highway Code, this means stop, the same as a red light. 'Amber-gamblers' should also beware the traffic-light cams, 'cos they'll get you one day. Unlike (a few) points for speeding, points for traffic light offences will really hurt your insurance premiums, so watch it.

SPECS

Yikes - this really is Big Bro stuff. This system uses digital cameras (no film needed), mounted high on special gantries - these are a set distance apart, and create a speed monitoring zone. When you 'enter the zone', your number plate is recorded digitally, with a date and time stamp (regardless of whether you're speeding). When you leave the zone, another camera does the same thing. Because you've travelled a known distance between the two cameras, it's possible to calculate your average speed - if you're over the limit for the stretch of road, the computer spits out a fine in your direction.

What's really worrying about this technology is that it can be used to cross-check you and your car for other offences (whether your car's taxed and MoT'd, for instance). Anything dodgy, and the next time you pass by those cameras at that time of day, you could be in for a jam-sandwich surprise. Still, it could also catch the crims making off with your motor...

Mobile or temporary speed traps

These are either Gatso, Mini-Gatso, or laser type.

The potential Gatso sites are easy enough to spot - look for three shiny strips across the road, with a sturdy grey metal post alongside, on the pavement. Mr Plod comes along, sets up his camera (which uses sensors in the road strips not radar to detect your speed), catches his daily quota of speeders, and moves on. Don't give him a short day by being one of his victims.

Mini-Gatsos are just smaller, mobile versions of the UK's least-favourite roadside 'furniture', operated out of cop-cars and anonymous white vans - to get you, you have to be driving away from them.

More sinister (and much on the increase) are the laser cameras, which are aimed at your number plate (usually the front one) and record your speed on video. Often seen mounted on tripods, on bridges overlooking busy roads, or hidden inside those white 'safety camera partnership' vans. Lasers have quite a range (1000 metres, or over half a mile), so by the time you've spotted them, they've spotted you speeding. It's up to the operator to target likely speeding vehicles - so will they pick on your maxed motor? You bet!

Achtung!
Do you live in, or regularly drive through, Northamptonshire or North Wales? We've got two words for you. Oh, dear. Northamptonshire is the area with the most cameras, and where new camera technology is often first tried out, while North Wales has one of the most active safety cam partnerships, with many roaming vans. But don't feel too bad, guys - the way it's going, the rest of us will soon catch you up.

Beating the system

No-one's condoning regular speeding, but these days, it's just too easy to get 'done' for a fairly minor speed infringement. Which hardly seems fair. There must be some way of fighting back, surely?

Cheap and legal

Don't. Ever. Speed. Simple, but not easy in the real world. Next!

Neither cheap nor legal

The James Bond option

One of 007's older cars had self-changing number plates - this may have been the inspiration for a highly-illegal speed camera dodge. Since all the detection systems rely heavily on your number plate, some skankers drive round with false plates - they might even have copied yours. Worth remembering if you ever get accused of speeding in the Outer Hebrides. Getting caught on false plates could be a £1000 fine, so is it worth the risk?

For ages now, companies have been advertising 'photo-reflective' plates (they're not illegal, but the dibble take a dim view). Most are a rip-off, but some do appear to work – on traps which flash. Speed cameras take very high-res pictures, however - even if your plates don't give you away, the coppers might i.d. your motor from its non-standard features. Money wasted, then.

Cloaking device?

The mobile laser speed trap is one of the most common, and most hated, in the UK. It sends out a laser beam which targets your front number plate. Wouldn't it be great if you could buy something to mess up its signal, so it couldn't 'lock on'? You can - it's called a laser diffuser (sometimes marketed under the guise of a remote garage door-opener). And yes, they do work - but careful fitting is needed, and the lenses need regular cleaning. If you're caught using it for speed trap evasion, you can be done for obstruction, or perverting the course of justice - it pays to have a well-placed 'off' switch.

Gatso-beating radar 'scramblers' are said not to work, while radar jammers are an illegal transmitter - using one could see you inside for much longer than a speeding conviction.

A sound investment?

Laser detectors

The makers say this is essential kit to combat the roaming camera van threat, but be careful. We said earlier that laser cams have a range of up to 1000 metres, but most operators don't trigger theirs until you're much, much closer than that. Which means you have far less time to react. As long as you're not the first car along, your laser detector may pick up laser 'scatter' from cars in front, but there isn't much scatter with a laser. It's said that some laser detectors will only go off if your car's already been targeted - and of course, it's too late by then.

Radar detectors

These have been around for ages, and started life in the US. They're good for detecting radar-based speed cameras (most Gatsos), and any old police radar guns still in use, but that's all. Don't buy an old one (you'll get lots of false alerts if it's not meant for Euro/UK use), or a cheap one (it might not have enough range to give you a chance). *Stop press: Looks like laser and radar detectors are finally going to be made illegal later this year (2004) — only GPS systems will be legal after this.*

GPS systems

Using Global Positioning Satellite technology, these devices are really speed camera site locators, not detectors. Using an onboard database of camera locations, they constantly monitor your car's position, and warn when you're approaching a 'danger area'. Providing you keep your dash-mounted podule updated (by downloading the latest camera/blackspot info from the maker's website), these will warn you of virtually every potential camera in the country, including Truvelo and SPECS. The only limitations are a lack of laser detection, and it won't get all the mobile sites.

You must download new info regularly, and this costs (you buy a subscription to the website). Also, if your system hasn't been in use for a while, it can take quite a few minutes for the pod to pick up the satellites it needs - during this time, you're unprotected. Don't buy secondhand units with no subscription left, as the makers sometimes can't (won't?) re-activate them.

A final word

Don't rely too heavily on even the best anti-camera technology - try and drive within the spirit, if not the letter, of the Law, with a detector as backup.

Road **Angel**

The most effective way to 'detect' a camera is to know where it is. Yeah – obviously! But with cameras still being hidden behind road signs and bridges, and increasing numbers of camera-kitted white vans, knowing where the cams are ain't easy.

A GPS locator monitors your car's position relative to known camera sites, and warns you when you're getting close. The latest offerings also warn when you're approaching schools and other areas where extra care is needed. These devices are definitely not illegal. They increase road safety, by telling you where 'accident blackspots' are – not when to brake…

tricks 'n' tips
Don't leave the mounting cradle fitted when you leave the car – it's all the clue a thief needs that there's some serious money's worth hidden in your glovebox. Even if it's not there (because you've sensibly taken it with you) you're still making it too tempting.

This latest Road Angel offers two main mounting options – a sticky-backed magnetic mount directly on the dash, or this rather neat screen-mounted cradle (also with a mag mount).

01 Either way, make sure the wipers don't obscure the unit's 'view', or the laser detection function won't stand a chance.

02 A GPS unit like this is only as good as the info it's working from – update it regularly by downloading the latest camera locations, or it's worse than useless. If you can use a PC well enough to download stuff from the Internet, you've got no worries.

03 Plug the unit into its lighter socket power supply (assuming it's not already taken by your phone charger or hands-free kit), then fit the unit to its bracket. First, you're greeted by a friendly message, then the unit starts searching for its satellites. While this is going on, remember that you're not protected.

04 Depending which system you've got, when you're getting near a camera site (sorry – accident blackspot), you'll get a warning beep or message, and the display will flash. If you miss all that lot, you probably need to downgrade your ICE install.

Look Mum, no hands!

As of December 2003 (okay, March 2004 really) it became illegal to hold your mobile while driving. Well, brilliant - something new to get done for. Like we were really getting short of that kind of thing. But you have to say, yipping and driving always was a pretty dodgy pastime, with driving coming off worse - if only all the UK's traffic legislation made this much sense.

Of course, the people who really benefit are the ones making hands-free car phone kits - you're looking at upwards of £50 (for a conventional kit) to get anything worth fitting. Which one do I go for? Will I have to make holes in my dash? Good questions. But we're jumping ahead - let's deal first with what the new law means in the real world.

Points of law
First, fitting a hands-free kit is merely a way of getting round part of the new legislation. They're not 'fully-legal', they're just 'not prohibited'. Even using a hands-free set-up is a distraction while you're piloting your machine, and if you start weaving about, carve up a cyclist, or run a red light, you're still likely to face

a 'driving without due care' charge, or worse. The best solution for making a call is to stop where it's safe - have voicemail enabled if you get called while you're driving.

Answering a call, even with hands-free, might not be safe in all circumstances. Let it ring. As for what you're allowed to do with the phone itself - it's just pressing the buttons (and no, this doesn't mean it's ok 2 txt). Holding the phone in any way is not permitted. Even if you're stuck in traffic, completely stationary, the engine would have to be off before you can use your mobile normally - only then could you really say you weren't 'driving'.

At the moment, getting caught using a phone on the move only carries a fixed fine. But it looks like this hasn't worked, because it's soon going to be a bigger fine, and points on the licence. Use your moby sensibly (better still, don't use it, in the car at least), or it could mean re-sitting your driving test. Paying attention now, aren'tcha?

Achtung!
Don't just pull over and screech to a stop when the phone rings. If you do this somewhere stupid, you're just as likely to get fined as you would for using the phone on the move.

tricks 'n' tips
If you've got a passenger in the car, it's perfectly legal for them to use a mobile, so if yours rings, let them answer it, and relay the message to you - can't be done for that.

What's available?

Conventional kits

The new law has brought a whole range of new product to the market, so there's no need to settle for the old-style in-car kits, which leave holes all over your dash. Most of the latest kits have adhesive pads, and just plug into your fag lighter. The most essential item, to comply with the rules, is a phone holder or 'cradle' (holding phone bad - cradle good).

As no-one keeps the same phone for very long, it's worth looking for a kit which you can convert from one make of phone to another - by buying a different adapter lead, for instance.

Look for kits offering 'full duplex' operation - this means you can talk and listen at the same time. Just like real life. What it really means is conversations are easier and more natural - to understand fully why you need this feature, try one without it. Non-duplex kits cut out the speaker when they pick up any sound - this could be you talking (as intended), or it could just be noise inside the car. Very irritating, especially in an area where you've already got poor reception to deal with.

Some kits feature 'infra-red technology', which means you can answer/end calls by waving your hand in front of the phone. Proper hands-free operation, and great for impressing your passengers. Maybe not so good if you make lots of hand gestures while driving?

Car stereo kits

One of the newest ideas, and catching on fast. Uses a radio transmitter clipped over the phone speaker to transmit calls over a radio channel on your car stereo. When the phone rings, flick on the radio to the preset channel, speak into the phone's mike as normal, and hear your caller through your car speakers (since it's your stereo, you have easy control over call volume). They're cheap, and they appear to work, though there are potential problems with interference. Remember, this is a developing technology - it pays to buy the latest model you can find.

Bluetooth headsets

Bluetooth offers wireless operation, so get yourself a headset with mike, and you can chat away without having the phone up to your ear. Most modern handsets are Bluetooth-capable, and really new ones also have voice-activated dialling, which offers true hands-free operation in the car. Downsides? Some doubts over sound quality, and do you really want to wear a headset all the time you're driving?

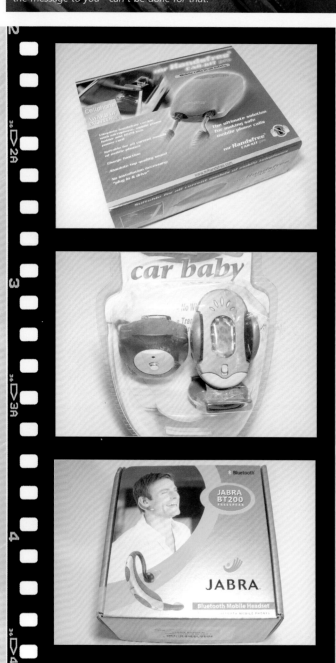

Kit fitting

Fitting details are obviously going to vary, depending on what you've bought – the main trick is to get one which doesn't require you to go drilling holes in your dash. Luckily, this is now so unpopular that most modern kits don't even offer hole-drilling as an option.

Mr Handsfree

Insurance & The Law

01 All these kits (apart from the Bluetooth headset) need power, usually conveniently taken from the fag lighter socket. Umm, yeah... right... Not easy getting the adapter in the socket, with the ashtray in place, is it?

02 If you're not going to drill holes, you'll be sticking stuff on. If you want things to stay stuck (and you usually only get one shot at this) a little cleaning is in order first.

03 Mostly, it's Velcro pads you get for sticking the various kit bits in place (so they can be easily ripped off and stashed when you leave the car). Leave the two 'halves' of Velcro stuck together while fitting. With the mounting area clean, it's peel . . .

04 . . . and press firmly. This is the main unit, which contains the speaker. We thought the centre console was too good a spot to ignore. You only have to ensure the two curly-cords will reach the lighter socket and the phone.

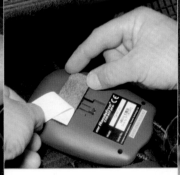

05 Not all fitting is quite this simple, though. With a little clever thinking, you can do a much neater fitting job than one which leaves all the wires hanging out. Take this little mike which comes with the Mr Handsfree kit – by prising out one of the blank switches, we hid the wire inside the dash and stuck the mike to the switch, right where it's needed. Result.

06 For mounting the phone itself, we have a magnetic bracket, again stuck with sticky pads. It's only an old Nokia, but we'd still better make sure it doesn't hit the deck, by making sure it's firmly attached.

07 And there it is – the phone's nice and handy, the mike's discreetly mounted, and the speaker unit's tucked in the console. And this is the first one of these we've fitted!

Pama Plug n Go

This is one neat unit – no dangling wires, a well-designed mounting bracket with a huge sucker for sticking to the windscreen, and a built-in speaker which faces the glass, so sound is 'reflected' back. The unit is self-contained, with a built-in battery (car charger supplied), so it can be used anywhere, not just in-car. Looks sweet, works a treat.

01

Jabra Bluetooth headset

Only any good to you if your phone's got Bluetooth, but like the Pama unit we fitted earlier, there's no mess. The headset needs charging before use, but after that, you just 'pair' your phone and headset together, and start jabbering. If your phone's trendy enough to have voice-activated dialling, this is about as hands-free as you'll get. You don't even need a cradle for your mobile with this one!

01

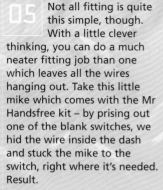

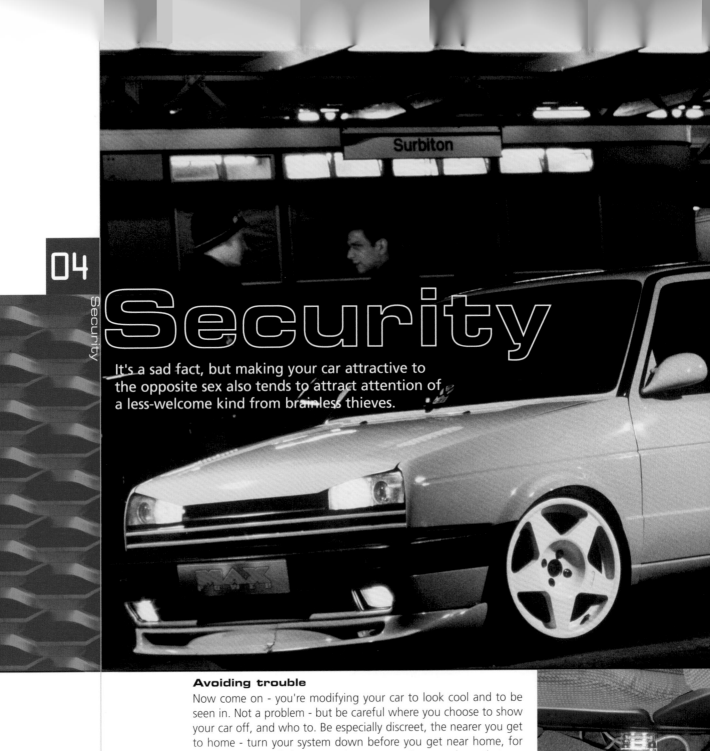

Surbiton

Security

It's a sad fact, but making your car attractive to the opposite sex also tends to attract attention of a less-welcome kind from brainless thieves.

Avoiding trouble

Now come on - you're modifying your car to look cool and to be seen in. Not a problem - but be careful where you choose to show your car off, and who to. Be especially discreet, the nearer you get to home - turn your system down before you get near home, for instance, or you'll draw unwelcome attention to where that car with the loud stereo's parked at night.

If you're going out, think about where you're parking - somewhere well-lit and reasonably well-populated is the best bet.

Hands up, who doesn't lock their car when they get petrol? Your insurance company has a term for this, and it's "contributory negligence". In English, this means you won't get a penny if your car goes missing when you haven't locked it.

If you're lucky enough to have a garage, use it and fit extra security to the garage door.

Always use all the security you have, whenever you leave the car, even if it's a bit of a chore fitting a steering lock, just do it.

A word about your stereo

From the moment you bolt on those nice alloys, it's taken as read that you've also got stereo gear that's worth nicking - and the thieves know it. All the discreet installation in the world isn't going to deter them from finding out what's inside that nice motor.

If you have a CD player, don't leave discs or empty CD cases lying around inside the car. 6x9s on the rear shelf are also very inviting to thieves, and very easy to steal. When you're fitting your system, give some thought to the clues you could accidentally leave in plain view. Oxygen-free speaker cable is great stuff, but it's also a bit bright against dark carpets, and is all the clue necessary that you're serious about your speakers.

Most modern sets are face-off or MASK, so if they've got security features like this, use them - take your faceplate off when you leave the car, and take it with you rather than leaving it in the door pocket or glovebox (the first places a thief will look).

Things that go beep in the night

Don't skimp on an alarm, it may never even be put to the test, but if it is, you'll be glad you spent wisely …

The simplest first step to car security is to fake it. It's obviously risky if the thief calls your bluff, but if you really can't afford an alarm just an LED is cheap to buy and easy to fit, and can be rigged to a discreet switch inside the car (we show you how, later on).

Don't overlook the value of so-called "manual" immobilisers, such as steering wheel locks. These are a worthwhile deterrent - a thief not specifically after your car (and yours alone) may move on to an easier target. Some of the items offered may be "Sold Secure" or Thatcham Cat 3, accolades well worth checking out, as it means they've withstood a full-on brute force attack for a useful length of time.

The only way to combat the more determined thief is to go for a well-specified and intelligently-installed alarm. Immobilisers alone have their place, but a pro-fitted immobiliser alone won't stop someone pinching your wheels, or breaking in for the stereo gear.

Finally, one other scam which you might fall victim to. If you find that your alarm is suddenly going off a lot at night, when previously it had been well-behaved, don't ignore the problem. It's an old trick for a thief to deliberately set off your alarm several times, each time hiding when you come out to investigate, then to wait until the fifth or sixth time when you don't reset, leaving him a clear run. If your alarm does keep false-alarming without outside assistance, find out the cause quickly, or your neighbours will quickly become "deaf" to it.

Thatcham categories and meanings:

1 **Cat 1.** For alarms and electronic immobilisers.

2 **Cat 2.** For electronic immobilisers only.

3 **Cat 2-1.** Electronic immobilisers which can be upgraded to Cat 1 alarms later.

4 **Cat 3.** Mechanical immobilisers, eg snap-off steering wheels, locking wheel bolts, window film, steering wheel locks/covers.

5 **Q-class.** Tracking devices.

Other alarm features

Two-stage anti-shock - means that the alarm shouldn't go off, just because the neighbour's cat jumps on your car roof, or because Little Johnny punts his football into your car. Alarm will only sound after a major shock, or after repeated shocks are detected.

Anti-tilt - detects any attempt to lift or jack up the car, preventing any attempt to pinch alloys. Very unpopular with thieves, as it makes the alarm very sensitive (much more so than anti-shock). Alarm may sound if car is parked outside in windy conditions (but not if your suspension's rock-hard!).

Anti-hijack - immobiliser with built-in delay. If your motor gets hi-jacked, the neanderthals responsible will only get so far down the road before the engine cuts out.

Rolling code - reduces the chance of your alarm remote control signal from being "grabbed" by special electronic equipment.

Total closure - module which connects to electric windows or sunroof and central locking, which closes all items when alarm is set.

Pager control - yes, really - your alarm can be set to send a message to your pager (why not your mobile?) if your car gets tampered with.

Current-sensing disable - very useful feature on some cars which have a cooling fan which can cut in after the ignition is switched off. Without this feature, your alarm will be triggered every time you leave it parked after a long run - very annoying.

Volumetric-sensing disable - basically allows you to manually disable the interior ultrasonics, leaving the rest of the alarm features active. Useful if you want to leave the sunroof open in hot weather - if a fly gets in the car, the alarm would otherwise be going off constantly.

Talking alarms - no, please, please no. Very annoying, and all that'll happen is you'll attract crowds of kids daring each other to set it off again. Unfortunately, these are becoming more popular, with some offering the facility to record your own message!

The knowledge

What people often fail to realise (at least, until it happens to them) is the level of violence and destruction which thieves will employ to get your stuff - this goes way beyond breaking a window.

It comes as a major shock to most people when they discover the serious kinds of tools (weapons) at many professional thieves' disposal, and how brutally your lovingly-polished car will be attacked. Many people think, for instance, that it's their whole car they're after, whereas it's really only the parts they want, and they don't care how they get them (this means that these parts are still attractive, even when fitted to a basic car which has yet to be fully modded). Obviously, taking the whole car then gives the option of hiding it to strip at leisure, but it won't always be the option chosen, and you could wake up one morning to a well-mangled wreck outside.

Attack 1 The first option to any thief is to smash glass - typically, the toughened-glass side windows, which will shatter, unlike the windscreen. Unfortunately for the thief, this makes a loud noise (not good), but is a quick and easy way in. The reason for taking this approach is that a basic car alarm will only go off if the doors are opened (voltage-drop alarm) - provided the doors aren't opened, the alarm won't go off.

Response 1 A more sophisticated alarm will feature shock sensing (which will be set off by the impact on the glass), and better still, ultrasonic sensing, which will be triggered by the brick coming in through the broken window.

Response 2 This kind of attack can also be stopped by applying security film to the inside of the glass, which holds it all together and prevents easy entry.

Attack 2 An alternative to smashing the glass is to pry open the door using a crowbar - this attack involves literally folding open the door's window frame by prising from the top corner. The glass will still shatter, but as long as the door stays shut, a voltage-drop alarm won't be triggered.

Response This method might not be defeated by a shock-sensing alarm, but an ultrasonic unit would pick it up.

Incidentally, another bonus with ultrasonic alarms is that the sensors are visible from outside - and act as a deterrent.

Attack 3 The next line of attack is to disable the alarm. The commonest way to kill the alarm is either to cut the wiring to the alarm itself, or to disconnect the battery after taking a crowbar to your bonnet catch.

Response 1 If your alarm has extra pin-switches, be sure to fit one to the bonnet, and fit it in the bonnet channel next the battery, so that it'll set off the alarm if the bonnet is prised up. Also make sure that the wire to the pin-switch cannot be cut easily though a partly-open bonnet.

Response 2 Make sure that the alarm module is well-hidden, and cannot be got at from underneath the car.

Response 3 Make the alarm power supply connection somewhere less obvious than directly at the battery terminal - any thief who knows his stuff will immediately cut any "spare" red wires at the battery. Try taking power from the fusebox, or if you must source it under the bonnet, trace the large red battery lead to the starter motor connections, and tap into the power there.

Response 4 Always disguise the new alarm wiring, by using black insulating tape to wrap it to the existing wiring loom. Tidying up in this way also helps to ensure the wires can't get trapped, cut, melted, or accidentally ripped out - any of which could leave you with an alarm siren which won't switch off, or an immobiliser you can't disable.

Response 5 An alarm which has a "battery back-up" facility is best. Even if he's successfully crow-barred your bonnet and snipped the battery connections, the alarm will still go off, powered by a separate battery of its own. A Cat 1 alarm has to have battery back-up.

Fitting a basic LED

All you need for this is a permanent live feed, an earth, a switch if you want to be able to turn it on/off, and the flashing LED itself (very cheap, from any car accessory shop).

An LED draws very little current, so tap into almost any live feed you fancy. If you've wired in your ICE, take a live feed from the permanent (radio memory supply) wire at the back of your head unit, or go into fusebox with your test light (as featured in the alarm fitting procedure). An earth can easily be tapped again from your head unit, or you can make one almost anywhere on the metal body of the car - drill a small hole, fit a self-tapping screw, then wrap the bared end of wire around and tighten it.

The best place to mount an LED is into one of the blank switches the makers love fitting. The blank switch is pried out, and a hole can then be drilled to take the LED (which comes in a separate little holder). Feed the LED wiring down behind the dashboard to where you've tapped your live and earth, taking care not to trap it anywhere, nor to accidentally wrap it around any moving parts.

Connect your live to the LED red wire, then rig your earth to one side of the switch, and connect the LED black wire to the other switch terminal. You should now have a switchable LED! Tidy up the wiring, and mount the switch somewhere discreet, but where you can still get at it. Switch on when you leave the car, and it looks as if you've got some sort of alarm - better than nothing!

Wiring
basics

If you were thinking of taking an alarm live supply direct from the battery - don't. It's better to trace the red lead down to the starter motor, and tap in there.

If a thief manages to get past your bonnet switch, his first thought will be to cut every additional live feed at the battery - of course, if he cuts all the battery leads, you're stuffed (without a battery back-up alarm), but at least you tried…

With your wires identified, how to tap into them?

The best options are:

Soldering - avoids cutting through your chosen wire - strip away a short section of insulation, wrap your new wire around the bared section, then apply solder to secure it. If you're a bit new to soldering, practice on a few offcuts of wire first.

Bullet connectors - cut and strip the end of your chosen wire, wrap your new one to it, push both into one half of the bullet. Connect the other end of your victim wire to the other bullet, and connect together. Always use the "female" half on any live feed - it'll be safer if you disconnect it than a male bullet, which could touch bare metal and send your motor up in smoke.

Block connectors - so easy to use. Just remember that the wires can come adrift if the screws aren't really tight, and don't get too ambitious about how many wires you can stuff in one hole (block connectors, like bullets, are available in several sizes).

Steer clear of connectors like the one below – they're convenient but can give rise to problems.

With any of these options, always insulate around your connection - especially when soldering, or you'll be leaving bare metal exposed. Remember that you'll probably be shoving all the wires up into the dark recesses of the under-dash area - by the time the wires are nice and kinked/squashed together, that tiny bit of protruding wire might just touch that bit of metal bodywork, and cause a fire…

Alarm fitting

In order to try and make this section as useful as possible, we won't show in detail how one particular alarm is fitted, but instead pick out some of the highlights and tips, in case your chosen alarm is different to ours.

Tricks 'n' tips
Drill ONE hole first, and fit the bolt loosely, then drill the second hole. If you drill all the holes at once, you might get one off-centre - this way, it'll definitely line up.

01 Disconnect the battery negative lead, and move the lead away from the battery. Might screw up your stereo settings, but it's better than having sparks flying and your new alarm going mental the minute it's rigged up.

02 Decide where you're going to mount the alarm/siren. Choose somewhere not easily reached from underneath, firstly. On the Corsa, the main problem could be lack of space! Try the siren in position before deciding. It's also best to pick a location away from where you'll be topping up washers, oil or coolant.

03 Loosely fit the alarm to the bracket, to help you decide how well it'll fit in your chosen spot, then take the alarm away. Mark the position of the first mounting hole.

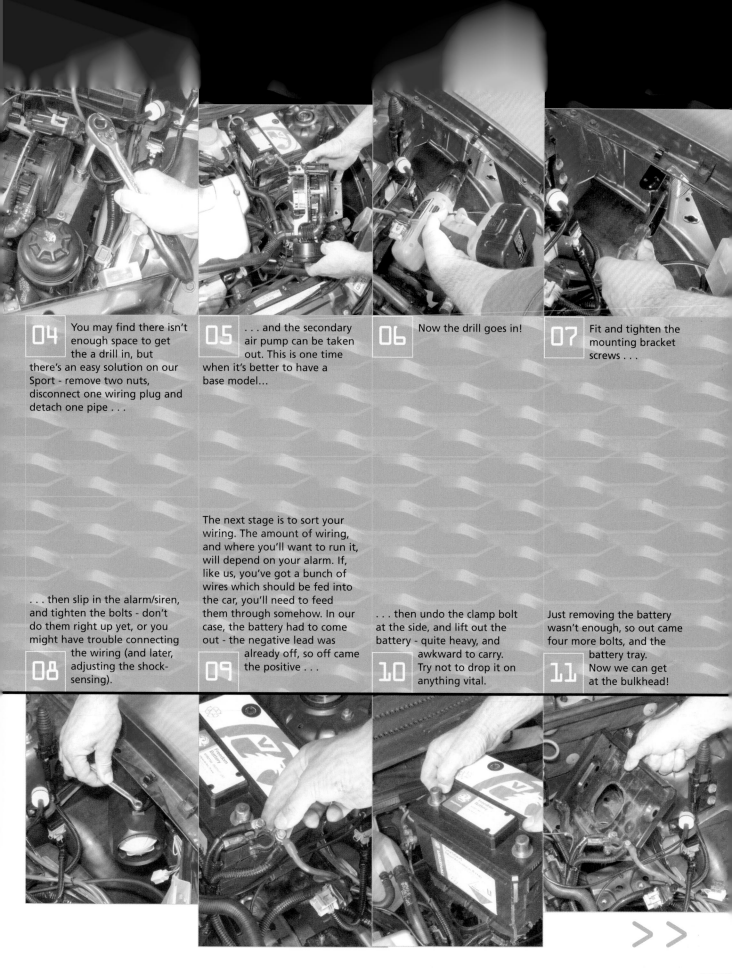

04 You may find there isn't enough space to get the a drill in, but there's an easy solution on our Sport - remove two nuts, disconnect one wiring plug and detach one pipe . . .

05 . . . and the secondary air pump can be taken out. This is one time when it's better to have a base model...

06 Now the drill goes in!

07 Fit and tighten the mounting bracket screws . . .

08 . . . then slip in the alarm/siren, and tighten the bolts - don't do them right up yet, or you might have trouble connecting the wiring (and later, adjusting the shock-sensing).

09 The next stage is to sort your wiring. The amount of wiring, and where you'll want to run it, will depend on your alarm. If, like us, you've got a bunch of wires which should be fed into the car, you'll need to feed them through somehow. In our case, the battery had to come out - the negative lead was already off, so off came the positive . . .

10 . . . then undo the clamp bolt at the side, and lift out the battery - quite heavy, and awkward to carry. Try not to drop it on anything vital.

11 Just removing the battery wasn't enough, so out came four more bolts, and the battery tray. Now we can get at the bulkhead!

>>

Achtung!
When trying to make holes, avoid the very centre of the bulkhead, low down, as this is where the heater matrix is located - put a screwdriver through that, and you won't be a very happy bunny.

12 Choosing a point in the bulkhead where another wire went through, we cut away some of the foam with a sharp knife . . .

13 . . . and, after moving inside the car, made a hole (removing the passenger shelf first, held by one screw and some clips). With the help of a mate, the alarm wiring was soon poked through. It's worth sealing any holes you make in the bulkhead (with silicone), to reduce the chance of water getting in, if you're ever a tad over-eager with the hosepipe!

14 Routing the wires across the inside of the car to the fusebox is easier if you tape them up - just a short bit of tape every six inches or so will hold them nicely bundled, and stop stray ones wandering off. Keeping the wires clear of the pedals might mean drilling the odd hole - there's a handy flange beside the heater, perfect for drilling for feeding wires through. If you're not as brave as this, generous use of cable-ties will make do.

19 Most alarms require you to link into the indicator circuit, so the lights flash on arming and disarming. One obvious place to tap into the indicators is at the indicator stalk, which means removing the steering column shrouds. First, remove three cross-head screws from the lower shroud.

20 Turn the wheel 90° one way, then prise out the trim cap and remove the screw behind. Turn the wheel back straight, then 90° the other way, and repeat the screw-removal process on the other side of the shrouds.

21 With a bit of persuasion, the lower shroud will now come down. Pull the shroud outwards over the ignition switch, and take out the rubber grommet which sits round the switch.

15 Now the wiring's more-or-less in the right place, it's time to start connecting it up. Lives and earths can be sourced from the fusebox - unclip the cover, then remove two screws below the rows of fuses, and it should be possible to lower the fusebox out from the dash. Refer to the wiring diagrams in the Haynes manual, so you know which fuse to aim for in the fusebox, and which colour wire you're after. Most of it can be deduced without major brainwork - honest!

16 Use a 12V circuit tester to locate the wires. Temporarily reconnect the battery. Find an ignition live by connecting the tester to the wire and the croc clip to a good earth (like a door pin switch screw) - check that it's a switched live, not permanent, by turning the ignition on and off. To check for an earth, use the same method, but connect the croc clip to a 12V supply. It's best to tap into the fused side of any wire - to check for this, pull the fuse from the fusebox, and make sure your chosen wire goes dead.

17 Most alarms are wired into the interior light circuit, which is operated by push-switches mounted on the door pillars. To get to the wiring, remove the screw holding the driver's door switch in place, and pull the switch out.

18 Disconnect the wiring plug from the switch, then use a circuit tester to identify which of the two wires is live, and which is earth. Different alarms require you to wire into the interior light circuit on one wire or the other - check the instructions with your system.

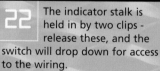

22 The indicator stalk is held in by two clips - release these, and the switch will drop down for access to the wiring.

23 Use a circuit tester to see which wires are live when the indicators are switched on - check both left- and right-hand indicators. You should find it's a black/white wire for left live, and a black/green wire for the right.

24 The best way to connect to any existing wiring without cutting it is to solder on your new alarm wires. It's permanent, won't come loose, and doesn't screw up the original circuit. Strip a little insulation off your target wire, and bare the end of the alarm wire. Twist one round the other, if possible.

25 Now bring in the soldering iron, and join the wires together (preferably, without burning yourself, the dash or the surrounding wires...)

41

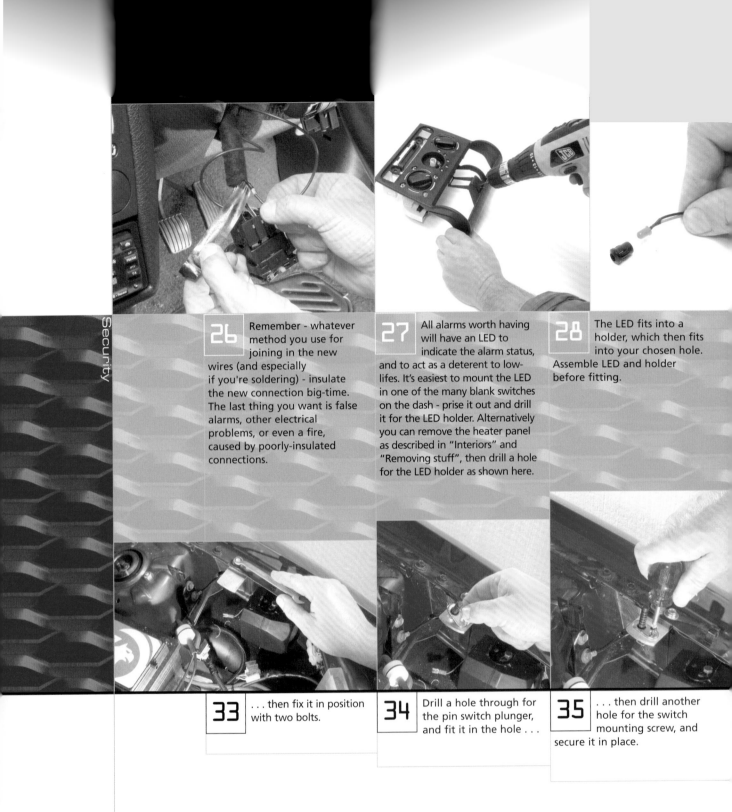

26 Remember - whatever method you use for joining in the new wires (and especially if you're soldering) - insulate the new connection big-time. The last thing you want is false alarms, other electrical problems, or even a fire, caused by poorly-insulated connections.

27 All alarms worth having will have an LED to indicate the alarm status, and to act as a deterent to low-lifes. It's easiest to mount the LED in one of the many blank switches on the dash - prise it out and drill it for the LED holder. Alternatively you can remove the heater panel as described in "Interiors" and "Removing stuff", then drill a hole for the LED holder as shown here.

28 The LED fits into a holder, which then fits into your chosen hole. Assemble LED and holder before fitting.

33 . . . then fix it in position with two bolts.

34 Drill a hole through for the pin switch plunger, and fit it in the hole . . .

35 . . . then drill another hole for the switch mounting screw, and secure it in place.

29 Here's the LED holder being fitted. We cut our LED wiring off the main loom, partly to make fitting to the heater panel easier, and partly because the standard wiring wouldn't reach. Once the panel was refitted, the wires were lengthened (by splicing-in an extra piece) and joined back together - you might find this approach useful too, depending on where you're fitting your LED.

30 You must protect your bonnet with a "pin switch". It's wise to protect your boot this way too. Fit your pin switch close to the battery, to protect the battery connections. First, make up a rough platform to mount your pin switch on, then hold a pen vertically on it and have a mate slowly close the bonnet. Mark where the pin switch needs to be, to work, bearing in mind the "contours" on the bonnet.

31 Your finished platform for the pin switch must be made of something pretty tough (metal seems obvious), otherwise it'll bend when the bonnet's shut. We used a nice thick bit of ally and trimmed it to size.

32 Drilling holes in your wing isn't usually a good idea. Here, it's essential. Drill through the flange at the top of the inner wing, and through your plate . . .

36 The only things left to do now are to connect the wiring from your alarm, and then to test the switch operation. The switch should be set very sensitive - the alarm should go off the minute the bonnet catch is pulled. The switch plunger is usually made of plastic, and can be trimmed with a knife if necessary. If you need to lengthen the plunger, fit a fat self-tapping screw into the top.

37 Now we're nearly there. Connect up the wiring plugs to the alarm/siren, and test it according to its instructions. Most require you to "programme in" the remotes before they'll work. Test all the alarm features in turn, remembering to allow enough time for the alarm to arm itself (usually about 30 seconds).

38 Set the anti-shock sensitivity with a thought to where you live and park - will it be set off every night by the neighbour's cat, or by kids playing football.

39 When you're happy all is well, go round and tidy up the wiring with tape and cable-ties. There's a bit of a dilemma on the alarm fuses - if, like ours, yours are right next to the alarm module, do you tape them up, so a thief can't simply rip them out? But if you've buried them too well, you won't be able to fit a new one so easily if it blows.
Finally - next time you park up, remember to set it!

43

Fitting an auxiliary fusebox

You'll need plenty of fused live feeds from the battery during the modifying process, for stereo gear, neons, starter buttons - and alarms, and it's always a pain working out where to tap into one. If you make up your own little fusebox, mounted somewhere easy to get at, you'll never have this problem again - and it's easy enough to do.

The first job is to run a main supply cable from the battery positive terminal, to inside the car - but don't connect the wire up to the battery terminal just yet. Make sure that the main cable is man enough for all the loads you're likely to put on it - starting with eight-gauge wire (available from all good ICE suppliers) will mean you're never short of current.

Make a note of which fuse is for which circuit, and carry the paper around in the glovebox (along with some spare fuses). If a fuse ever blows, you won't end up with your head stuck under the dash, trying to remember where you tapped in, and where the fuse is. You'll just pull the cover off, and replace the fuse. Who would've thought electrical safety could be so cool?

01 Inside the car, we decided our fusebox would go in the driver's kick panel, in the footwell. To improve access, we first removed the driver's side oddments shelf above the pedals (two screws - one each end).

02 Peel back the door weatherstrip . . .

07 Now the box is taken care of, we need some volts inside the car, from the battery. Having done a little 'research' up behind the dash, we return to the engine compartment, and drill a hole through next to the battery. A strip of masking tape stops the drill bit skating about.

08 Feeding our thick new wire through. The most important detail to notice here is the rubber grommet we fitted to the newly-drilled hole - an essential fitment. Any live wire in contact with a sharp metal edge is a fire waiting to happen - be safe.

09 Make a neat job of fitting the main live feed to your battery terminal, too. This is the proper way, with a ring terminal.

10 We could just have joined the single live feed to the six wires from our fusebox, using a large bullet connector, or a terminal block. Both these are a bit 'bodgy'. We bought a junction box from the same place as the fusebox - this simply gives you two nut-and-bolt connection terminals, and is a much neater solution.

03 . . . remove a screw or two from the front of the sill trim panel . . .

04 . . . then push through the pin securing the side panel . . .

05 . . . and slide the side panel out from the footwell. Removing this panel also gives you access to run wires through into the doors (central locking and ICE). For now, we're going to make up an alloy panel, to take our new fusebox.

06 Make up a suitable panel by trimming up a card template first (or use the old side panel as a guide to the right shape). This is the back of our fusebox (we bought ours from our local Lucas branch), with all six live 'in' feed wires attached - to get a live feed, fit your new wire to the other side of the 'box, and plug in a fuse.

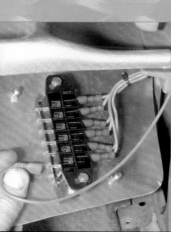

11 With all the connections made for now, the fusebox's alloy panel can be mounted to the car. Don't make too good a job of this - you'll want to get that panel off again, to connect your new feeds as you need them.

12 Here's our first customer - we needed a live feed for our interior neons. All we do is fit a feed wire (off to the neon tubes) to one of our new fusebox terminals . . .

13 . . . plug in a suitable fuse (10A in this case) . . .

14 . . . and clip on the fusebox cover. See how easy it is, to get at the new fuses if they should blow in future? A very well-engineered solution, and far better than tapping into the wiring at random.

 Achtung!
Disconnect the battery negative (earth) lead before starting work, and only reconnect it when all live leads and terminals have been securely connected.

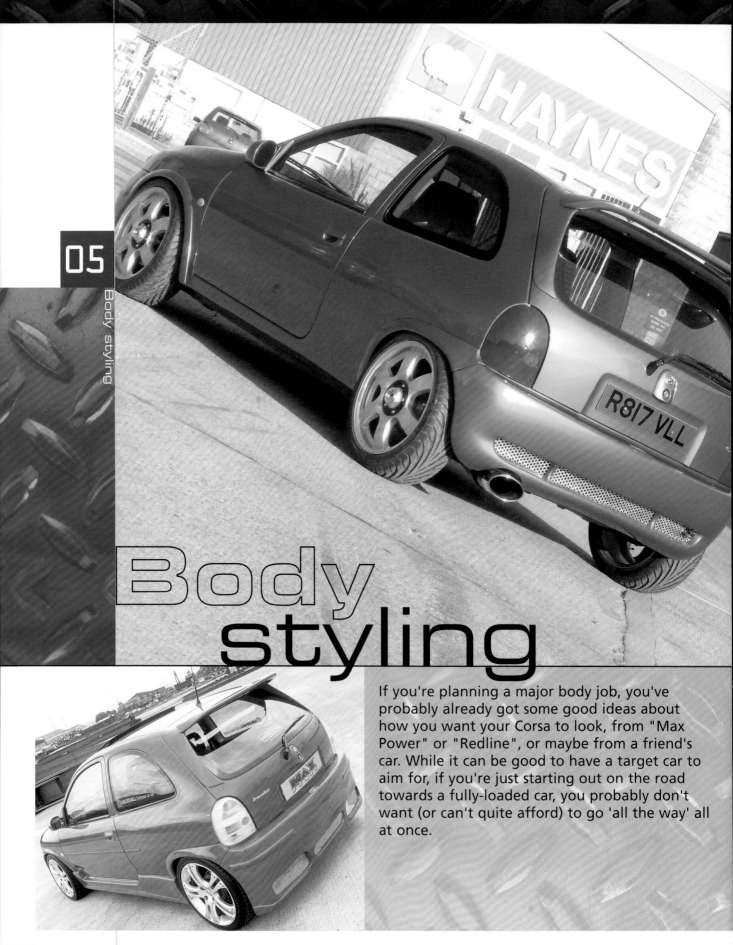

Body styling

If you're planning a major body job, you've probably already got some good ideas about how you want your Corsa to look, from "Max Power" or "Redline", or maybe from a friend's car. While it can be good to have a target car to aim for, if you're just starting out on the road towards a fully-loaded car, you probably don't want (or can't quite afford) to go 'all the way' all at once.

If you're new to the world of modifying, it's a good idea to start with smaller jobs, and work up to the full body kit gradually, as your skills increase; spending loads on a body kit is a pretty dumb idea if you then make a mess of fitting it! There's plenty of small ways to improve the look of your Corsa, which don't cost much, and which are simple enough to fit; start with some of these before you go too mad!

One golden rule with any body mods is to plan what you're going to do, and don't rush it. It's better that the car looks a bit stupid for a week (because you couldn't get something finished) than to rush a job and have the car look stupid forever. Read through the instructions (if any), then see what we say, and plan each stage. Have you got all the tools, screws or whatever before you start, or will you have to break off halfway through? If you get stuck, is there someone you can get to help, or have they gone off for the weekend? Above all, if something goes wrong - don't panic - a calm approach will prove to be a huge bonus.

If a piece of trim won't come off, don't force it. If something feels like it's going to break, it probably will - stop and consider whether to go on and break it, or try another approach. Especially on an older car, things either never come off as easily as you think, or else have already been off so many times that they break or won't fit back on properly. While we'd all like to do a perfect job every time, working on an older car will, sooner or later, teach you the fine art of 'bodging' (finding valid alternative ways of fixing things!). Bodging is fine (if you've no choice) with interior and exterior trim, but make sure there are no safety implications - gluing an exterior mirror on might just about work with the car stood still, but it's going to fall off half a mile down the road, isn't it? Any Tips 'n' Tricks we give in our procedures are things we've tried ourselves, which we know will work. Also, don't assume that you'll have to bodge something back on every time - if a trim clip breaks when you take something off, it might be easier and cheaper than you think to simply go to your Vauxhall dealer, and buy a new clip.

New grille, anyone?

One of the first places anyone's going to look at on your Corsa (after the wheels, maybe) is the front, which can set the tone for the rest of the "look" of your Corsa. As with everything else in the world of modifying, grille fashions change quickly - hopefully, though, this will at least give you some good ideas, and a helping hand to what's involved in fitting.

The standard Vauxhall grilles have got to go if you're serious about modding any Corsa. Be warned - taking off the grille without removing the bumper first will probably bust most of the grille clips. It doesn't come off without a fight.

One of the most common options is to mesh the resulting hole - assuming you're going for a new bodykit (or front/rear bumper combo), then the best time to mesh the hole is when the bumper's off. Most bodykits come with a form of grille built into the front bumper, or you can get aftermarket grilles.

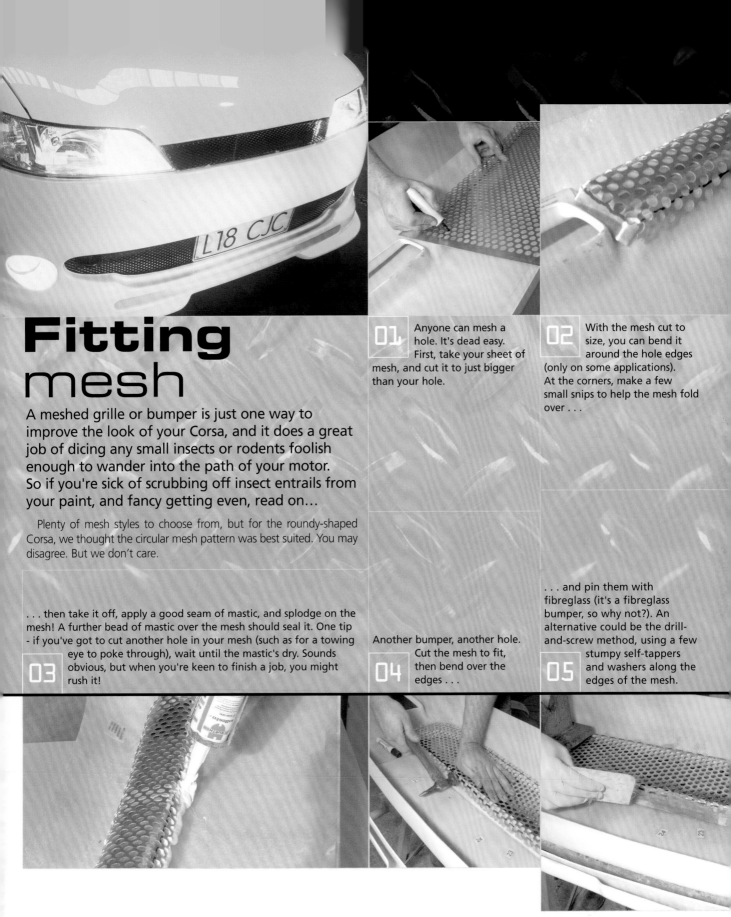

Fitting mesh

A meshed grille or bumper is just one way to improve the look of your Corsa, and it does a great job of dicing any small insects or rodents foolish enough to wander into the path of your motor. So if you're sick of scrubbing off insect entrails from your paint, and fancy getting even, read on...

Plenty of mesh styles to choose from, but for the roundy-shaped Corsa, we thought the circular mesh pattern was best suited. You may disagree. But we don't care.

01 Anyone can mesh a hole. It's dead easy. First, take your sheet of mesh, and cut it to just bigger than your hole.

02 With the mesh cut to size, you can bend it around the hole edges (only on some applications). At the corners, make a few small snips to help the mesh fold over . . .

. . . and pin them with fibreglass (it's a fibreglass bumper, so why not?). An alternative could be the drill-and-screw method, using a few stumpy self-tappers and washers along the edges of the mesh.

03 . . . then take it off, apply a good seam of mastic, and splodge on the mesh! A further bead of mastic over the mesh should seal it. One tip - if you've got to cut another hole in your mesh (such as for a towing eye to poke through), wait until the mastic's dry. Sounds obvious, but when you're keen to finish a job, you might rush it!

04 Another bumper, another hole. Cut the mesh to fit, then bend over the edges . . .

05

Mirror, mirror

Another simple-to-fit essential accessory, the DTM- or M3-style door mirror is well-established on the modified car circuit. Most aftermarket mirrors are supplied in either carbon-look, or (more often) in black for spraying. A cheaper option is to buy carbon-look mirror covers - nowhere near as cool as the real thing, but it might sort you out if funds are tight.

Like so much else, with mirrors, you get what you pay for. Cheapest option is the "universal-fit" mirror. Bear in mind that "universal-fit" does not mean "easy-fit", and almost always means a lot of work is involved cutting and shaping to suit. One problem with the Corsa is that the mirror bases blend into the curves of the front wings. The standard "universal" mirrors come with a flat base, and the fitted effect is not good. Different to standard, sure, but not all it could be - study a few show cars, and decide for yourself. If you can afford it, go for mirrors specifically designed for your Corsa - they'll be much easier to fit, and chances are, they'll end up looking better too, no matter how long you take fitting the cheapies. Your call.

01 Inside the car, prise off the triangular trim panel for access to the mirror mounting bolts. If you're lucky enough to have electric mirrors, disconnect the mirror wiring plug. Might be as well to tape the plug up at some point, rather than just leaving it dangling.

02 The mirror's held on by three bolts - hang onto the mirror while the last one's being removed . . .

03 . . . and you'll remove the mirror in a controlled fashion from outside, rather than picking the bits up off the floor.

04 This next bit won't tax the grey cells too much - fit the new mirror to its base . . .

Fitting **DTM mirrors**

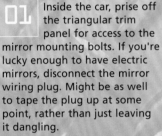

05 . . . and secure with the three small self-tappers. Having had bad experiences with universal-fit mirrors in the past we went for some Corsa-specific DTM mirrors. If you like the easy life, so should you - simple to fit, and look great.

06 Try the assembled mirror in place on the door - it's held on by the three original bolts. When you're happy it fits, it'll need prepping for spraying. If there's any rough edges or seams in the plastic which you're not happy with, this is a good time to sand them out. For more info on painting plastics, see "Painting by numbers" later.

07 To avoid the possibility of rain leaking into the car around the mirror base, apply a bead of mastic to the outside of the door, where the mirror bolts on, before offering up the new mirror. Secure with the three original bolts, and refit the trim panel. Simple. Here's our new mirror in place, with Ed refitting the mirror glass (which he took out prior to spraying).

Racing-style
fuel filler

Ah, the humble fuel filler flap. Not much to it, really - just a hinged metal cover which hides the unsightly filler cap below. At least the Corsa filler flap is round, unlike a few cars (Golfs, for example), so it's easier to re-create the "racing" look. If you don't want to make too much of the flap, there are stick-on fuel cap covers available. Easy to fit, but a bit tacky. For those who want to impress, it's got to be a complete race-style filler, which does away with the flap and the dull black filler cap below, in favour of a fully-functional alloy item to grace the Corsa flanks.

01 First, get rid of the old flap - that's easy. Two screws inside the flap to remove . . .

02 . . . and the flap's history.

> **Achtung!**
> Fuel vapour is explosive. No smoking and no naked lights anywhere near the open fuel filler, please. Even power tools (see step 10) are not strictly allowed - drill slowly to avoid sparks.

It's the same trick to remove the catch, on the opposite side of the hole - remove two screws. If your Corsa has central locking, the filler flap's part of the system - be careful when removing the catch to slide it off the operating rod behind it.

03

Again with the central locking, you'll need to disconnect the flap motor wiring. You can get at this by removing the trim panel inside the boot. We took out the rear light for a view of the wiring plug in question.

04

Now it's time to try the new filler surround in the hole. Our filler needed a little reshaping to fit.

05

By careful sanding-down and repeated trial fittings we got the shape right. Although there's still lots to do yet, now is a good time to spray the surround up - the next step is where it gets glued into the car, and after that, you'll need lots of masking to spray it up.

06

07 Before applying the mastic supplied in the kit, clean up the hole with a suitable degreaser.

08 The mastic should be petrol-resistant (of course). Apply a decent, continuous bead to the hole edge, and to the inside edge of the surround, where it fits over the filler neck.

09 Make sure you get the surround aligned accurately before you press it firmly in place. Pin it in place with a few strips of tape, and leave it for a good few hours to set firm (ideally, overnight).

10 With the mastic fully set, offer up the metal surround and the cap, and decide which way you want the cap to sit, when it's finished. Remove the cap, then mark and drill through the first of the screw holes. As we've said before, don't drill all the holes at once - get at least two screws in before you do the rest.

There's a cork gasket to go on, before finally fitting the metal surround.

11

Secure the metal surround with the screws . . .

12

. . . then fit the cap, and admire the finished result. Except - ours isn't finished, because we knew Ed would be spraying it for us.

13

See what we mean by lots of masking, if you don't spray the surround before the mastic stage?

14

Smoothly does it

If you've bought a basic Corsa, it's understandable that you might not want to declare this fact loudly from the rear end of your car. Badges also clutter up the otherwise clean lines, and besides - you've got a sexy Corsa, so who needs a badge? Most Corsas also come with admittedly-useful but ugly side rubbing strips of some sort - lose these if you're at all serious about raising your game.

General bodywork smoothing takes an awful lot of time and skill, and is probably best done on a car which is then getting a full respray. There's no doubt, however, that it really looks the business to have a fully-smoothed tailgate, or even to have those rather ugly roof gutters smoothed over. Probably best to put the pros at a bodyshop to work on this. De-stripping and de-badging is the next best thing, though, and this can be done at home.

01 Removing the side rubbing strips themselves is easy - heat them up with a hot-air gun, to soften the glue, and peel them off.

02 The same is true of the side badges, and the ones on the tailgate.

03 The problems start when you try removing the industrial-strength double-sided tape underneath. No solvents would touch the glue on this tape. The pros use a drill! You can buy a circular sanding block specifically designed for removing tape and stripes. Try a bodyshop or motor factors. Ours worked a treat, and even buffed up the dulled paint under where the rubbing strip had been.

Fitting a sunstrip

The modern sunstrip - where did it come from? Could it be a descendant of the eye-wateringly naff old shadebands which were popular in the 70s - you know, the ones which had "DAVE AND SHARON" on? If so, things have only got better...

A really wide sunstrip imitates the "roof chop" look seen on American hot rods, and colour-coded, they can look very effective from the front - plus, of course, you can use the space to advertise your preferred brand of ICE (no, no, no! Not a good idea!). As it's fitted to the outside of the screen, the sunstrip has a good chance of seriously interfering with your wipers (or wiper, if you've been converted). If this happens to the point where the wipers can't clean the screen, Mr MOT might have a point if he fails your car... The wiper blades may need replacing more often, and the sunstrip itself might start peeling off - still sound like fun?

There are two options to make your car look (and maybe even feel) cooler:

a The sunvisor, a screen tint band inside the screen, which is usually a graduated-tint strip. As this fits inside, there's a problem straight away - the interior mirror. The Corsa mirror is bonded to the screen, and it seriously gets in the way when trying to fit a wet and sticky (nice!) strip of plastic around it. Go for a sunstrip instead.

b The sunstrip, which is opaque vinyl, colour-matched to the car, fits to the outside of the screen. Much more Sir.

01 This is only stuck to the outside, so do a good job of cleaning - any dirt stuck under the strip will ruin the effect.

02 Spray the screen with water . . .

03 . . . then peel off the backing. The next step is much easier if you get a mate to help out.

04 With one of you either side of the car, check the strip's level - use the top corners of the windscreen rubber as a guide for measuring from. Squeegee out any bubbles, and trim the strip up to the windscreen rubber. You'll make a tidier job of the corners with a really sharp knife, and by cutting in one movement, rather than lots of little nicks.

Legal eagle:
Tinting a windscreen is strictly forbidden, and although it's not illegal to fit a sunstrip, if it comes too far down the screen you could fall foul of the law. If you want to play on the safe side don't make the strip come down below the level of the sunvisors. After all, they're not illegal, so the sunstrip can't be? Some police and MOT testers may disagree, so be warned.

Travelling incognito

As with so much in modifying, window tinting is a matter of personal taste - it can look right with the right car and colour. There are also a wide variety of films available including coloured films, security films and films which reflect UV rays. The only downside is that it might not be legal to use some tints on the road, which is why many are advertised as "for show cars only".

Kits fall into two main groups - one where you get a roll of film, which you then cut to shape, or a pre-cut kit where the film pieces are supplied to suit your car. In theory, the second (slightly more expensive) option is better, but it leaves little margin for error - if you muck up fitting one of the supplied sections, you'll have to buy another complete kit. The roll-of-film kit may leave enough over for a few false starts... Check when buying how many windows you'll be able to do - our Foliatec blue tint kit was only good for three Corsa windows.

The downside to tinting is that it will severely try your patience. If you're not a patient sort of person, this is one job which may well wind you up - you have been warned. Saying that, if you're calm and careful, and you follow the instructions to the letter, you could surprise yourself.

In brief, the process for tinting is to lay the film on the outside of the glass first, and cut it exactly to size. The protective layer is peeled off to expose the adhesive side, the film is transferred to the inside of the car (tricky) and then squeegeed into place (also tricky). All this must be done with scrupulous cleanliness, as any muck or stray bits of trimmed-off film will ruin the effect (tricky, if you're working outside). The other problem which won't surprise you is that getting rid of air bubbles and creases can take time. A long time. This is another test of patience, because if, as the instructions say, you've used plenty of spray, it will take a while to dry out and stick... just don't panic!

Legal eagle:
The law on window tinting currently is that you're allowed up to 25% reduction in light transmission through the windscreen, and up to 30% on all other glass. Many cars come with tinted glass as standard, which has to be taken into account before the tint film is fitted. If in doubt, ask before you buy, and if you can, get a letter from the company to support the legality of the kit, to use in your defence. Some police forces now have portable test equipment they use at the roadside - if your car fails, it's an on-the-spot fine.

Tinting
windows

First, pick your day, and your working area, pretty carefully - on a windy day, there'll be more dust in the air, and it'll be a nightmare trying to stop the film flapping and folding onto itself while you're working. Applying window tint is best done on a warm day (or in a warm garage), because the adhesive will begin to dry sooner. Don't try tinting when it's starting to get dark! It's a good idea to have a mate to help out with this job too.

Step one is to get the window being tinted clean, really clean, inside and out. Don't use glass cleaners (or any other product) containing ammonia or vinegar, since both these will react with the film or its adhesive, and muck it up. It's also worth cleaning the working area around the window, because it's too easy for stray dirt to attach itself to the film - and by the time you've noticed it, it could be too late. On door windows, wind them down slightly, to clean all of the top edge, then **01** close them tight to fit the film.

Before you even unroll the film, take note - handle it carefully. If you crease it, you won't get the creases out. Unroll the film, and **02** cut it roughly to the size of the window.

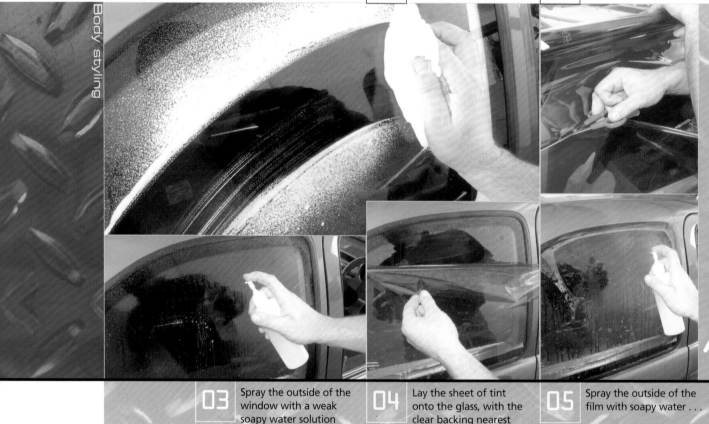

03 Spray the outside of the window with a weak soapy water solution (Foliatec supply a small bottle of Joy fluid in their kit, but you could use a few drops of ordinary washing-up liquid). Get one of those plant sprayers you can buy cheap in any DIY store, if your kit doesn't contain a sprayer.

04 Lay the sheet of tint onto the glass, with the clear backing nearest you. Check this by applying a small bit of really sticky tape to the front and back side - use the tape to pull the films apart, just at one corner. Once apart, the identity of the films will be obvious.

05 Spray the outside of the film with soapy water . . .

07 Using a sharp knife (and taking care not to damage your paint or the window rubber), trim round the outside of the window. On the Corsa rear and tailgate glass, there are wide black bands at some edges of the glass - your tint should be cut just inside these, and NOT to the window rubbers, or the tint won't fit when you transfer it inside. Using a straight-edge to cut to is a big help here.

08 Now go inside, and prepare for receiving the tint. We water-proofed our side trim panel in anticipation of the water which will be used, by taping on some plastic sheet - when doing a door window, it's a good idea to remove the door trim panel first (refer to "Interiors" for door trim panel removal). Spray the inside of the glass with the soapy solution.

09 Back outside, it's time to separate the films. Use two pieces of sticky tape to pull the films slightly apart at one corner.

06 . . . and use a squeegee to get out the air bubbles, sticking the film to the outside of the glass.

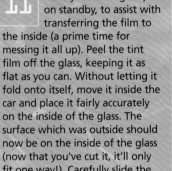

10 As the films come apart, spray more solution onto the tinted piece underneath, to help it separate cleanly. Try not to lift the tint film too much off the glass when separating, as this increases the risk of creasing.

11 Have your willing helper on standby, to assist with transferring the film to the inside (a prime time for messing it all up). Peel the tint film off the glass, keeping it as flat as you can. Without letting it fold onto itself, move it inside the car and place it fairly accurately on the inside of the glass. The surface which was outside should now be on the inside of the glass (now that you've cut it, it'll only fit one way!). Carefully slide the film into the corners, keeping it flat.

12 Spray the film with the soapy water, then carefully start to squeegee it into place, working from top to bottom. We found that, to get into the corners, it was easier to unscrew the blade from the squeegee, and use that on its own for some of it.

13 You'll end up with a few strips at the bottom, which seemingly won't stick to the glass. Don't panic. First, soak up any excess water at the base of the film with paper towels. Now using a hot-air gun to very gently warm the film should help to finish drying, and encourage the film to stick. Be careful squeegee-ing the film when it's dry - risk of damage. Don't lift the film off the glass - the adhesive will stick, given time. Persistence pays off.

Single **wiper**

Another racing-inspired item, the single wiper conversion is a really smart way to make your Corsa stand out from the crowd. Many Corsa owners fit the single wiper because it helps to remove the clutter from the classic Corsa lines - put two Corsas side by side, and the one with one less wiper looks much better. It's a fairly "neutral" mod, too - unlike some, it works well no matter what look you're aiming for.

01 Unsurprisingly, the first job is to remove your old wiper arms. Make sure that the wipers are in their "parked" position, if necessary by flicking the wipers on, then quickly off. Flip up the cap at the base of each arm, and unscrew the 13 mm nut . . .

02 . . . take off the washers, and pull the arms off their splined fittings.

03 Now open the bonnet, and remove a total of five screws which secure the two halves of the plastic scuttle panel . . .

04 . . . the panel halves are clipped under the screen glass - remember for when you're refitting.

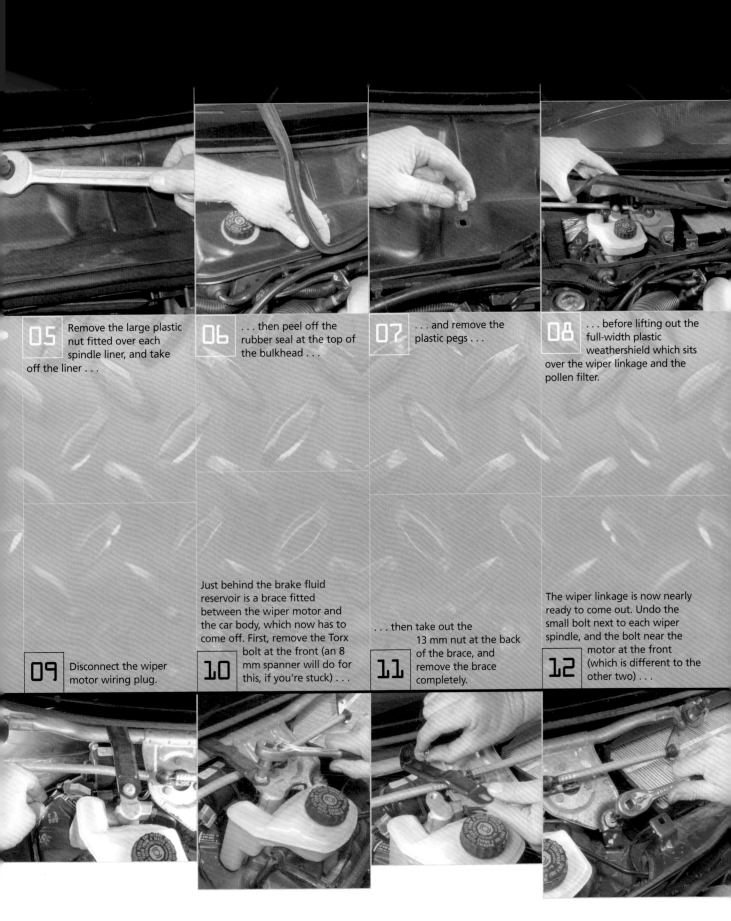

05 Remove the large plastic nut fitted over each spindle liner, and take off the liner . . .

06 . . . then peel off the rubber seal at the top of the bulkhead . . .

07 . . . and remove the plastic pegs . . .

08 . . . before lifting out the full-width plastic weathershield which sits over the wiper linkage and the pollen filter.

09 Disconnect the wiper motor wiring plug.

10 Just behind the brake fluid reservoir is a brace fitted between the wiper motor and the car body, which now has to come off. First, remove the Torx bolt at the front (an 8 mm spanner will do for this, if you're stuck) . . .

11 . . . then take out the 13 mm nut at the back of the brace, and remove the brace completely.

12 The wiper linkage is now nearly ready to come out. Undo the small bolt next to each wiper spindle, and the bolt near the motor at the front (which is different to the other two) . . .

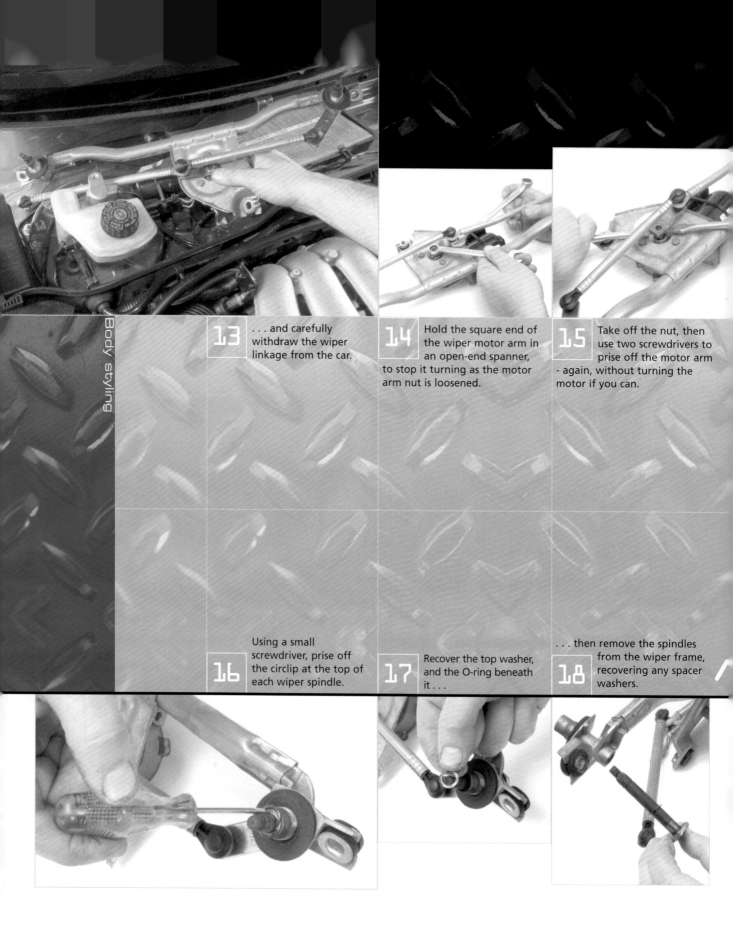

13 . . . and carefully withdraw the wiper linkage from the car.

14 Hold the square end of the wiper motor arm in an open-end spanner, to stop it turning as the motor arm nut is loosened.

15 Take off the nut, then use two screwdrivers to prise off the motor arm - again, without turning the motor if you can.

16 Using a small screwdriver, prise off the circlip at the top of each wiper spindle.

17 Recover the top washer, and the O-ring beneath it . . .

18 . . . then remove the spindles from the wiper frame, recovering any spacer washers.

19 All that's left of the original wiper linkage is now just the frame and the wiper motor. As you won't be needing it again, now's the time to cut off the threaded section of the driver's-side spindle. Trim it neatly down to the flat section. Oh - and make sure you cut the correct one, or you'll be very unhappy!

20 At last - it's time to start fitting the new linkage! First, remove the circlip from the top of the new spindle, then apply some grease to the spindle shaft.

21 The new spindle has to be fitted to the central hole (passenger wiper hole) in the old wiper frame, with the washers and circlips in the right order - check your kit's instructions. On ours, fit the first circlip and an original spring washer, then slip the spindle into its hole.

22 Now add the spindle liner, followed by the O-ring, washer, and a circlip.

Fit the motor arm back onto the motor shaft, noting that, if the motor's still in the parked position, the motor arm should **23** lie directly under the operating arm of the new linkage.

Hold the square end of the motor arm with an open-end spanner, and tighten **24** the shaft nut securely.

Before you forget, it's worth oiling the linkage joints **25** with a spot or two of oil.

Temporarily take out the pollen filter - it's quite likely that the filter will be crushed by **26** the new linkage if you don't.

27 Place the new linkage in position . . .

28 . . . and secure with the three bolts, remembering that the one nearest the motor is different to the other two. Connect the wiper motor wiring plug, and run the motor.

29 You may find that some part of the linkage catches on something - in the case of our kit the rear edge of the pollen filter housing, had to be trimmed up before the knocking noises stopped.

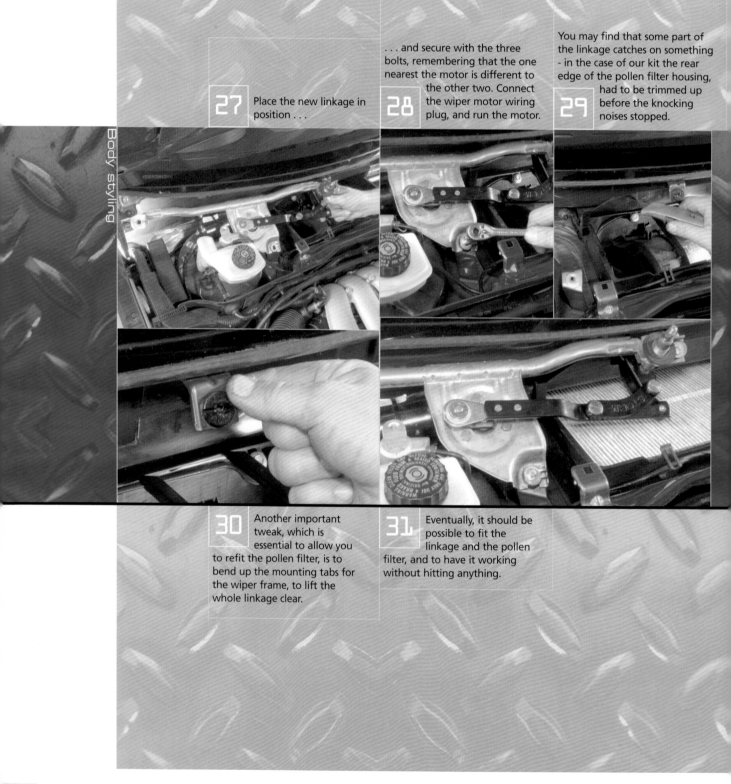

30 Another important tweak, which is essential to allow you to refit the pollen filter, is to bend up the mounting tabs for the wiper frame, to lift the whole linkage clear.

31 Eventually, it should be possible to fit the linkage and the pollen filter, and to have it working without hitting anything.

Our kit was initially set to park the wiper on the passenger side of the screen, so the new wiper was fitted on the splines in that position.

32

The new wiper arm also has a new serrated washer and nut - don't tighten it fully until you've tested the system with the wiper arm attached. If the wiper sweep is not satisfactory, move the arm by one spline and re-test.

33

If you fancy having your wiper arm park in the middle of the screen, in a DTM-style, you'll need to reset the position of the motor arm on its shaft. The motor itself should always be in the parked position before you move the motor arm. Some trial-and-error is unavoidable before you get the perfect result for you. Try not to have it blocking your view too much.

34

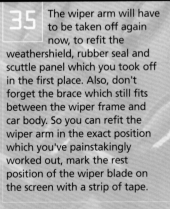

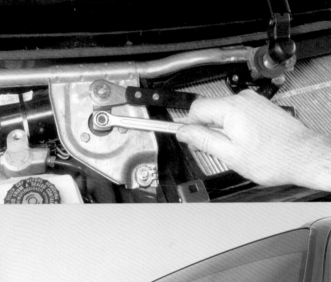

35 The wiper arm will have to be taken off again now, to refit the weathershield, rubber seal and scuttle panel which you took off in the first place. Also, don't forget the brace which still fits between the wiper frame and car body. So you can refit the wiper arm in the exact position which you've painstakingly worked out, mark the rest position of the wiper blade on the screen with a strip of tape.

36 And now - the final photo. After finally tightening your wiper arm nut, it only remains to blank off the hole for the departed driver's-side wiper arm, with this grommet.

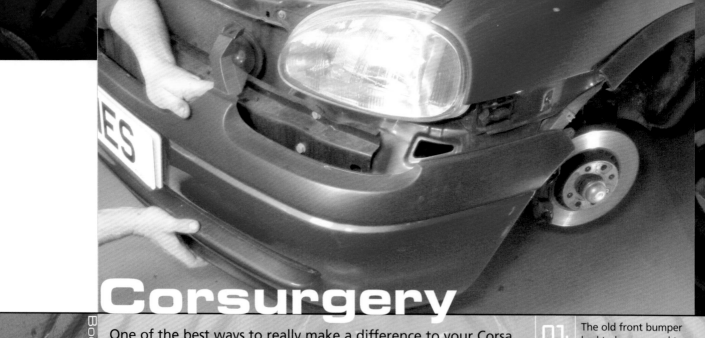

Corsurgery

One of the best ways to really make a difference to your Corsa is to go for a full-on bodykit, but not everyone wants (or can afford) one. So popular is the Corsa, that there are loads of different front and rear bumpers which can be fitted. We decided to be a little bit different, and went for the RS bumper kit, which is now proving popular with owners wanting to re-create the "Euro" look (mega-slammed, with smallish alloys). It looks great and is well-suited to the cars's sexy curves.

01 The old front bumper had to be removed to fit our Morette headlights, so have a look in "Lights & bulbs" for how it was done.

RS bumper kit

02 In theory, if your new bumper's any good, it should go straight on, and line up beautifully. But life's not like that. Ours went on okay in the end, but care had to be taken, especially to get the bumper to clip under our previously-fitted Morettes.

03 Finally, it was possible to get the screw holes to line up, and to start tacking the bumper on loosely. It's vitally important to get the fit dead right before you even think about prepping the bumper for spraying, never mind getting the paint out. The idea is that your freshly-painted (and still easily-damaged) bumper will glide effortlessly into position - or that at least you'll know which bits are tricky to fit, beforehand.

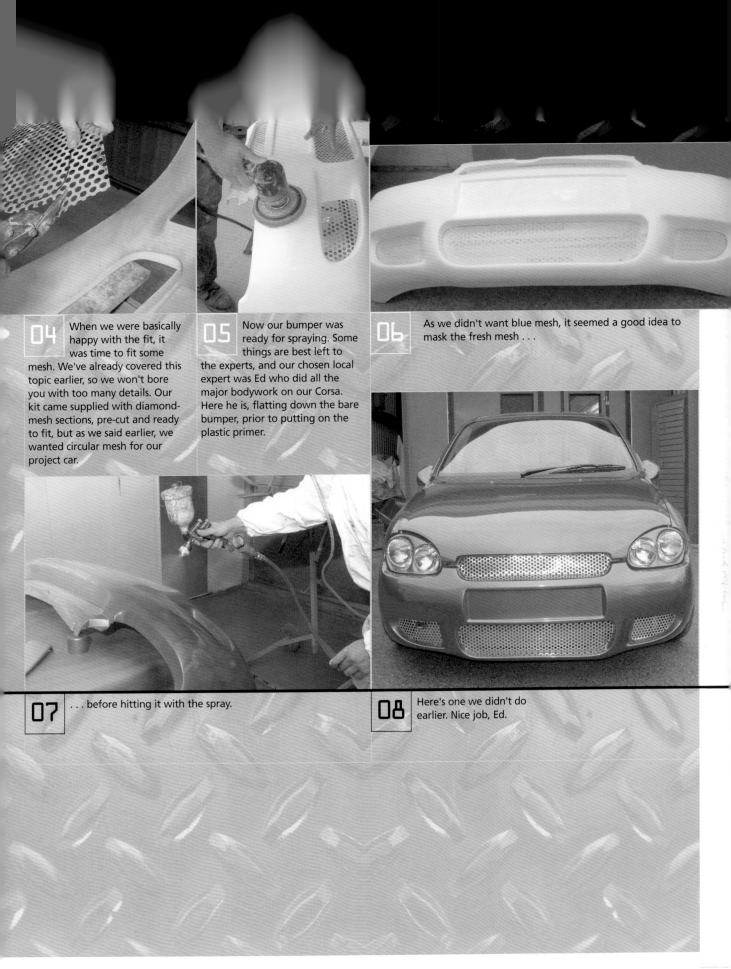

04 When we were basically happy with the fit, it was time to fit some mesh. We've already covered this topic earlier, so we won't bore you with too many details. Our kit came supplied with diamond-mesh sections, pre-cut and ready to fit, but as we said earlier, we wanted circular mesh for our project car.

05 Now our bumper was ready for spraying. Some things are best left to the experts, and our chosen local expert was Ed who did all the major bodywork on our Corsa. Here he is, flatting down the bare bumper, prior to putting on the plastic primer.

06 As we didn't want blue mesh, it seemed a good idea to mask the fresh mesh . . .

07 . . . before hitting it with the spray.

08 Here's one we didn't do earlier. Nice job, Ed.

First job is to take off the rear wheelarch trims. Quite simple, but best done with the rear wheels off, so loosen the rear wheel bolts and jack up the back of the car (see "Wheels & tyres" for jacking info). The arch trims are held on by six plastic nuts, all on the inside edge of the wheelarch, with a clip securing them to the bumper at the back.

Rear **bumper**

01 First job is to take off the rear wheelarch trims. Quite simple, but best done with the rear wheels off, so loosen the rear wheel bolts and jack up the back of the car (see "Wheels & tyres" for jacking info). The arch trims are held on by six plastic nuts, all on the inside edge of the wheelarch, with a clip securing them to the bumper at the back.

02 Under the car, the bumper lower edge has four screws to remove.

03 Unscrew the rear bumper by removing the three screws along its top edge.

04 If necessary trim and cut your bumper to shape.

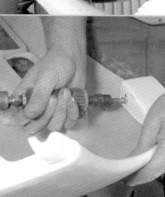
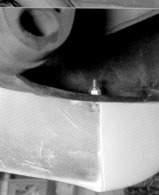

05 It's wise to add a couple of extra bumper mountings at the back of the wheelarches. Drill through the body and the bumper . . .

06 . . . to take an M6 nut and bolt. That's much more solid.

07 We took off our previously-fitted back box, before fitting the new bumper, because we knew the two would collide. Now with the bumper provisionally fitted, it's time to get the tailpipe nestling into the bumper. Offer up the back box, and mark the centre of the tailpipe on the bumper. Now measure the overall width of the tailpipe . . .

08 . . . and mark this either side of the centre point on the bumper, with two x's. Make up a cardboard template of the shape of your tailpipe (in our case, an oval), making it bigger than actual size, to allow a decent clearance around the pipe (say 10 mm, to stop any meltdowns). Use the template to mark out a curve around the two x's.

09 Now get brave, and get out the chopping tools.

10 After possibly some final trimming, your tailpipe should be sitting snugly in your new rear bumper.

11 Time to mesh those unsightly holes, next. We showed you the basics of doing this earlier, so here's an almost-finished shot of our nicely-meshed apertures.

12 This may be a matter of personal taste, but we felt our mesh would look more effective if you couldn't see the blue bodywork behind it. So we sprayed the back end of the car black, below the bumper.

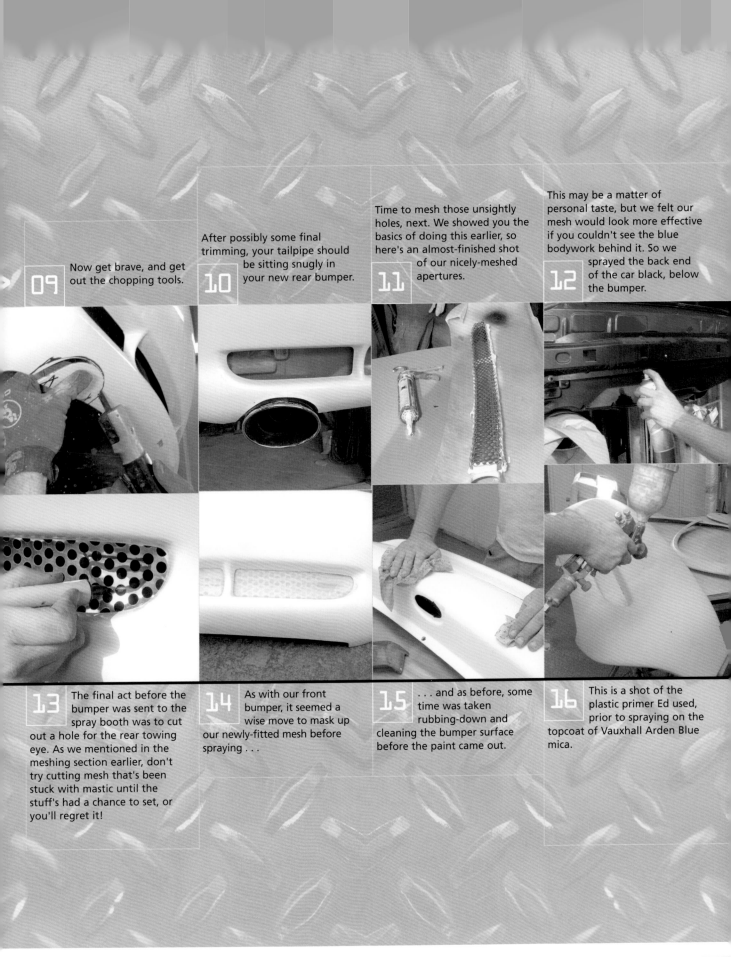

13 The final act before the bumper was sent to the spray booth was to cut out a hole for the rear towing eye. As we mentioned in the meshing section earlier, don't try cutting mesh that's been stuck with mastic until the stuff's had a chance to set, or you'll regret it!

14 As with our front bumper, it seemed a wise move to mask up our newly-fitted mesh before spraying . . .

15 . . . and as before, some time was taken rubbing-down and cleaning the bumper surface before the paint came out.

16 This is a shot of the plastic primer Ed used, prior to spraying on the topcoat of Vauxhall Arden Blue mica.

Painting by numbers

This is not the section where we tell you how to respray your entire Corsa in a weekend, using only spray cans. This bit's all about how to spray up your various plasticky bits before final fitting - bits such as door mirrors, light brows, spoilers, splitters - and even bumpers if you like. As we've no doubt said before, with anything new, fit your unpainted bits first. Make sure everything fits properly (shape and tidy up all parts as necessary), that all holes have been drilled, and all screws, etc, are doing their job. Then, and only when you're totally, completely happy with the fit - take them off, and get busy with the spray cans.

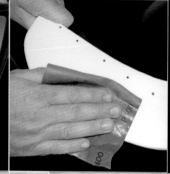

01 The first job is to mask off any areas you don't want painted. Do this right at the start, or you could be sorry; on these door mirrors, we decided to mask off just at the lip before the glass, to leave a black unpainted edge - if we hadn't masked it as the very first job, we would've roughed up all the shiny black plastic next, and wrecked the edge finish.

02 Remove any unwanted "seams" in the plastic, using fine sandpaper or wet-and-dry. Some of these seams look ok, others don't - you decide. Also worth tidying up any other areas you're not happy with, fit-wise, while you're at it.

Especially with "shiny" plastic, you must rough-up the surface before spray will "bite" to it, or it'll just flake off. Just take off the shine, no more. You can use fine wet-and-dry for this (used dry), but we prefer Scotch-Brite. This stuff, which looks much like a scouring pad, is available from motor factors and bodyshops, in several grades - we used ultra-fine, which is grey. One advantage of Scotch-Brite is that **03** it's a bit easier to work into awkward corners than paper.

Once the surface has been nicely "roughened", clean up the surface using a suitable degreaser (one which won't dissolve plastic!). Generally, it's ok to use methylated spirit or cellulose thinners, but test it on **04** a not-so-visible bit first, so you don't have a disaster.

Before you start spraying (if it's something smaller than a bumper) it's a good idea to try a work a screw into one of the mounting holes, to use as a "handle", so you can **05** turn the item to spray all sides.

Another good trick is to use the screw to hang the item up on a piece of string or wire - then **06** you can spin the item round to get the spray into awkward areas.

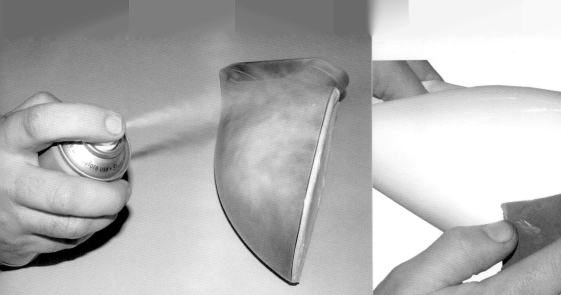

07 Be careful when painting outdoors. If it's at all windy, you'll end up with a really awful finish and overspray on everything (which can be a nightmare to get off). Even indoors, if it's damp weather, you'll have real problems trying to get a shine - some kind of heater is essential if it's cold and wet (but not one with a fan - stirring up the dust is the last thing you want). Give the can a good shake.

08 If you're a bit new at spraying, or if you simply don't want to foul it up, practice your technique first. Working left-right, then right-left, press the nozzle so you start spraying just before you pass the item, and follow through just past it the other side. Keep the nozzle a constant distance from the item - not in a curved arc. Don't blast the paint on too thick, or you'll have a nasty case of the runs - hold the can about 6 inches away - you're not trying to paint the whole thing in one sweep.

09 Once you've got a patchy "mist coat" on (which might not even cover the whole thing) - stop, and let it dry (primer dries pretty quickly). Continue building up thin coats until you've got full coverage, then let it dry for half an hour or more.

10 Using 1000- or 1200-grade wet-and-dry paper (used wet), very lightly sand the whole primered surface, to take out any minor imperfections (blobs, where the nozzle was spitting) in the primer. Try not to go through the primer to the plastic, but this doesn't matter too much in small areas.

13 Especially with a colour like red (which fades easily), it's a good idea to blow on a coat or two of clear lacquer over the top - this will also give you your shine, if you're stuck with a very "dry" finish. It's best to apply lacquer before the final top coat is fully hardened. The spraying technique is identical. Lacquer also takes a good long while to dry - pick up your item too soon for that unique fingerprint effect!

11 Rinse off thoroughly, then dry the surfaces - let it stand for a while to make sure it's completely dry, before starting on the top coat.

12 Make sure once again that the surfaces are clean, with no bits left behind from the drying operations. As with the primer, work up from an initial thin mist coat, allowing time for each pass to dry. As you spray, you'll soon learn how to build a nice shine without runs - any "dry" (dull) patches are usually due to overspray landing on still-wet shiny paint. Don't worry if you can't eliminate all of these - a light cutting polish will sort it out once the paint's hardened (after several hours).

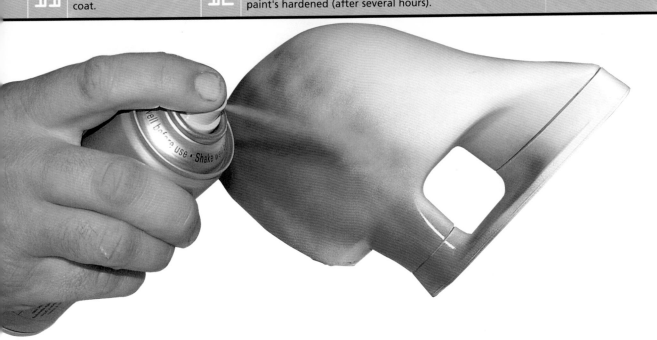

Tailgate
smoothing

Achieving the complete "smooth-tailgate" look isn't too involved
a procedure, providing you know someone who can weld, and
are handy with filler and spray. Completely smoothing the
tailgate is a logical extension of de-badging - the first thing to go
is the rear wiper. Remove the rear wiper arm, motor and washer
jet, and the lock/trim, and fill over the holes - easy, eh?

Well, yes, except that most of the holes are too
big to just fill over, and will probably need
glassfibre matting or welding. The final act of
smoothing is to weld a plate over the rear number
plate recess (cutting the recess out would weaken
the panel), and finish with filler and spray. The
number plate then takes pride of place, nestling
in your new bumper, rear diffuser or bodykit -

though it will need to be lit at night, remember.

If you're going to de-lock the tailgate as well,
you'll need to devise a means of opening it
afterwards. Options range from attaching a cable
to the lock itself, feeding it through for manual
operation, or fitting a solenoid kit and wiring it up
to a convenient switch.

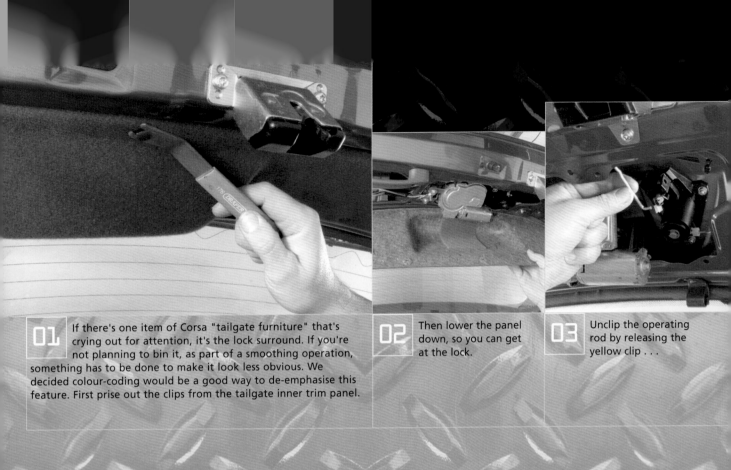

01 If there's one item of Corsa "tailgate furniture" that's crying out for attention, it's the lock surround. If you're not planning to bin it, as part of a smoothing operation, something has to be done to make it look less obvious. We decided colour-coding would be a good way to de-emphasise this feature. First prise out the clips from the tailgate inner trim panel.

02 Then lower the panel down, so you can get at the lock.

03 Unclip the operating rod by releasing the yellow clip . . .

Tailgate
button surround

04 . . . then remove the three nuts . . .

05 . . . take off the lock from the inside . . .

06 . . . and the surround from the outside. Easy!

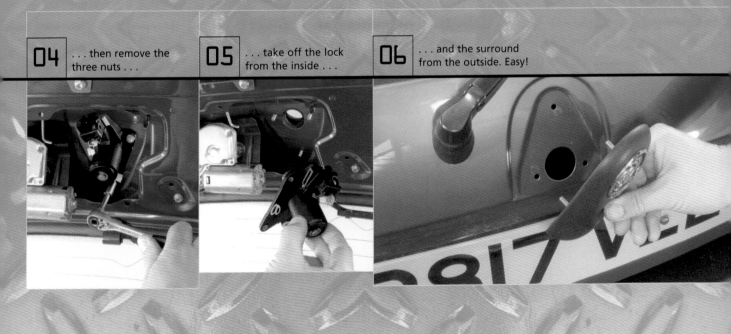

07 With care, the Vauxhall badge can be prised off intact, to be used again - if you like.

08 Clean up the surface, then hit it with a few coats of plastic primer. If you don't want the Vauxhall badge back on, fill the two small holes before spraying.

09 When the primer's dry, spray on the top coat . . .

10 . . . followed by a generous coat of lacquer.

11 We kept our Vauxhall badge - looks alright against the blue paint.

12 Gluing the badge back on's easy, if you use a couple of blobs of glue on the inside, spread out using a small screwdriver.

13 That looks so much better, it's a wonder they don't do it at the factory.

De-locking

One very popular way to tidy up the Corsa lines is to do away with the door locks, and even the door handles - but be careful. Removing the rear door handles (on 5-door models) is okay, legally/MOT-speaking, but removing the front door handles will land you in trouble, come MOT time. Don't spend loads of time (or money, at a bodyshop) having cool mods done, which you then have to spend more money undoing!

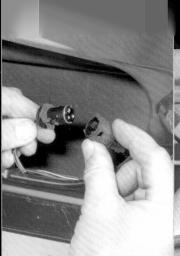

The easiest route to de-locked standard handles is to fit a pair of rear door handles from a 5-door Corsa to the front doors - these look identical to the front handles, but have no locks. And they're pretty cheap, even brand new from a Vauxhall dealer. For a really cleaned-up look, why not colour-code the handles too, so they blend in.

01 First, the door trim panel has to come off. Look in "Removing stuff", in "Interiors" for door trim panel removal. On our Corsa, we had an alarm system wiring plug cable-tied to the base of the door, which had to be removed and separated first.

02 Reach inside the door, and remove the two nuts securing the inner part of the door handle. With these nuts removed, the handle is loose, but it won't come out.

Make sure the door window's wound up for this next bit. **03** Remove the two nuts at the base of the door . . .

04 . . . then pull the window rear guide channel forwards and down, to release the clip at the top, and work it out from the door panel.

05 Again inside the door, use a small screwdriver to release the yellow clip which secures the handle operating rod . . .

06 . . . then the inner handle can be dropped down through the door, and removed. Release any wiring from its clips, as needed.

07 The outer handle is just clipped into the door, and can be prised out from the outside.

08 Before the new outer handle can be fitted, the lock barrels have to be removed from the inner handles. First, prise off the top circlip . . .

09 . . . and take off the operating rod/linkage. You won't be needing that again.

10 After taking off a washer and a spring, you're left with the inner handle and the lock barrel. The barrel is secured by a tiny rollpin - either tap it out, or if that proves difficult drill it out. After this, the lock barrel's history, and the inner handle can now be refitted to the inside of the door.

11 We colour-coded our new handles, and to do this successfully means dismantling the handle. The hinge has to come out first, but it won't just slide out, due to the punch-flattened sections at either end - file these off . . .

12 . . . and the hinge can slide free.

13 There's now a small spring and the white plastic clip for the handle operating rod to take off - note carefully how these fit beforehand. Don't worry - it's only a simple door handle. At last, the handle part comes off the surround. Before starting any spray work, note that there's a couple of rubber handle stops clipped into the surround - makes sense to remove these first.

14 For more details on spraying, see "Painting by numbers" earlier in the section. Even brand-new handles should be treated with Scotchbrite, to improve the chances of paint adhesion.

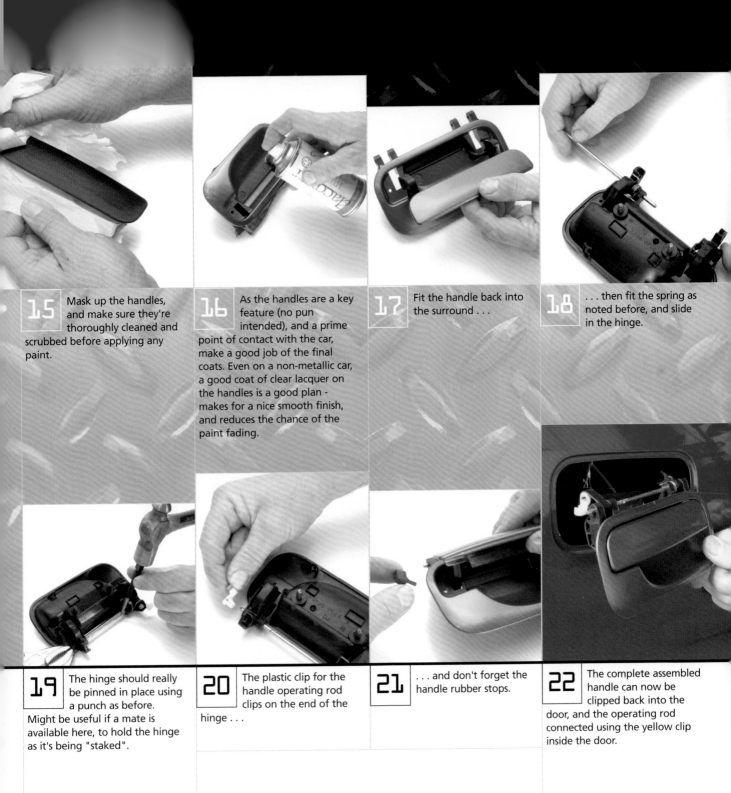

15 Mask up the handles, and make sure they're thoroughly cleaned and scrubbed before applying any paint.

16 As the handles are a key feature (no pun intended), and a prime point of contact with the car, make a good job of the final coats. Even on a non-metallic car, a good coat of clear lacquer on the handles is a good plan - makes for a nice smooth finish, and reduces the chance of the paint fading.

17 Fit the handle back into the surround . . .

18 . . . then fit the spring as noted before, and slide in the hinge.

19 The hinge should really be pinned in place using a punch as before. Might be useful if a mate is available here, to hold the hinge as it's being "staked".

20 The plastic clip for the handle operating rod clips on the end of the hinge . . .

21 . . . and don't forget the handle rubber stops.

22 The complete assembled handle can now be clipped back into the door, and the operating rod connected using the yellow clip inside the door.

Remote locking

So you can lock and unlock your freshly de-locked doors, you'll need to buy and fit a remote central locking kit, which you can get from several Corsa parts suppliers (our Microscan kit is really an extension kit for our chosen alarm, but is pretty typical of what you'll get). If your Corsa already has central locking, you're in luck - the Vauxhall system is the one most compatible with the alarms out there, so you shouldn't even need to buy a central locking interface.

To wire up your alarm interface, the best advice is to follow the instructions with the kit - it's impossible to second-guess detailed instructions like this.

For what it's worth, though, one piece of advice to bear in mind when tracking down the locking trigger wires is not to disconnect the wiring plugs inside the driver's door, for testing - the locking system won't work at all if you do, and you won't learn anything! On our Corsa, the lock and unlock trigger wires were brown/white and brown/red. Our interface's green wire went to the brown/white, and the blue wire to the brown/red.

When you come to test the operation, first make sure at least one window's open, in the unlikely event you lock yourself out. Also check that the doors are locked when the alarm's armed, and not the other way round!

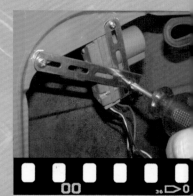

Central locking kit

If your Corsa doesn't have central locking as standard, don't despair - there's several kits out there to help you towards your goal.

Our project Corsa already had central locking, so regrettably there are no Corsa-specific photos to show you, but hopefully, the details below, together with your kit's instructions, will help you out.

Before you start fitting your new lock solenoids, it makes sense to test them. Connect them all together as described in your kit's instructions - with power connected to all the solenoids, pull up on the operating plunger of one, and all the rest should pop up too.

Decide where you're going to mount the lock control unit, then identify the various looms, and feed them out to the doors.

The new lock solenoids must be mounted so they work in the same plane as the door lock buttons. What this means is it's no good having the lock solenoid plungers moving horizontally, to work a button and rod which operate vertically! Make up the

mounting brackets from the metal bits provided in the kit, and fit the solenoids loosely to the brackets, and to the doors.

The kit contains several items which look uncannily like bike spokes - these are your new lock operating rods, which have to be cut to length, then joined onto the old rods using screw clamps. It's best to join the old and new rods at a straight piece of the old rod, so feed the new rod in, and mark it for cutting.

Cut the new rod to the marked length, fit the cut rod to the solenoid, then slip the clamp onto it. Fit the solenoid onto its bracket, and offer the rod into place, to connect to the old rod. Join the new rod and old rod together, and fasten the clamp screws tight. If the clamp screws come loose, you're basically going to be locked out.

Now you can connect up the wires - the easy bit is joining up inside the door. Hopefully, your kit's instructions should be sufficient, but if not, you'll have to resort to the Haynes manual wiring diagrams.

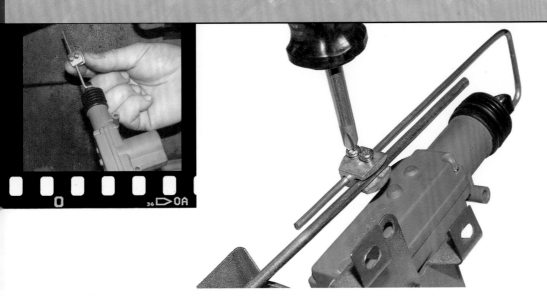

Roof **spoilers**

No Corsa looks complete without a rear spoiler - even if it's just a Sport/GSi standard rear window type, fitted to a basic model. But we don't want to give you that. One popular option for a rear wing for the Corsa is an item of kit fitted to the Citroen Saxo VTS. Add this spoiler to the "tailgate surround" item you probably already have (SRi/Sport/GSi), and you're well on the way to toning up your rear end. So to speak.

There are many other options for a rear spoiler. There are several aftermarket options and there's nothing stopping you adapting one from a different car to make something original.

01 This is one item it'll pay you to take time over fitting - get it off-centre, and it just won't look right. Get a mate to help you hold the spoiler up in place, and establish exactly where your existing bodywork has to be drilled. You need two holes. Measure and establish where the centre of the car is, then measure the gap between the two holes in your new spoiler, and mark the car up for drilling.

02 With the holes drilled, it's fairly straightforward. The spoiler comes with two threaded holes, to accept M6 threaded bar. Cut off a length of this (should be provided with the kit, but it's easy enough to get hold of, if not), and screw it tightly into the spoiler.

03 Offer the spoiler into place, and if your drilling calculations were accurate, the bolt threads should slip effortlessly into your new holes.

Saxo VTS spoiler

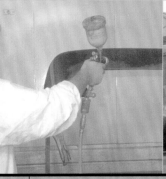

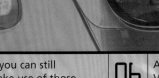

04 All that remains then is to fit some large washers and nyloc (plastic-insert) nuts to the bolts, and tighten up (not too tight, or plastic things will start to protest and crack). When you're happy with the fit, the spoiler can be taken off again, for spraying.

05 This is how the professionals do it, but you can still learn a few tricks here. For instance, make use of those bolts sticking out of the spoiler, for hanging it up so you can spray all round it - even if it is just with cans, at home in the garage.

06 And this is the finished VTS spoiler.

Bum notes
The rear spoiler we were originally supplied with didn't get fitted. Why? Well, it didn't take a bodywork expert to spot that the thing was bent. Now this could, of course, have been down to unsympathetic handling in the post - it happens. The spoiler we actually fitted also came in the post, and wasn't bent.

Wheelarch mods

The law states that not one smidgeon of rubber shall protrude from outside your wheelarches, and the MOT crew will not be impressed if your new rubber's rubbing, either. This presents something of a problem, if you're fitting 8-inch wide 17s, especially to a car that's also had a severe drop job (like our Corsa, on coilovers). If you've exhausted all possibilities with spacers (or wheels with a more friendly offset - see "Wheels & tyres"), those arches are gonna have to be trimmed.

Our wheelarch mods were done at a bodyshop - but if you're brave and reasonably talented, there's nothing to stop you having a go yourself. You won't be doing much trimming with the wheels on - have a look in "Wheels & tyres" for info on jacking the car up, if you need to.

01 The first thing to go is the wheelarch liner - for good. It's held in place by six clips and one bolt. One downside to removing the liner altogether is that it exposes the engine bay to muck thrown up by the tyres - the inner wings are not complete by any means. You might want to trim up a section of the liner, to plug the resulting hole.

02 Next, the wheelarch trim can come off - it's held on by five nuts on the edge of the arch.

03 With the trim removed, mark a line on the arch for cutting, just below the edges of the bolt holes . . .

04 . . . then it's out with the cutting apparatus, and lose some metalwork.

05 Watch your hands and sand down the sharp metal edges, as much as possible.

06 To avoid rust, seal the cut edges of metal with paint or underseal. You know it makes sense.

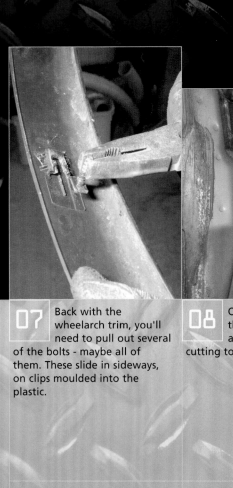

07 Back with the wheelarch trim, you'll need to pull out several of the bolts - maybe all of them. These slide in sideways, on clips moulded into the plastic.

08 Offer the trims up to the newly-cut arches, and mark them up for cutting to the required profile.

09 Cut the arch, in this case with an airsaw, but a hacksaw will do. Don't forget to de-burr the edges, after cutting.

10 Other unfriendly wheelarch features shouldn't be overlooked, either. Any sharp edges or protruding objects should be dealt with. Severely.

Even our new bumper wasn't immune to the treatment, requiring several re-shaping operations with the air hacksaw.

Where you had to remove any bolts, you should now fit "speed clips" in their place . . .

. . . to take self-tapping screws when you come to refit the arch trims.

Having butchered your arch trims, it's only fair to treat them to a little paint. Colour-coding's a good way to cover up any over-enthusiastic cutting or de-burring, too. Here's a pair of our arch trims, roughed-up and prepped for spraying.

11

12

13

14

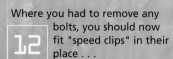

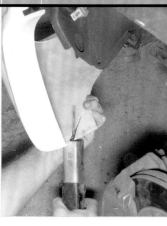
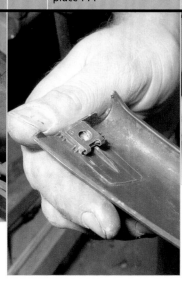

Rear arches

01 Trimming-up the rear arches is essentially the same procedure as for the fronts, with one important difference. To accommodate wide rear rubber, the metal edge of the arch has to be flared outwards. This can be done by a bodyshop, or in the absence of proper tools, you could always "dolly" out the arch edge using a hammer and block of wood. One piece of advice - heat the arch edge thoroughly before you start - this helps the metal to bend without cracking the paint.

02 Again, mark a line below the bolt holes, and trim off the excess metal . . .

The rest of the operations are as for the front arches, except that the bolts used on the rear arch trims have to be cut off - it shouldn't be necessary to cut more than just the top bolts. When you come to refit the trim, use the original bolts where you can - at the back, we glued in two longer bolts.

Otherwise, use mastic/sealant (or even No-Nails) to glue the trims on . . .

03 . . . then de-burr the edges, and paint to prevent corrosion.

04

05

06 . . . and invest in some clamps. Good luck!

Bonnet vents

Once you've got your bodykit on, you may well want to fit some kind of bonnet vent. This is a very tricky job to tackle yourself, unless you're really that good, or that brave. Leave it in the hands of the professionals, is our advice. Plenty of options - you can get little louvres stamped in as well, to complement your Evo, Impreza, Integrale or Celica GT4 vent. You could even go for something more original. There are even people using the bonnet scoop from a Kia Sedona people carrier! Truly, anything goes.

Water features

This is all about giving you a couple of highly-visible features up front. Forget Charlie Dimmock. Do not even think Charlie Dimmock. Washer jet lights are now almost expected at a cruise, and it's such a simple feature to fit, it's nearly a crime not to. Course, our friendly fellas in blue uniforms don't see it quite that way - showing anything other than a white light up front is illegal, and plenty of people get stopped for it. The best answer? Fit them by all means, but rig them into a well-placed switch for emergencies.

01 Removing the boring standard washer jets is easy, and will take no time at all. On the underside of the bonnet, peel back the rubber sleeve at the base, then pull off the clear tubing. Our pyromaniac mechanic couldn't resist getting his fag lighter out on this – provided you stop short of melting the tube, a bit of heat helps it off.

02 To remove the jet from the bonnet, use a small screwdriver to release the plastic securing tab, and it's history. Try not to break it - you might be refitting it one day.

03 Slide the rubber base gasket up the wire and onto the bottom of the new washer jet. On a Corsa bonnet, all this washer really does is save your paint from getting scratched.

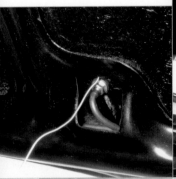

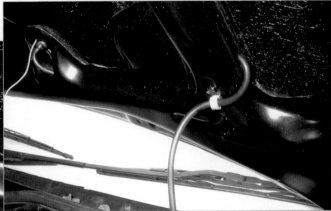

04 Pop the new jet into the bonnet and slide the rubber washer up the wire. The rubber washer has a small recess cut out to stop the retaining nut crushing the wire.

05 Add the metal washer and retaining nut and tighten. With the old washer pipe refitted, the end result should look something like this.

06 This next bit is really fiddly, so take your time. The wires from the jets need to be routed into the engine bay, where they will be passed through the bulkhead to the switch on the dash. Use a length of welding wire and attach the end of each wire to it, then pull them through behind the bonnet braces. Using cable-ties attach the two wires to the existing washer pipe until you reach the battery.

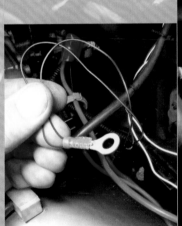

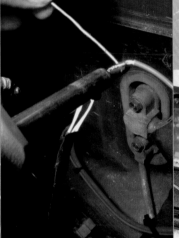

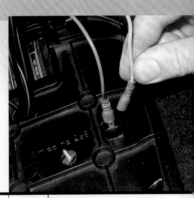

07 Each jet has a black and a white wire - according to the instructions, the blacks are earths. Using a ring terminal, connect the two black wires together, then fit them to a convenient earth point (should be lots available under the bonnet, or make your own by drilling a hole in the metalwork).

08 Now to the two white wires (the live feeds). At this point, we have to add a length of our own wire, as the wire supplied is not long enough to get it to its final resting place inside the car. Solder the two white wires to the new wire, remembering to insulate the joint afterwards. Or you could use crimps.

09 We've decided to add a switch to the jets (good idea, seeing as they're for show use only, thus illegal). So the next job is to mount the switch to a suitable area inside the car. After removing your chosen panel, mark and cut out a hole for the switch to sit in.

10 Feed the new wire through the bulkhead, under the dash and into the driver's footwell, where a female connector will join the wire to the back of the switch. The final stage of the wiring is to find yourself a live feed. We've taken one from our fusebox, but a fused feed from the battery will be fine. Another female crimp joins our yellow live wire to the switch and completes the circuit.

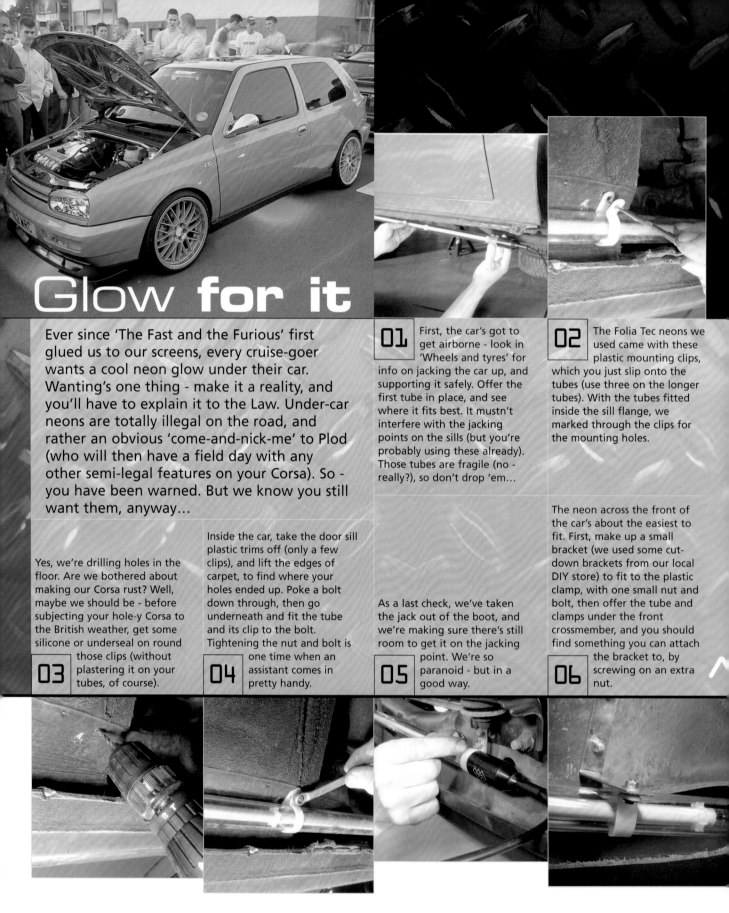

Glow for it

Ever since 'The Fast and the Furious' first glued us to our screens, every cruise-goer wants a cool neon glow under their car. Wanting's one thing - make it a reality, and you'll have to explain it to the Law. Under-car neons are totally illegal on the road, and rather an obvious 'come-and-nick-me' to Plod (who will then have a field day with any other semi-legal features on your Corsa). So - you have been warned. But we know you still want them, anyway...

01 First, the car's got to get airborne - look in 'Wheels and tyres' for info on jacking the car up, and supporting it safely. Offer the first tube in place, and see where it fits best. It mustn't interfere with the jacking points on the sills (but you're probably using these already). Those tubes are fragile (no - really?), so don't drop 'em...

02 The Folia Tec neons we used came with these plastic mounting clips, which you just slip onto the tubes (use three on the longer tubes). With the tubes fitted inside the sill flange, we marked through the clips for the mounting holes.

The neon across the front of the car's about the easiest to fit. First, make up a small bracket (we used some cut-down brackets from our local DIY store) to fit to the plastic clamp, with one small nut and bolt, then offer the tube and clamps under the front crossmember, and you should find something you can attach the bracket to, by screwing on an extra nut.

03 Yes, we're drilling holes in the floor. Are we bothered about making our Corsa rust? Well, maybe we should be - before subjecting your hole-y Corsa to the British weather, get some silicone or underseal on round those clips (without plastering it on your tubes, of course).

04 Inside the car, take the door sill plastic trims off (only a few clips), and lift the edges of carpet, to find where your holes ended up. Poke a bolt down through, then go underneath and fit the tube and its clip to the bolt. Tightening the nut and bolt is one time when an assistant comes in pretty handy.

05 As a last check, we've taken the jack out of the boot, and we're making sure there's still room to get it on the jacking point. We're so paranoid - but in a good way.

06 The neon across the front of the car's about the easiest to fit. First, make up a small bracket (we used some cut-down brackets from our local DIY store) to fit to the plastic clamp, with one small nut and bolt, then offer the tube and clamps under the front crossmember, and you should find something you can attach the bracket to, by screwing on an extra nut.

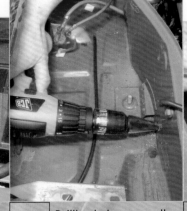
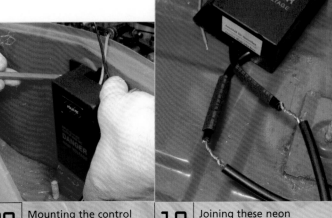

07 Tubes nicely mounted, but plenty of heavy cables dragging on the floor? Time to wire it all up, then. Decide where the control box is going (ours went next to the battery), and start feeding the two nearest tube cables in towards the battery (okay, so this isn't a Corsa. but you get the idea).

08 Drilling holes may well be necessary as part of the wire-routing process - for this one, we were lucky to get our cordless back out! The most important bit is fitting a grommet to the new hole. If you study the neon's control box, you'll see it mentions something about 6000 volts. If one of those cables rubs through on a sharp-edged hole - we'll leave the rest to your imagination.

09 Mounting the control box somewhere near the battery seems a good move - lots of lives and earths close to hand. However, if you remove the battery (like we did) to give yourself more room, check before finally fitting the box that the battery will go back in. That's what we call a Homer moment.

10 Joining these neon cables together requires a special technique - strip about an inch off the thick insulation of each wire, and twist the bared ends together. Do not use solder. Do not use bullets, terminal blocks, or any other joiners. Do not pass Go. Apparently, any method other than the wires-twisted-together one might cause the tubes to malfunction. So there.

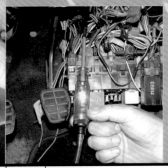

11 You are allowed to tape up the joint - which is just as well, with all those volts going through it. Don't be shy with the tape. And tidy all that wiring up, with some cable-ties – we don't want a high-voltage wire flapping around in the engine bay…
Two more wires to go now, at

12 the control box - a red live, and a black earth. We've got the battery earth lead right in front of us - shame not to use it. Unbolt it from the car, and fit the black wire to the earth lead mounting bolt, using a ring terminal.

13 You must be able to control under-car neons - a switch is essential. Run the red wire from the control box into the car, and feed it to one side of your new switch (this red wire became a blue wire by the time it reached the switch). Here, we're joining on another red wire, which is going to be our live feed. We fitted our switch in the centre console, on a new alloy plate.

14 To get a live feed, you have two options. You can poke about behind the fusebox with a test light and your Haynes wiring diagrams for an existing wire to join onto (tricky, but check out the section on de-locking), or you can run one into the car from the battery (easy).

Lights
& bulbs

Being scene

Lights - one of the easiest and coolest ways to trick up your Corsa. Several options here, so we'll start at the front, and work back.

Headlights

Almost nothing influences the look of your Corsa more than the front end, so the headlights play a crucial role.

What's available?

For most people, there's essentially four popular routes to modding the Corsa headlights - two cheap, and two rather less cheap (but more effective).

The popular cheap option is stick-on headlight "brows", which do admittedly give the rather cute Corsa front end a tougher look. The brows are best sprayed to match the car, before fitting - some have sticky pads, others can be fitted using mastic.

Another cheap option is again stick-on - this time, it's stick-on covers which give the twin-headlight look. This is basically a sheet of vinyl (shaped to the headlights, and colour-matched to your car) with two holes cut in it. Dead easy to fit, but a bit of a style no-no.

Getting more expensive, we're looking at complete replacement lights. Cheapest option here are replacements with smoked or colour-tinted glass - most people go for the smoked. Combine these with light brows, and the car will look a lot better. When you're buying lights, make sure they're UK-legal - they must be E-marked, and for right-hand-drive (any advertised as LHD will cause you trouble at MOT time, because the dipped beam pattern will be wrong).

The most expensive option is to go for "proper" twin-headlights, available as a kit from the French company Morette. Typically around £300 a set at time of writing, these are by no means cheap. The light surrounds have to be sprayed to match your car, and fitting is not without some difficulties, but the finished result is worth it. Did we say "most expensive"? For those with money to burn, why not try fitting the increasingly-popular Golf Mk4 lights, which really suit the curvy Corsa. Mk4 Astra lights look great, too.

Did you know?

The popular twin-headlight look was derived from a cunning tweak first employed in the Touring Cars, years ago. Some teams homologated a twin-headlight unit, but for racing, turned one pair of the "headlights" into air inlets, to direct air from the front of the car to brake ducts or into the engine air intakes, as required. Think about it - why else would the touring cars bother with headlight mods? Until recently, there were no night races!

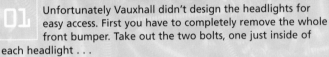

01 Unfortunately Vauxhall didn't design the headlights for easy access. First you have to completely remove the whole front bumper. Take out the two bolts, one just inside of each headlight . . .

02 . . . then remove the screw each side, just inside the front of the wheelarch.

03 There's five screws altogether along the front bottom edge of the bumper . . .

Morette twin headlights

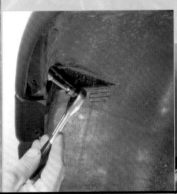

04 . . . then inside the top of the wheelarch, flick out the plastic cover and remove one plastic nut each side. You should now have a very wobbly bumper.

05 The back edge of the bumper is pegged to the wheelarch trim by a stud - the plastic nut for which, you've just removed. Pull the wheelarch trim out from the bumper . . .

06 . . . and (ideally with the help of a mate), your bumper can now be gently dumped on the ground.

07 At last - we can take out the headlights. Two bolts per light, one at the inside, one at the top . . .

08 . . . then the light can be pulled forward to release the clip at the bottom, and you can start disconnecting the wiring plugs. There could be as many as four plugs to remove - sidelight, indicator, main/dipped beam, and headlight levelling (if you have it). Might be an idea to label the plugs as they come off. Eventually, the headlight can be removed completely. Also remove the white plastic clip fitted at the base of the headlight hole.

Tips 'n' tricks
Before we go any further, it's worth mentioning that the Corsa Morette lights come in two flavours - pre-1996, and 1997-on, with or without electric levelling. That's four flavours, then. Make sure you get the right kit for your car.

09 Corsa headlights have indicators built into them. Morette lights for the Corsa do not. Therefore, new front indicators are provided, to be fitted into the front bumpers - we'll show how to do this to the standard bumpers. To start with, the metal bumper bar has to be cut at either end, to make room for the new light units. Measure the distance given in the instructions . . .

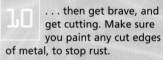

10 . . . then get brave, and get cutting. Make sure you paint any cut edges of metal, to stop rust.

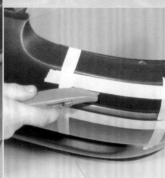

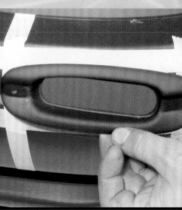

11 Before cutting the two holes in the plastic bumper, you'll need to establish where the exact centre of the bumper is (looks better if the new indicators are evenly spaced!). There's a handy central join in the bumper bottom lip, but take other measurements as well, to double-check. With a centre-line marked, you can measure out to the sides . . .

12 . . . then measure and mark the positions for the indicator light holes . . .

13 . . . before getting Stanley out to cut the holes. You might need more than one new blade, before you're finished. If you're more of a dab hand with a jigsaw, this might be less effort.

14 Try the indicator surrounds in the holes, and trim up as needed.

15 Now take the new indicators, fit centrally into the holes, and drill the screw holes. The screw holes must be fitted with the metal clips provided, to give the self-tappers something to bite into - the clips slide into the edges of the main hole, aligning with the screw holes.

16 Fit the indicator and surround into the bumper, and secure with the self-tapping screws. When the bumper's finally refitted, feed the old indicator wiring plug (blue/white) down to the new indicator, and connect both sides up.

17 Of course, if you don't like the new indicators supplied with the kit, you could always go your own way. Using the same methods to establish the bumper centre-line, drill a hole either end, and fit some oval side repeaters into the bumper. Ours were clear (you could go smoked or coloured), and had a self-adhesive backing. Fitting couldn't be much easier, but the wiring plugs might need to be chopped and spliced.

18 It's about time we sorted the Morettes themselves. If your Corsa's got electric-levelling lights, prise the motors out of the old headlights, releasing the balljoint fitting, then clip into the new lights with a bayonet fitting. The motors will sit in various positions in their brackets - wait 'til the lights are in before deciding this. The length of the motor operating rod can be adjusted if necessary using the thumbwheel on the back of the motor.

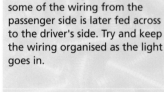

19 Now the new lights can be fed in - do the passenger side first, as some of the wiring from the passenger side is later fed across to the driver's side. Try and keep the wiring organised as the light goes in.

20 Connect up the sidelight first (black/blue plug), then the large square main/dipped beam socket (shown here) and the levelling motor plug (black/green plug).

21 The inner lights on the Morettes are the main beams, operated through a relay. They're wired up by splicing the relay wire (provided) onto the white wire on the square main/dipped beam socket. Many people don't approve of this type of connector - they're thought to be unreliable in service. If you must, at least do the job properly - clip round your target wire . . .

22 . . . and crush the connector to make the joint. Close up the plastic clip to seal the connector. If you want a more reliable joint, strip and solder the wires, remembering to insulate the joint afterwards. Even bullets or blocks are preferable…

Vauxhall Corsa

23 Now the passenger-side light can be bolted in. Use this arrangement of oversized washers, toothed washers and a nut to fix the light through the square hole at the base. When the light's in the hole, access to put the nut on is awkward. Depending on how crowded your Corsa underbonnet area is, some further minor dismantling might be required…

24 With the bottom fixing tightened, the two upper ones can be sorted - the original bolts and holes are re-used. No worries.

25 Before going any further, sort out the remaining wires. First, there's a black wire with an in-line fuse and a ring connector, which goes to the battery positive terminal. Connect it up, and find a secure place for the fuse holder (either tape or cable-tie it in position).

26 Next, the shorter grey wire with a ring connector should be fitted to a good earth point on the passenger side of the car (we chose one of the radiator bracket bolts).

27 The remaining wires have spade connectors (and there's another grey with a ring connector) - these have to be fed across the car, to the driver's-side headlight. Make sure the wires are routed so they can't get trapped, cut, or melted. Connect the wires as per instructions (finding another earth point for the other grey wire) before fitting the right-hand headlight, using the same procedure as for the left.

28 Before the headlight shells are sprayed, this is what you should have. The shells are secured by five screws, and by one of the light mounting bolts, so at least the light doesn't have to come off again, for spraying. Like the oval indicator? At least it's probably legal, unlike what we did next…

29 When our Corsa went to Ed for spraying, he had another idea for our front indicators - mount them inside the headlights. Taking out the indicator bulbholder from the old headlights, he then removed the sidelight bulbholder from the new Morette outer light, and fitted the indicator in its place.

30 Now lacking a sidelight, he made a new hole in the inner Morette light, fitted a grommet, and gave the sidelight bulbholder a new home. Looks sweet, but is it legal? Probably not at night, with the dipped beams interfering with the indicators. How observant is your MOT tester?

Headlight **bulbs**

Currently very popular, the new high-power and "blue" headlight bulbs are an excellent way to boost headlight performance, and to give more of a unique "look". However, fitting these bulbs is not without its pitfalls. First, some of the bulbs on sale are in fact illegal for use in this country - too powerful - and as with all other non-standard lights, the boys in blue will love pulling you over for a word about this, so ask before you buy and choose a reputable brand.

Even if you're not bothered about the legality of over-powerful bulbs there are various problems associated with monster bulbs (and we're talking about those in excess of 60W/55 power here). It's almost too easy to fit mega-powerful bulbs, not realising the dangers.

These bulbs give off masses of heat, and plenty of people have melted their headlights before they found this out. The excessive heat these bulbs generate will damage the headlights eventually, either by warping the reflector or by burning off the reflective coating. Or both.

The increased current required to work these bulbs has also been known to melt wiring (this could lead to a fire) and will almost certainly burn out your light switch. There's no headlight relay fitted as standard, so the wiring and switch were designed to cope only with the current drawn by standard-wattage bulbs; if you're going for high power, a relay must be fitted (much as you'd have to, to fit foglights or spots).

01 To get at the driver's side headlight, on some Corsas, you'll find an air inlet duct in the way (that's if you haven't already got your induction kit fitted). Turn this plastic fastener through 90° . . .

02 . . . then lift the duct away, unclipping it as necessary.

03 At the back of the headlight, pull off this plug . . .

04 . . . then whip off the rubber.

Blue headlight bulbs

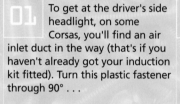

Tips 'n' tricks
Put the old bulbs in the glovebox - carrying spare bulbs is a good way to get a let-off from Plod, if they stop you for having a bulb gone. "Yes, officer, I'll replace it right now!"

05 You'll now find a wire clip with two prongs on it, which you squeeze together, and hinge down . . .

06 . . . and now the bulb falls out - if it hasn't already. If you've any plans to re-use it or sell it, hold it only by the metal bits, not the glass.

07 Now to fit our blue bulbs (H4 type). The bulb packaging makes it very easy to pull the bulb out by the glass, which will instantly ruin it. The correct way to open this box is from below. If you touch the bulb glass, wipe it clean with a little meths (methylated spirit - colour purple, not white spirit - colourless). Otherwise, your new bulb will burn out even faster than stated on the packet.

08 Fit the new bulb, secure with the wire clip, fit the rubber boot over the bulb connectors, and plug in. Simple.

Front fog/spotlights

If you're fitting fogs, they must be wired in to work on dipped-beam only, so they must go off on main beam. The opposite is true for spotlights. Pop out the main light switch (or pull down the fusebox) and check for a wire which is live only when the dipped beams are on. The Haynes wiring diagrams will help here - on our Corsa, it was a white and yellow wire we needed.

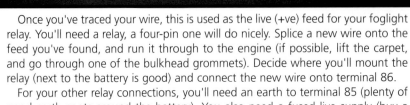

Once you've traced your wire, this is used as the live (+ve) feed for your foglight relay. You'll need a relay, a four-pin one will do nicely. Splice a new wire onto the feed you've found, and run it through to the engine (if possible, lift the carpet, and go through one of the bulkhead grommets). Decide where you'll mount the relay (next to the battery is good) and connect the new wire onto terminal 86.

For your other relay connections, you'll need an earth to terminal 85 (plenty of good earth spots around the battery). You also need a fused live supply (buy a single fuseholder, and a 15 or 20 amp fuse should be enough) and take a new feed straight off the battery connection - this goes to terminal 30 on your relay.

Terminal 87 on your relay is the live output to the fogs - split this into two wires, and feed it out to where the lights will go. Each foglight will also need an earth - either pick a point on the body next to each light, or run a pair of wires back to the earth point you used earlier for your relay. Simple, innit?

With the wiring sorted, now fit the lights. Most decent foglights come with some form of mounting brackets. To look their best, hopefully your new lights can slot into pre-cut holes in your new front bumper/bodykit.

To connect the wiring to the lights, splice the terminal 87 wires to the new light's wiring plugs.

Rear light clusters

Available in as many colours as the front and side indicators, coloured rear light clusters are also very popular among the modded Corsa fraternity. Smoked or clear/white lights are probably the most popular, but there's no reason not to colour-code. You can always save your dosh, and spray-tint your rear lights.

One cool option is the "Lexus-style" clusters. Such style comes at a price, but it's not excessive, considering the finished effect. When buying rear light clusters, it's not a good idea to go for the cheapest you can find, as they may be for left-hand-drive fitment. The problem concerns rear foglights and rear reflectors, both of which your rear lights must have, to be legal. Getting around this problem can cause loads of grief, so it's best to only go for UK-legal lights.

01 Removing and refitting the rear light clusters shouldn't tax your brain too much, but it is a bit fiddly. First, open the tailgate and release the big bulbholder from the back of the light by squeezing the tabs.

02 If you like, you can now unplug the bulbholder, by pulling off this wiring plug. This isn't essential, but it gets the bulbholder out of the way.

03 The light cluster itself is held in by four very small, very awkward-to-get-at bolts. It's also remarkably easy to drop them down into the depths of the boot/side trim, well beyond the reach of your fingers. Investing in a telescopic magnetic pick-up tool will never make more sense. It's also a good plan to hold onto the light while the last bolt's being loosened, or new clusters will no longer be optional!

04 After the light comes out you can fit whatever replacement clusters take your fancy. Or - you can spray-tint your lights. First, give them a good clean - any silicone polish that's been used will ruin the paint. Meths is a pretty safe bet for cleaning purposes, but give the lights a good wipe with a clean, dry rag or towel even after this.

05 The trick with light-tinting this way is to put the paint on evenly. You'll need more than the suggested two coats to get the lights really blue, but you can already see the effect of one light coat, on the previously-white reversing light lens. Obviously, it helps if both rear lights get the same number of coats... Don't go too dark with any colour - you still have to let the lights shine through!

06 The effect you're after is something like this. Not remotely difficult to achieve, and at a fraction of the cost of new lights. Why not also spray-tint the number plate light, while you're there? The lens just prises out of the bumper.

Side **repeaters**

These provide one of the first and best ways to start colour-coding your Corsa, and you'll need to think long and hard about the final look you want before deciding which colour to go for. There seems to be no set rule for this - people try to mix n' match almost any combination of colours, and (with a few exceptions) they all seem to work. The key seems to be deciding on a colour scheme, and sticking to it religiously - the more wacky the scheme, the more determined you'll have to be!

There is a range of "standard" colours that indicators come in (clear, red, smoked, green and blue), and again, it would probably make sense to buy as many of your lights as you can from the same manufacturer, for greater chance of getting the same shade. The clear lenses can be coloured using special paint, if the particular shade you want isn't one of the "standard" ones. The paint must be applied evenly to the lens, or this will invite an easily-avoided MOT failure.

One potential problem here is that the indicators must still show an orange light when the indicators are on, and they must be sufficiently bright (not easy to judge this point, and no two coppers will have the same eyesight!). Providing you buy good-quality lenses, and use the recommended bulbs with them, there should be no problem.

Especially if you've decided on the clear lenses, note that you'll have to change the bulbs too, to orange ones. Unfortunately, of course, you can then see the orange bulbs through the lenses, leading to what's known as the "fried egg" effect. To get round this, there are special bulbs available which provide the orange light without being as obviously orange from outside.

Besides the various colour effects, side repeater lights are available in different shapes. Any shape goes, really. For something a bit different, try some Focus-style triangular repeaters.

01 Fitting side repeaters, in theory, is easy - as long as you've bought the right units! Some "universal" types don't actually have the right wiring plug to connect to the standard wiring.

02 Remove the old repeater by prising it forwards and out at the rear edge.

03 Disconnect the wiring plug from the light, and that's about it for removal! Don't let the wiring fall back inside the wing, or a 5-minute job could turn into a half-hour one. If you've bought the right units for the car, connect up the wiring plug to the new light . . .

04 . . . then fit the new light into the front edge of the hole, and secure by pressing forwards and in at the rear edge. The Corsa look, only better!

Bum notes

If you have trouble fitting the driver's side repeater, chances are you're up against the charcoal canister. The what? Fitted just inside the rear of the front wheelarch is a large plastic can for fuel tank fumes. Some aftermarket repeaters poke through the wing, and interfere with this.

If you have this trouble, don't force your lights in (the retaining clips will break). Instead, take out the plastic wheelarch liner, remove the canister and its bracket, and move it to the front of the wheelarch. This process might involve getting hold of a few sections of petrol pipe, and some new clips. There's several holes at the front for mounting (or even cable-tying) the canister to. Make sure none of the pipes is kinked or squashed, and that all the pipe clips are done tight. Oh, and no, you shouldn't just take the canister out...

Wheels & tyres

Your most important decision?

Alloy wheels are the most important styling decision you'll make. No matter how good the rest of your car is, choose the wrong rims and your car will never look right. Choose a good set and you're already well on the way to creating a sorted motor. Take your time and pick wisely - wheel fashions change like the weather, and you don't want to spend shedloads on a set of uncool alloys.

None of the standard alloys cut it, and should very quickly be dumped. Advice on which particular wheels to buy would be a waste of space, since the choice is so huge, and everyone will have their own favourites - for what it's worth, though, we reckon Mille Miglia's range (Spider, Revenge especially) is a safe bet at the time of writing, although it's arguably better to go for something a little more original. Beyond those words of dubious wisdom, you're on your own - car colour and your own chosen other mods will dictate what will look right on your car.

One "problem" with the Corsa, and with many other Vauxhalls, is the wheel offset. Most normal cars fall somewhere in the mid-30s to early 40s, but the Corsa has a peculiar offset of 49. This can limit your choice of wheels somewhat, so make sure you mention they're for a Corsa at an early stage in negotiations. Having said that, it seems many wheel manufacturers don't actually recognise the 49 offset, and insist on supplying Corsa wheels in something like a 45 or 46. Fitting 17s or 18s will be a great deal less stressful if you get wheels with exactly the right offset - otherwise, your arches won't just have to be "trimmed" - they'll be butchered! Fitting wheels with the wrong offset may also do unpleasant things to the handling.

Alloys and insurance

Before we go any further into which wheels are right for you, a word about insurance and security. Fitting tasty alloys to your Corsa is one of the first and best ways to make it look cool. It follows, therefore, that someone of low moral standing might very well want to unbolt them from your car while you're not around, and make their own car look cool instead.

Since fitting a set of alloys is one of the easiest, and most popular bolt-on mods, it's no surprise that the market in stolen alloys is as alive and kicking as it currently is. It's not unknown for a set of wheels to go missing just for the tyres - if you've just splashed out on a set of Yokohamas, your wheels look even more tempting, especially if you've got a common-size tyre.

Tell your insurance company what you're fitting. What will probably happen is that they'll ask for the exact details. Provided you're happy to then accept that they won't cover the extra cost of the wheels if they get nicked (or if the whole car goes), you'll most likely find you're not charged a penny more, especially if you've fitted some locking wheel nuts/bolts. Not all companies are the same, though - some charge an admin fee, and yes, some will start loading your premium. If you want the rims covered, it's best to talk to a company specialising in modified cars, or you could be asked to pay out the wheel cost again in premiums. Don't say nothing, and hope they don't find out - the insurance company is likely to not pay out altogether, purely on the basis of undeclared alloy wheels.

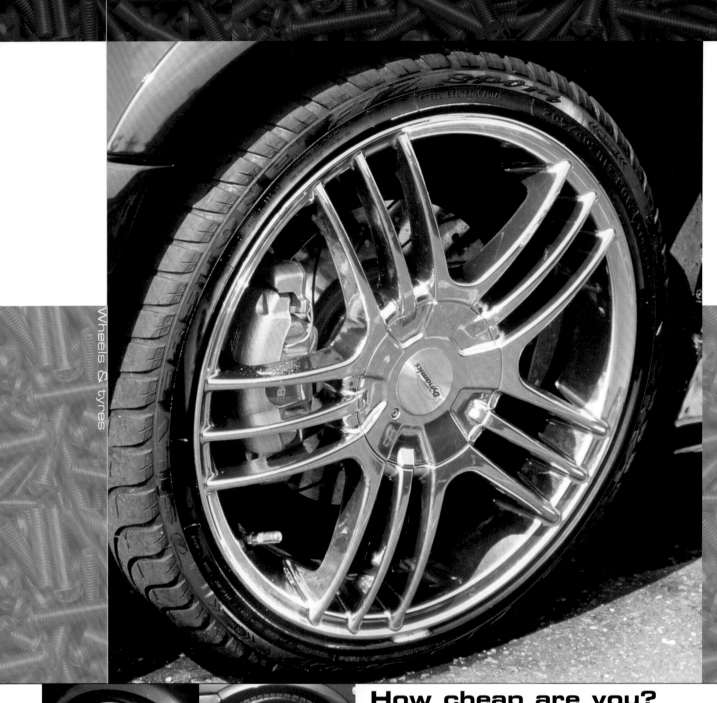

How cheap are you?

Hopefully, you'll be deciding which wheels to go for based on how they look, not how much they cost, but inevitably, price does become a factor. Some of the smaller manufacturers recognise this, and offer cheaper copies of more expensive designs - this is fine as far as you're concerned, but what's the catch? Surely buying a cheaper wheel must have its pitfalls? Well, yes - and some of them may not be so obvious.

Inevitably, cheaper wheels = lower quality, but how does this manifest itself? Cheap wheels are often made from alloys which are more "porous" (a bit like a sponge, they contain microscopic holes and pockets of air). Being porous has two main disadvantages for a wheel, the main one being that it won't be able to retain air in the tyres. The days of tyres with inner tubes are long gone (and it's illegal to fit tubes to low-profile tyres), so the only thing keeping the air in are the three "walls" of the tyre, with the fourth "wall" being the inside of the wheel itself. If you like keeping fit by pumping up your tyres every morning, go ahead - the rest of us will rightly regard this as a pain, and potentially dangerous (running tyres at low pressure will also wear them out quicker)

Porous wheels also have difficulty in retaining their paint or lacquer finish, with flaking a known problem, sometimes after only a few months. This problem is compounded by the fact that porous wheels are much harder to clean.

The final nail in the coffin for cheap wheels is that they tend to corrode (or "fizz") more readily than more expensive types. This not only looks bad if visible from outside, but if you get corrosion between the wheel and the hub, you could find yourself faced with a wheel that simply won't come off.

Buying wheels from established, popular manufacturers with a large range has another hidden benefit, too. It stands to reason that choosing a popular wheel will mean that more suppliers will stock it, and the manufacturers themselves will make plenty of them. And if you're unlucky enough to have an accident which results in non-repairable damage to one wheel, you're going to need a replacement. If you've chosen the rarest wheels on the planet, you could be faced with having to replace a complete set of four, to get them all matching... A popular wheel, even if it's a few years old, might be easier to source, even second-hand.

Cleaning wheels

It's a small point maybe, but you'll obviously want your wheels to look as smart as possible, as often as possible - so how easy are they going to be to clean?

Some designs are hell to clean - a fiddly toothbrush job - do you really want that much aggro every week? The simpler the design, the easier time you'll have.

Other options

If you're on a really tight budget, and perhaps own a real "basic" model Corsa, don't overlook the possibility of fitting a discarded set of standard alloys, possibly from another Vauxhall entirely - check that the stud pattern's the same, obviously.

If the Vauxhall range of wheels is too limiting, don't be too quick buying (for instance) BMW or VW alloys - they might appear to bolt on alright, but the offset is often different. In the case of some alloys, the pitch circle diameter (or PCD, see "Jargon explained") may be only fractionally different, but if you bolt these on, the strain on the bolts is too great, and they can fracture or work themselves loose...

Jargon explained

PCD – Is your Pitch Circle Diameter, which relates to the spacing of your wheel bolt holes, or "stud pattern". It is expressed by the diameter of a notional circle which passes through the centre of your wheel bolts, and the number of bolts. If, for instance, the PCD is 100 mm with four bolts, it's given as 100/4.

ROLLING RADIUS – is the distance from the wheel centre to the outer edge of the tyre, or effectively, half the overall diameter.

OFFSET - this is determined by the distance from the wheel mounting face in relation to its centre-line. The offset figure is denoted by ET (no, I mustn't), which stands for einpress tiefe in German, or pressed-in depth (now I know you're asleep). The lower the offset, the more the wheels will stick out. Fitting wheels with the wrong offset might bring the wheel into too-close contact with the brake and suspension bits, or with the arches. Very specialised area - seek advice from the wheel manufacturers if you're going for a very radical size (or even if you're not). The correct offset for Corsas of all sizes is ET 49.

Tricks 'n' tips

It's worth applying a bit of car polish to the wheels - provided it's good stuff, and you can be sure of getting the residue out of the corners and edges, a polished wheel will always be easier to clean off than an unpolished one.

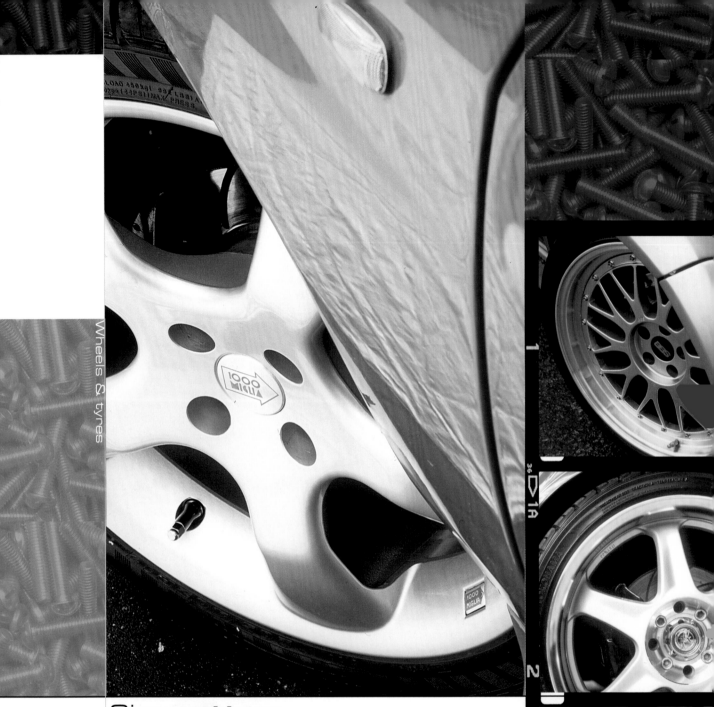

Size **matters**

The trend in wheel size is an interesting one. It seems that, for us Brits, biggest is best - there are Corsas out there with 18s and up. But in general it's safe to say that you can't be seen with anything less than 17-inchers.

In Europe, meanwhile, they're mad for the small-wheel look, still with seriously dropped suspension of course, but on 14- and 15-inch rims - strange how only a small drop in wheel size can have so marked an effect. On many cars (the Corsa included), 16-inch rims are the biggest you can sensibly fit before you really have to start looking at sorting the arches, and they will improve the handling (unlike 17s, which often have the opposite effect!). In fact, on the Corsa, we wouldn't rule out the possibility of some rear arch massaging, even on 16s, especially if you're determined to slam the car down.

What most of you are going to want to know is what work is necessary to get 17s on?

Width is the key

Successfully fitting big wheels in combination with lowered suspension is one of the major challenges to the modifier.

At least the Corsa has reasonably roomy front arches (or they can be made to be easily, by taking out the plastic wheelarch liners). As much as anything, it seems that tyre width is what ultimately leads to problems, not so much the increased wheel diameter.

If the tyres are simply too wide (or with wheels the wrong offset), they will first of all rub on the suspension strut (ie on the inside edge of the tyre). Also, the inside edges may rub on the arches on full steering lock - check left and right. Rubbing on the inside edges can be cured by fitting offsets or spacers between the wheel and hub, which effectively pull the wheel outwards, "spacing" it away from its normal position (this also has the effect of widening the car's track, which may improve the on-limit handling - or not). Fitting offsets must be done using special longer wheel bolts, as the standard ones may only engage into the hubs by a few threads, which is highly dangerous (also check that your locking bolts are long enough).

Rubbing on the outside edges is a simple case of wheelarch lip fouling, which must be cured by rolling out the wheelarch return edge, and other mods. If you've gone for really wide tyres, or have already had to fit spacers, the outer edge of the tyre will probably be visible outside the wheelarch, and this is a no-no (it's illegal, and you must cover it up!).

The other trick with fitting big alloys is of course to avoid the "4x4" look, which you will achieve remarkably easily just by bolting on a set of 17s with standard suspension. Overcoming this problem by lowering is essential (see "Suspension").

Speedo error? Or not?

One side-effect of fitting large wheels is that your car will appear to go slower, due to the mechanically-driven speedometer.

As the wheel diameter increases, so does its circumference (distance around the outside) - this means that, to travel say one mile, a large wheel will turn less than a smaller wheel. Therefore, for a given actual speed, since the method for measuring speed is the rate of wheel rotation, a car with larger wheels will produce a lower speedo reading than one with smaller wheels - but it's not actually going any slower in reality.

With the ever-increasing number of Gatsos, spare a thought to what this speedo error could mean in the real world. If (like most people) you tend to drive a wee bit over the posted 30s and 40s, your real speed on 17s or 18s could be a bit more than the bit more you thought you were doing already, and you could get an unexpected flash to ruin your day. Actually, the speedo error effect on 17s and 18s really is tiny at around-town speeds, and only becomes a factor over 70.

Did you know?

Modern cars with fuel injection and engine management run electronic speedos, but since most of these are fed by gearbox-driven sensors, the problem with big wheels remains. Incidentally, the latest German luxury cars use the ABS wheel sensors to drive the speedometer - but these sensors measure wheel rotation too, and so are no more help than before!

Hold on to your wheels

The minute you bolt on your alloys, your car becomes a target. People see the big wheels, and automatically assume you've also got a major stereo, seats and other goodies - all very tempting, but that involves breaking in, and you could have an alarm. Pinching the wheels themselves, now that's a doddle - a few tools, some bricks or a couple of mates to lift the car, and it's easy money.

Tricks 'n' tips

If you're keeping a steel wheel as your spare (or even if you're keeping an original alloy), keep a set of your original wheel bolts in a bag inside the spare wheel. Locking bolts especially might be too long when fitted to a thin steel wheel, and might jam up your brakes!

The trouble with fitting big wheels is that they are bolted on, and are just as easily bolted off, if you don't make life difficult. If you're unlucky enough to have to park outside at night, you could wake up one morning to a car that's literally been slammed on the deck! Add to this the fact that your car isn't going anywhere without wheels, plus the damage which will be done to exhaust, fuel and brake pipes from dropping on its belly, and it's suddenly a lot worse than losing a grand's worth of wheels and tyres…

The market and demand for stolen alloys is huge, but most people don't bother having them security-marked in any way, so once a set of wheels disappears, they're almost impossible to trace.

When choosing that car alarm, try and get one with an "anti-jacking" feature, because the thieves hate it. This is sometimes called "anti-tilt", to avoid confusion with anti-hijacking. Imagine a metal saucer, with a metal ball sitting on a small magnet in the centre. If the saucer tilts in any direction, the ball rolls off the magnet, and sets off the alarm. Highly sensitive, and death to

anyone trying to lift your car up for the purpose of removing the wheels - the crims are not fond of this feature at all. Simply having an alarm with anti-shock is probably not good enough, because a careful villain will probably be able to work so as not to create a strong enough vibration to trigger it - mind you, it's a whole lot better than nothing, especially if set to maximum sensitivity.

Locking wheel bolts

Locking wheel bolts will be effective as a deterrent to the inexpert thief, but will probably only slow down the pro.

What so many people don't realise is that thieves want to work quickly, and will use large amounts of cunning and violence to deprive you of your stuff. If you fit a cheap set of locking bolts, they'll use a hammer and thin chisel to crack off the locking bolt heads. Some bolts can easily be defeated by hammering a socket onto the bolt head, and undoing the locking bolt as normal, while some of the key-operated bolts are so pathetic they can be beaten using a small screwdriver. So - choose the best bolts you can, but don't assume they'll prevent your wheels from disappearing. Insurance companies do like you to fit them though.

There seems to be some debate as to whether it's okay to fit more than one set of locking bolts to a car - some people value their wheels so highly that they've fitted four or five sets of bolts - in other words, they've completely replaced all the standard bolts! The feeling against doing this is that the replacement locking bolts may not be made to the same standard as factory originals, and while it's okay to fit any set on security grounds, fitting more than that could be dangerous on safety grounds (bolt could fail, wheel falls off, car in ditch, owner in hospital…).

Obviously, you must carry the special key or tool which came with your bolts with you at all times, in case of a puncture, or if you're having any other work done, such as new brakes or tyres. The best thing to do is rig this onto your keyring, so that it's with you, but not left in the car. The number of people who fit locking bolts and then leave the key to them cunningly "hidden" in the glovebox or the boot - if only the low-lifes out there were as daft! You don't leave a spare set of car keys in your glovebox as well, do you?

Tricks 'n' tips

A word of warning about re-using your existing wheel bolts, should you be upgrading from steel wheels. Most steel-wheel bolts are not suitable for use with alloy wheels (and vice-versa). Make sure you ask about this when buying new wheels, and if necessary, bargain a set of bolts into the price.
Another point to watch for is that the new wheel bolts are the correct length for your fitment, taking into account whether you've fitted spacers or not. Bolts that are too short are obviously dangerous, and ones that are too long can foul on drum brakes, and generally get in the way of any turning activities. If in doubt ask the retailer for advice. Always check that the wheels turn freely once they've been put on, and investigate any strange noises before you go off for a pose.

Changing a set of wheels

You might think you know all about this, but do you really? Okay, so you know you need a jack and wheelbrace (or socket and ratchet), but where are the jacking points? If you want to take more than one wheel off at a time, have you got any axle stands, and where do they go?

If you've only ever had wheels and tyres fitted by a garage, chances are you're actually a beginner at this. It's surprising just how much damage you can do to your car, and to yourself, if you don't know what you're doing - and the worst thing here is to think you know, when you don't...

Our standard alloys had an anti-theft cover fitted over the bolts. It's not impenetrable but it's a start. You'll need the special key to remove this cover

What to use

If you don't already have one, invest in a decent hydraulic (trolley) jack. This is way more use than the standard car jack, which is really only for emergencies, and which isn't stable enough to rely on. Lifting and lowering the car is so much easier with a trolley jack, and you'll even look professional. Trolley jacks have a valve, usually at the rear, which must be fully tightened (using the end of the jack handle) before raising the jack, and which is carefully loosened to lower the car - if it's opened fully, the car will not so much sink as plummet!

Axle stands are placed under the car, once it's been lifted using the jack. Stands are an important accessory because once they're in place, there's no way the car can come down on you - remember that even a brand new trolley jack could creep down (if you haven't tightened the valve), or could fail completely under load (if it's a cheap one, or knackered, or both).

Under no circumstances use bricks, wooden blocks or anything else which you have to pile up, to support the car - this is just plain stupid. A Corsa weighs plenty for a "small" car - if you want to find out just how solidly it's built, try crawling under it when it's resting on a few bricks.

Where to use it

Only ever jack the car up on a solid, level surface (ideally, a concrete or tarmac driveway, or quiet car park). If there's even a slight slope, the car's likely to move (maybe even roll away) as the wheels are lifted off the ground. Jacking up on a rough or gravelled surface is not recommended, as the jack could slip at an awkward moment - such as when you've just got underneath…

How to use it - jacking up the front

Before jacking up the front of the car, pull the handbrake on firmly (you can also chock the rear wheels, if you don't trust your handbrake). If you're taking the wheels off, loosen the wheel bolts before you start jacking up the car. It's easily forgotten, but you'll look pretty silly trying to undo the wheel bolts with the front wheels spinning in mid-air.

We'll assume you've got a trolley jack. The next question is - where to stick it? Vauxhall provide two nice support points at the front, on the square-section "outriggers" just behind the front wishbones. Put a nice flat offcut of wood on your jack head, and get it under there! You can jack on the sill jacking points (which are marked by little notches above the sill edges), but it's better to leave those for your axle stands.

Once you've got the car up, pop an axle stand or two under the front sill jacking points. These points are shown by having a notch cut in the bottom edge of the flange, and this is the only part of the sill it's safe to jack under or rest the car on. On the GSi, you'll have to unclip a cover for access to the sill jacking points, and even then, access to them might not be all you'd like. With the stands in place, you can lower the jack so the car's weight rests on the stands. Some people prefer to spread the weight between the stands and the jack.

Don't jack up the car, or stick stands under the car, anywhere other than kosher jacking and support points. This means - not the floorpan or the sump (you'll cave it in), not the suspension bits (not stable), and not under the brake/fuel pipes.

Tricks 'n' tips
Whenever you have your wheels off, clean off any hub corrosion with wet-and-dry paper, then coat the hub mating surfaces with copper (brake) grease - this "sticks" better than ordinary grease, and is temperature-resistant. There's no way you'll suffer stuck-on wheels again. "Proper" alloys come with a plastic collar which fits inside the wheel - this is an essential item which should not be discarded, as it centres the wheel properly and reduces wheel-to-hub corrosion.

How to use it - jacking up the rear

When jacking up the rear of the car, place wooden chocks in front of the front wheels to stop it rolling forwards, and engage first gear. If you're taking the wheels off, loosen the wheel bolts before lifting the car.

Jacking and supporting the rear is a little trickier. There's a decent support point provided just inside the sill jacking point at the back, ideal for an axle stand with a block of wood to spread the load. This still leaves the problem of where to jack up in the first place! One possible spot is to jack under the flat plates provided at each end of the rear "axle" - don't jack directly on the "edge" of the axle (at least the flat plates spread the load). An alternative is to jack up under the back end of the trailing arm, where the rear shock mounts on, which is okay unless you're working on the rear suspension!

Remember not to put your axle stands under any pipes, the spare wheel well, or the fuel tank, and you should live to see another Christmas.

Changing wheels

Off with the old wheels and on with the new? Nearly that simple, but there are a few points to watch.

01 Before fitting your new wheels, there's stuff to check - first, have you got a plastic ring (spigot) inside the hub? Even with the ring of plastic, the metal bits can still corrode on. Equip yourself with some copper brake grease, and smear some on the wheel boss, inside.

02 You'll be doing yourself a favour if some of the same copper grease also finds its way onto the wheel bolt threads. Make sure your bolts are long enough to bite into the hub sufficiently.

Always tighten the wheel bolts very securely (ideally, to the correct torque - 110 Nm). This can only be done properly with the wheel back on the ground. Don't over-tighten the bolts, or you'll never get them undone at the roadside, should you have a flat. If your wheels have a centre cap of some kind, make sure you fit it. Not only does it look better, but in certain cases, the Allen key needed to undo it might be all the theft-deterrent you need, to stop an opportunist…

03 Pop the wheel on, turning it to align the bolt holes . . .

04 . . . then in with the nicely-greased bolts, and tighten up as far as possible by hand. On the fronts (unless you've left it in gear) you won't be able to fully tighten the bolts anyway, as the wheels will spin.

05 Don't forget your locking wheel bolts. Keep your locking wheel bolt tool somewhere safe, but not obvious. The glovebox is obvious, so it's the wrong place!

06

Always nice to see a good brand of tyre on a decent alloy. How cool do cheap tyres look, on a car like the Corsa?

Tyres

To some people, tyres are just round and black, they're nearly all expensive, and don't last long enough. When you're buying a new set of wheels, most centres will quote prices with different tyres - this is convenient, and usually quite good value, too, but look carefully at what you're buying.

Some people try to save money by fitting "remould" or "re-manufactured" tyres. These aren't always the bargain they appear to be - experience says there's no such thing as a good cheap tyre.

Without wanting to sound like an old advert, choosing a known brand of tyre will prove to be one of your better decisions. Tyres are the only thing keeping you on the road, as in steering, braking and helping you round corners - what's the point of trying to improve the handling by sorting the suspension if you're going to throw the gains away by fitting naff tyres? Why beef up the brakes if the tyres won't bite? The combination of stiff suspension and cheap tyres is inherently dangerous - because the front end dives less with reduced suspension travel, the front tyres are far more likely to lock and skid under heavy braking.

Cheap tyres also equals more wheelspin - might be fun to be sat at the lights in a cloud of tyre smoke, but wouldn't you rather be disappearing up the road? Another problem with really wide tyres is aquaplaning - hit a big puddle at speed, and the tyre skates over the water without gripping - this is seriously scary when it first

Tricks 'n' tips
When buying tyres, look out for ones which feature a rubbing strip on the sidewall - these extend over the edge of the wheel rims, and the idea is that they protect the rim edges from damage by "kerbing". Our Toyo Proxes had these strips - discreet and very practical, we reckon.

happens. Fitting good tyres won't prevent it, but it might increase your chances of staying in control. The sexiest modern low profile tyres have a V-tread pattern, designed specifically to aid water dispersal, which is exactly what you need to prevent aquaplaning - try some, and feel the difference!

Finally, cheap tyres ruin your Corsa's appearance - a no-name brand emblazoned in big letters on your tyre sidewalls - how's that going to look? If you're spending big dosh on wheels, you've gotta kit 'em out with some tasty V-tread tyres, or lose major points for style. Listen to friends and fellow modifiers - real-world opinions count for a lot when choosing tyres (how well do they grip, wet or dry? How many miles can you get out of them?) Just make sure, before you splash your cash on decent tyres, that you've cured all your rubbing and scrubbing issues, as nothing will rip your new tyres out faster.

Marks on your sidewalls

Tyre sizes are expressed in a strange mixture of metric and imperial specs - we'll take a typical tyre size as an example:

205/40 R 17 V
for a 7-inch wide 17-inch rim
205 width of tyre in millimetres
40 this is the "aspect ratio" (or "profile") of the tyre, or the sidewall height in relation to tyre width, expressed as a percentage, in this case 40%. So - 40% of 205 mm = 82 mm, or the height of the tyre sidewall from the edge of the locating bead to the top of the tread.
R Radial.
17 Wheel diameter in inches.
V Speed rating (in this case, suitable for use up to 150 mph).

Pressure situation

Don't forget, when you're having your new tyres fitted, to ask what the recommended pressures should be, front and rear - it's unlikely that the Vauxhall specs for this will be relevant to your new low-low profiles, but it's somewhere to start from. If the grease-monkey fitting your tyres is no help on this point, contact the tyre manufacturer - the big ones might even have a half-useful website! Running the tyres at the wrong pressures is particularly stupid (you'll stand to wear them out much faster) and can be very dangerous (too soft - tyre rolls off the rim, too hard - tyre slides, no grip).

Speed ratings

Besides the tyre size, tyres are marked with a maximum speed rating, expressed as a letter code:

T up to 190 km/h (118 mph)

U up to 200 km/h (124 mph)

H up to 210 km/h (130 mph)

V inside tyre size markings (225/50 VR 16) over 210 km/h (130 mph)

V outside tyre size markings (185/55 R 15 V) up to 240 km/h (150 mph)

Z inside tyre size markings (255/40 ZR 17) over 240 km/h (150 mph)

If you've got marks on your sidewalls like this, you're in trouble - this has almost certainly been caused by "kerbing".

If your Corsa's still sitting on standard suspension, it's probably safe to say it doesn't cut it - yet. If you've decided you couldn't wait to fit your big alloys, the chances are your Corsa is now doing a passable impression of a tractor. An essential fitment, then - so how low do you go, and what nasty side-effects will a lowering kit have?

08 Suspension

Suspension

The main reason for lowering is, of course, to make your car look cool. Standard suspension nearly always seems to be set too soft and too high - a nicely lowered motor stands out instantly. Lowering your car should also improve the handling. Dropping the car on its suspension brings the car's centre of gravity closer to its roll and pitch centres, which helps to pin it to the road in corners and under braking - combined with stiffer springs and shocks, this reduces body roll and increases the tyre contact patch on the road. But if improving the handling is really important to you, choose your new suspension carefully. If you go the cheap route, or want extreme lowering, then making the car handle better might not be what you achieve…

As for what to buy, there are basically three main options when it comes to lowering, arranged in order of ascending cost below:

1 *Set of lowering springs*

2 *Matched set of lowering springs and shock absorbers*

3 *Set of "coilovers"*

Lowering springs

The cheapest option by far, but with the most pitfalls and some unpleasant side-effects.

Lowering springs are, effectively, shorter versions of the standard items fitted to your Corsa at the factory. However, not only are they shorter (lower), they are also of necessity uprated (stiffer) - if lowering springs were simply shorter than standard and the same stiffness ("rate"), you'd be hitting the bump-stops over every set of catseyes. With lowering springs, you just fit the new springs and keep the original shock absorbers ("dampers") - even if the originals aren't completely knackered, you're creating a problem caused by mis-matched components. The original dampers were carefully chosen to work in harmony with the original-rate springs - by increasing the spring rate without changing the dampers, you end up with a situation where the dampers will not be in full control of the spring motion. What this does before long is wreck the dampers, because they can't cope with the new springs, so you don't save any money in the end.

The mis-matched springs and dampers will have other entertaining side-effects, too. How would you like a Corsa which rides like a brick, and which falls over itself at the first sign of a corner taken above walking pace? A very choppy ride and strange-feeling steering (much lighter, or much heavier, depending on your

luck) are well-documented problems associated with taking the cheap option. Even if you don't object to a hard ride if your car looks cool, think on this - how many corners do you know that are completely flat (ie without any bumps)? On dodgy lowering springs, you hit a mid-corner bump at speed, and it's anyone's guess where you'll end up.

If cost is a major consideration, and lowering springs the only option for now, at least try to buy branded items of decent quality - some cheap sets of springs will eat their way through several sets of dampers before you realise the springs themselves have lost the plot. Needless to say, if riding around on mis-matched springs and shocks is a bit iffy anyway, it's downright dangerous when they've worn out (some inside 18 months!).

Assuming you want to slam your suspension so that your arches just clear the tops of your rims, there's another small problem with lowered springs - it takes some inspired guesswork to assess the required drop accurately, so be prepared for some arch work if you go for a big drop. Springs are generally only available in a very few sizes, expressed by the amount of drop they'll produce - most people go for around 45 mm or more, but there's options from 30 to 60 mm to chose from. Take as many measurements as possible, and ask around your mates - suppliers and manufacturers may be your best source of help in special cases.

Suspension kit

A far better choice is a matched set of springs and dampers. It's a genuine "upgrade", and well worth doing. There are several branded kits available, and most of the Vauxhall specialists do their own. With a properly-sorted conversion, your Corsa will handle even better, and you'll still be able to negotiate a set of roadworks without the risk of dental work afterwards. Actually, you may well be amazed how well the Corsa will still ride, even though the springs are clearly lower and stiffer - the secret is in the damping.

Some of the kits are billed as "adjustable", but this only applies to the damper rates, which can often be set to your own taste by a few minutes' work (don't mistake them for cheap coilovers). This Playstation feature can be quite a good fun thing to play around with, even if it is slightly less relevant to road use than to hillclimbs and sprints - but be careful you don't get carried away and set it too stiff, or you'll end up with an evil-handling car and a CD player that skips over every white line on the road!

Unfortunately, although you will undoubtedly end up with a fine-handling car at the end, there are problems with suspension kits, too. They too are guilty of causing changes to steering geometry (have it reset) and once again, you're into guesswork territory when it comes to assessing your required drop for big wheels. Suspension kits are generally available with a fairly modest drop, typically, 35 to 40 mm, but bigger drops are available.

Coilovers

This is the most expensive option, and it offers one vital feature that the other two can't - true adjustability of ride height, meaning that you can make the finest of tweaks to get the car low.

This also gives you more scope to fit those big rims. Lower it as far as poss, then wait 'til next month before you have the arches rolled, and drop it down to the deck. Coilovers are a variation on the suspension kit theme, in that they are a set of matched variable-rate springs (some have separate "helper" springs too) and shocks, but they achieve their adjustability in a way which might not guarantee as good a ride/handling mix as a normal kit.

A coilover set replaces each spring and shock with a combined unit where the coil spring fits over the shocker (hence "coil" "over") - nothing too unusual in this, because so far, it's similar to a normal front strut. The difference lies in the adjustable spring lower seat, which can lower the spring to any desired height (within limits). .

Unfortunately, you can't change the laws of physics, and coilovers are something of a compromise. Making a car go super-low is not going to be good for the ride or the handling. Coilover systems necessarily have very short, stiff springs, and this can lead to similar problems to those found with cheap lowering springs alone. If you go too far with coilovers, you can end up with a choppy ride, heavy steering and generally unpleasant handling. Combine a coilover-slammed car with big alloys, and while the visual effect may be stunning, the driving experience might well be very disappointing.

Coilover sets are developing all the time, and advances in progressive-rate springs mean that good-quality sets from known makers are well worth the extra over cheaper solutions.

Coilover conversion

Another cheaper option is the "coilover conversion". Offering as much potential for lowering as genuine coilovers (and at far less cost), these items could be described as a cross between coilovers and lowering springs, because the standard dampers are retained. What you get is a new spring assembly, with adjustable top and bottom mounts - the whole thing slips over your standard damper. Two problems with this solution:

1 Your standard dampers will not be able to cope with the uprated springs, so the car will almost certainly ride (and handle) like a pig if you go for a really serious drop.

2 The standard dampers are effectively being compressed, the lower you go. There is a limit to how far they will compress before being completely solid (and this could be the limit for your lowering activities). Even a partly-compressed damper won't be able to do much actual damping - the results of this could be dodgy.

Front Suspension

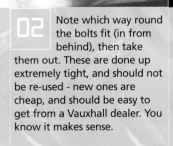

Tricks 'n' tips

Don't start this job without coil spring compressors, or you'll be sorry! A torque wrench is also pretty important. For safety, and to avoid the chance of the old nuts stripping when they're re-tightened (or coming loose again afterwards), you're supposed to use new strut-to-hub nuts/bolts, and a new strut top nut, each side - available cheap from a Vauxhall dealer.

01 Loosen the wheel bolts, jack up the corner of the car you're working on, and take off the wheel. Make sure you've got an axle stand under a solid part of the car (like the front chassis legs/outriggers) in case the jack gives out, and something else under the wishbone. Have a look in "Wheels & tyres" for more info on jacking up. Using two spanners (or a spanner and socket), loosen the two big strut-to-hub bolts.

02 Note which way round the bolts fit (in from behind), then take them out. These are done up extremely tight, and should not be re-used - new ones are cheap, and should be easy to get from a Vauxhall dealer. You know it makes sense.

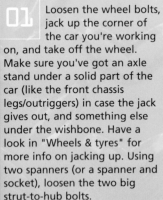

03 If it hasn't come apart on its own already (and yours might be rustier than ours), separate the hub from the base of the strut. All that's holding the strut in now are two small nuts on top, but it's worth just checking now that there's nothing else attached to the strut that would stop it dropping down. On some cars, for instance, the flexible brake hose is clipped to the strut. Unclip it.

04 Going back under the bonnet, it's time to loosen the two strut top mounting nuts. On the driver's side of our Corsa, there's a black plastic wiring conduit in the way, secured by two plastic nuts. Remove the plastic nuts . . .

05 . . . then lift the wiring clear, and loosen off the two (metal) nuts which secure the strut. Before these nuts are fully undone, reach under the wing and grab the strut, or it'll hit the deck.

06 Lower the strut out from under the wing, and take it to the workbench for surgery to begin.

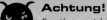

Achtung!
For the next bit, you must use coil spring compressors ("spring clamps"). Medical attention will be required if you don't! The spring's under tension on the strut, so even off the car it'll make a mess if it's not clamped properly.

07 There are two clamps, each with two hooks, which sit over one of the spring coils. You won't get the hooks over the top and bottom coils, but try the next nearest. Fit the two clamps opposite each other . . .

08 . . . then tighten the big bolt up the middle of each to compress one side of the spring - this must be done evenly, one side after the other, or the un-clamped side might fly off. Be very careful here.

09 Compress the spring carefully until the tension is off the top spring seat. Now undo the top nut, holding the piston rod with a small spanner on the flats provided on the rod. Spanner sizes for our Corsa? 18 mm and 9 mm - not what your average spanner set will contain, but don't be surprised if your car's different! You are now ready to dismantle your strut - soon you should have a pile of bits that looks like ours, most of which can be scrapped . . .

10 . . . except for these bits, which you'll need again, unless any of them appears to be knackered. Remember - use a new top nut on each strut.

11 Though it can be done at any time, we chose to set our lower spring seats roughly now - about halfway up the threaded section seemed as good a place as any. Setting them equal on both sides before fitting will make life easier, too, later on - measure the thread above or below the two rings to set it accurately.

12 If necessary, pull out the piston rod (central shiny bit) from the main body of the strut, to give you enough length to fit all the spring components on. The bump stop bottom plate goes on first . . .

13 . . . then the spring. If you're not sure which way up it goes, the printed writing on it should be readable with the strut upright. No compressors required now.

14 Fit the bump stop to its upper plate . . . then fit the pair onto the strut.

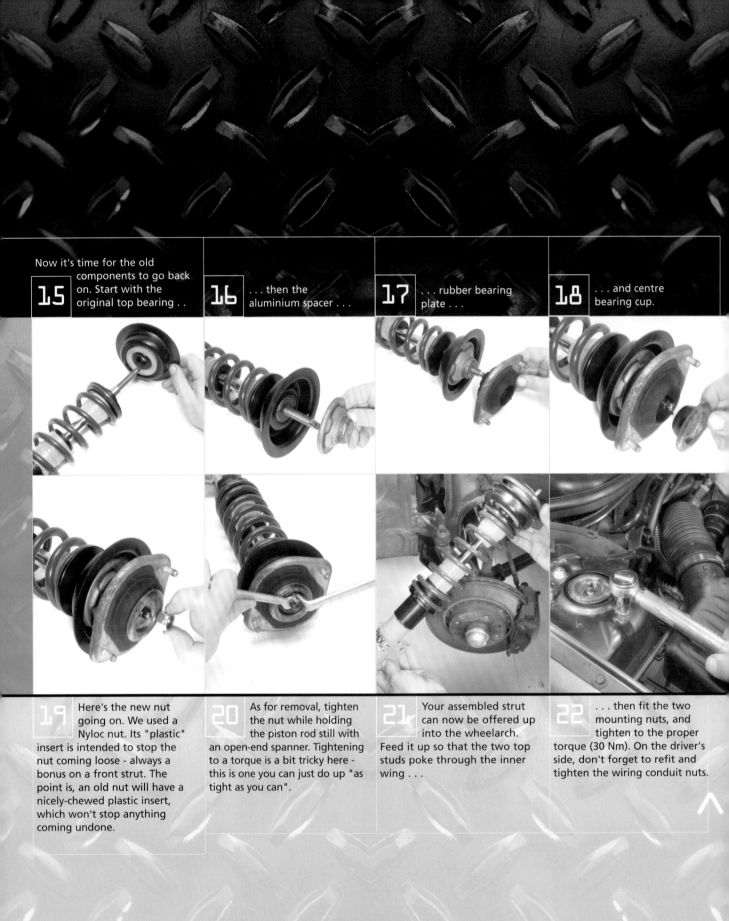

15 Now it's time for the old components to go back on. Start with the original top bearing . .

16 . . . then the aluminium spacer . . .

17 . . . rubber bearing plate . . .

18 . . . and centre bearing cup.

19 Here's the new nut going on. We used a Nyloc nut. Its "plastic" insert is intended to stop the nut coming loose - always a bonus on a front strut. The point is, an old nut will have a nicely-chewed plastic insert, which won't stop anything coming undone.

20 As for removal, tighten the nut while holding the piston rod still with an open-end spanner. Tightening to a torque is a bit tricky here - this is one you can just do up "as tight as you can".

21 Your assembled strut can now be offered up into the wheelarch. Feed it up so that the two top studs poke through the inner wing . . .

22 . . . then fit the two mounting nuts, and tighten to the proper torque (30 Nm). On the driver's side, don't forget to refit and tighten the wiring conduit nuts.

23 Now get down in the wheelarch, grab the brake disc, and engage the hub with the slot at the base of the strut. This might take some effort to get the hub high enough, now the shorter strut's been fitted. If you need to, use another small jack to raise the hub sufficiently.

24 When the hub's high enough, quickly slot in the two (new) strut-to-hub bolts from behind, to pin it in place.

25 Screw on the two (also new) nuts, then start tightening them up. Tightening is done in three stages - these are important nuts/bolts, after all (another reason why you should buy new ones). A torque wrench is an essential item here - if you don't have one, get one, somehow. First, tighten both nuts to 50Nm, holding the bolt heads with a spanner, to stop them turning. Then tighten both nuts some more, to 90Nm.

26 The final tightening stage is to turn both nuts through 45 to 60 degrees - or "angle-tightening". If you've forgotten, 90 degrees is a right-angle, 45 is half that, and 60 is two-thirds. Judging an angle is pretty easy - fit your socket handle on horizontal, and tighten until the handle's at the proper angle from horizontal. Use a protractor to mark the angle on some card, to hold behind your socket handle. To look more professional, buy or borrow an angle gauge.

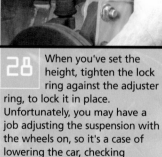

27 Setting the suspension height is a trial-and-error business. Our kit came with two C-spanners for use on the adjuster and lock rings, which is helpful.

28 When you've set the height, tighten the lock ring against the adjuster ring, to lock it in place. Unfortunately, you may have a job adjusting the suspension with the wheels on, so it's a case of lowering the car, checking height, raise car, take off wheel, adjust, refit wheel, lower car... But the results are worth it!

29 You also have a top-adjustable damper to play with. Our kit had a 10-position adjuster, which you start by setting at position 5 (five clicks). Follow the instructions with your kit, and don't be shy of ringing the company concerned for setting advice if you're not happy with the handling or ride.

30 A final piece of advice is to paint some rust-preventative stuff (eg Waxoyl) onto the adjuster threads. This will tend to gum up the threads, it's true, but this is way better than letting them go rusty. Your call. Just don't get any on the brake discs!

Rear Suspension

Tricks 'n' tips

Coil spring compressors aren't needed for the rear suspension, but at the back, it's all about support. As in supporting the rear suspension arms. Ideally, you should have two jacks of some description for this, and an assistant, as both sides have to be worked on at the same time. There's a risk of snapping the brake pipes if the rear suspension's just allowed to drop down unsupported. Without support, the rear arms will drop as soon as the shock absorber top mountings are removed. You have been warned!

01 Loosen all the rear wheel bolts, jack up each rear corner of the car in turn, and support using an axle stand under each rear jacking point. Have a look in "Wheels & tyres" for more info on jacking up. Remove both rear wheels, then using a jack directly under each suspension arm, raise the rear arms slightly, so they're both supported. Phew. Now go into the boot, and unclip the access panel from the rear shock upper mounting.

02 Pull off the rubber cap fitted over the top nut.

Back down below, and making sure that suspension arm's supported, loosen the shock lower mounting bolt. This has what's known as a "captive" (welded-in) nut at its other end, so it's only the bolt that comes off. Unfortunately, captive nuts can be prone to seizing - copious amounts of WD-40 might be needed to free the bolt!

Using a two-spanner technique similar to that used on the front suspension, loosen and remove the shock top locknut and the main nut underneath. This time it's 16 mm and 7 mm spanners we're using - two more unpopular sizes (but your Corsa may be different!).

03

With the nut removed, take off the top plate/washer and the mounting rubber below. Repeat this process on the other side.

04

05

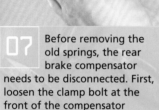
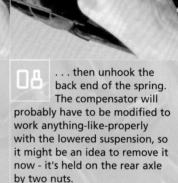
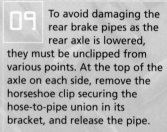
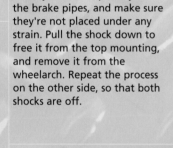

06 To remove the rear shock, it will be necessary to lower the suspension arm slightly until it's free. You shouldn't have to lower the arm very far for this, but if you do, keep an eye on the brake pipes, and make sure they're not placed under any strain. Pull the shock down to free it from the top mounting, and remove it from the wheelarch. Repeat the process on the other side, so that both shocks are off.

07 Before removing the old springs, the rear brake compensator needs to be disconnected. First, loosen the clamp bolt at the front of the compensator spring . . .

08 . . . then unhook the back end of the spring. The compensator will probably have to be modified to work anything-like-properly with the lowered suspension, so it might be an idea to remove it now - it's held on the rear axle by two nuts.

09 To avoid damaging the rear brake pipes as the rear axle is lowered, they must be unclipped from various points. At the top of the axle on each side, remove the horseshoe clip securing the hose-to-pipe union in its bracket, and release the pipe.

10 Follow the brake pipe down the axle and suspension arm, unclipping it from the plastic clips - if possible, do this by hand (without tools) to avoid damaging the pipe.

11 Slowly and carefully lower the jacks under the suspension arms. Stop every inch or so, and check that the brake pipes aren't getting caught up and strained. Eventually, the rear springs will virtually fall out.

12 When fitting the new springs, be guided by the writing printed on them as to which way up they go. Fit the springs to the moulded-in lower spring seat . . .

13 . . . then carefully raise both jacks, watching the brake pipes as before, and engage the spring tops with their top seats. If you don't get it right first go, lower the arm again, and have another bash. Just take care of those brake pipes.

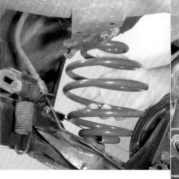

125

14 Okay, so the springs are in - let's get the shocks in place ASAP, so you can stop fretting about those brake pipes. First job, with these Spax shockers, is to fit the adjuster thumbwheel . . .

15 . . . tightening the screw with the Allen key provided.

16 Although the damper rate can obviously be adjusted when the shocks are on the car, it makes sense to put them to their basic recommended setting now. Refer to the instructions supplied, or ring the manufacturers if you're not sure where to set them. For safety, set both rears the same. These have twenty eight possible settings - count 'em!

17 Fit the bottom end of the shock into place on the suspension arm, and insert the bolt. It's not necessary to use a new bolt here, but if you had fun getting the old one out, it might not be a bad idea. At least clean the threads up with a wire brush, and use a spot of oil on them.

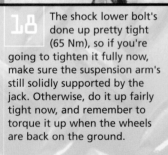

18 The shock lower bolt's done up pretty tight (65 Nm), so if you're going to tighten it fully now, make sure the suspension arm's still solidly supported by the jack. Otherwise, do it up fairly tight now, and remember to torque it up when the wheels are back on the ground.

19 Don't forget to clip the brake pipes back in place - remember, too, the horseshoe clip at the brake union on each side.

20 Raising the suspension arm as necessary, feed the shock absorber up into the wheelarch, and into its top mounting.

21 Back in the boot again, fit the mounting rubber, top plate/washer, and finally, the main nut and locknut, which must be tightened against each other. That is, screw on the main nut tight, then do up the locknut, then hold the main nut and give the locknut a final tweak. Simple. Stick the wheels back on, and see what sort of job you've done. You have just performed a Complete Overhaul of the Road Spring Assemblies. Oh dear.

But we're not finished yet. There's the small matter of the rear brake compensator to deal with. Now, if you've gone for a modest 35 to 40 mm drop, you might not need to modify your compensator. Our coilovers allow a major slam, though, and the adjustment available on the compensator wasn't enough. See "Nasty side-effects", later on. To get an idea of the

 22 required mods, here's the standard compensator.

Now, here's a pic of the bits needed to modify it (all locally-sourced, or easy to make). Two bolts, approx 100 mm, with matching nuts and washers, one piece of hollow bar, big enough diameter for one bolt to pass through, cut the same width as the compensator "frame" (to brace the assembly), and two extension plates, to elongate the compensator frame - holes drilled after offering the compensator up, to judge the extra reach required to

23 hook on the compensator spring.

And this is what the modified fella looks like. Because the first bolt (the one with the bracing sleeve) still sits in the original elongated slots in the compensator frame, there's still the same adjustment available when you get underneath to set it up.

 24 Which is what we'll do now.

With the car resting on its wheels, reach underneath and hook on the compensator spring first. Make sure the top/front nut and bolt are loose, to give

25 movement in the adjuster frame.

26 Now hook the compensator body over the rear axle, aligning the two studs with the holes . . .

27 . . . then fit the nuts from the front, and tighten them up.

28 Set the adjustment (using the sliding frame) so that the spring is only just under tension (no slack) . . .

29 . . . then tighten the top/front nut and bolt securely. Job done!

Techy stuff
The brake compensator shown here is fitted to the larger-engined Corsa. Smaller-engined models have compensator valves in the rear brake pipes - suspension height doesn't affect these.

Nasty side-effects
Camber angle and tracking

With any lowering "solution", your suspension and steering geometry will be affected - this will be more of a problem the lower you go. This will manifest itself as steering which either becomes lighter or (more usually) heavier, and tyres which scrub out their inner or outer edges in very short order - not funny, if you're running expensive low-profiles! Sometimes even the rear tyres can be affected in this way, but that's usually only after a serious slam. Whenever you've fitted a set of springs (and this applies to all types), have the geometry checked ASAP afterwards.

If you've dropped the car by 60 mm or more, chances are your camber angle will need adjusting. This is one reason why you might find the edges of your tyres wearing faster than you'd like (the other is your tracking being out). The camber angle is the angle the tyre makes with the road, seen from directly in front. You'll no doubt have seen race cars with the front wheels tilted in at the top, out at the bottom - this is negative camber, and it helps to give more grip and stability in hard cornering (but if your car was set this extreme, you'd kill the front tyres very quickly!). Virtually all road cars have a touch of negative camber on the front, and it's important when lowering to keep as near to the factory setting as possible, to preserve the proper tyre contact patch on the road. Trouble is, there's not usually much scope for camber adjustment on standard suspension, which is why (for some cars) you can buy camber-adjustable top plates which fit to the strut tops. Setting the camber accurately is a job for a garage with experience of modified cars - so probably not your local fast-fit centre, then.

Rear brake
pressure regulator
Some cars (Corsas included) have a rear brake pressure limiting valve fitted, which is linked to the rear suspension.

The idea is that, when the car's lightly loaded over the rear wheels, the braking effort to the rear is limited, to prevent the wheels locking up. With the boot full of luggage, the back end sinks down, and the valve lets full braking pressure through to the rear. When you slam the suspension, the valve is fooled into thinking the car's loaded up, and you might find the rear brakes locking up unexpectedly - could be a nasty surprise on a wet roundabout! The valves aren't generally intended to be easy to adjust, but they are quite simple devices - the best idea would be to get underneath and see how it looks when unloaded (on standard suspension), and try to re-create the same condition once the car's been dropped.

On the Corsa, the brake pressure regulator is under the car, in front of the right-hand rear wheel. The regulator linkage can be re-positioned on its mounting bracket, and does offer a limited amount of ride-height adjustability that way. The valve should be set so that, with the car resting on its wheels, the slack in the compensator spring has just been taken up. If the spring's under serious tension, the valve will already be letting too much braking effort through to the back wheels. Chances are, if your Corsa's been dropped by more than 35 to 40 mm, there won't be enough adjustment in the valve, and a small mod will be needed - more info on this mod in the section on fitting rear suspension.

Even with the compensator modified as we show you, the valve still won't work as the makers intended. The valve was meant to operate based on the full suspension travel originally available with the standard springs. Now the car's been lowered, the amount of travel will be less, so the valve will probably never be fully open, in fact. Just as well that 90% of the braking is done by the front wheels!

Suspension

The first thing to do is put the brace in its place! Lay it onto the strut tops, and see how much other stuff it interferes with. On our Corsa, it was obvious immediately that the wiring harness bracket attached to the driver's side strut top would need modifying, so we removed its plastic nuts and took it away.

01

Front
strut brace

Another item which is inspired by racing, the strut brace is another underbonnet accessory which you shouldn't be without.

The idea of the strut brace is that, once you've stiffened up your front suspension to the max, the car's body shell (to which the front suspension struts are bolted) may not be able to cope with the cornering forces being put through it, and will flex, leading to unsatisfactory handling. The strut brace (in theory) does exactly what it says on the tin, by providing support between the strut tops, taking the load off the bodyshell.

The strut brace can have an effect on handling, but the main reason to fit one is for show - and why not? Strut braces can be chromed, painted or anodised, and can be fitted with matching chromed/coloured strut top plates - a very tasty way to complement a detailed engine bay.

People also fit strut braces to the rear suspension mounts, usually on cars where the rear seats have been junked.

02 With the car resting on its wheels (quite important, if you don't want the struts to fall out), undo the two nuts securing the struts to the inner wings.

03 Fit just the brace end plates (easier than having the brace in the way, for now) onto the studs left sticking up through the strut tops, putting the nuts on just by hand for now.

04 Now for that wiring harness bracket mod we spoke of earlier. When the harness bracket was offered in place over the brace plate, part of it obscured the mounting for the brace bar itself - so we cut off the offending bit. Making sure you don't cut through the harness will prove to be a bonus here.

05 Offer the brace into position, and secure it on the driver's side with its nut and bolt, done up by hand for now. The next trick is to set the bar length so it fits into the plate on the passenger side, and the bolt will just go through (max tightness, in other words). There are two nuts either end of the brace, and the brace itself is what you turn to adjust its length. When you're happy, pop the other bolt in . . .

06 . . . and tighten it up securely. Now go back and tighten the nut/bolt on the driver's side, then do up the two strut top nuts on either side (if you've got a torque wrench, the setting's 30 Nm). Refit the wiring harness bracket, and secure it with the plastic nuts.

07 The final job is setting the brace bar fore-and-aft tilt, to clear (in our case) the filler cap for the coolant expansion tank. There's not much scope for movement, admittedly. Set the bar in its required position, and tighten the nuts at either end.

Brakes

The middle pedal

Uprating the brakes is actually a very easy bolt-on upgrade, but there are some points to consider. One of the strangest, given that improving the brakes should in theory also improve your chances of avoiding an accident, is that some insurance companies don't like performance brakes. You should still tell them anyway, and most specialist insurers won't up your premium.

Uprating the brakes will be a complete waste of time if you're a cheapskate on tyres. Cheap, no-name tyres or remoulds won't be able to translate extra braking power into actual vehicle-stopping power - they'll give up their grip on the tarmac and skid everywhere. Something like 90% of braking is done by the front wheels - ie the ones you steer with. If you consider that locked-up wheels also don't tend to steer very well, you'll begin to get an idea why good brakes and poor tyres are a dodgy mixture.

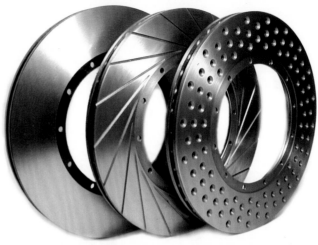

Performance discs

Besides the various brands of performance brake pads that go with them, the main brake upgrade is to fit performance front brake discs and pads. Discs are available in two main types - grooved and cross-drilled.

Grooved discs (which can be had with varying numbers of grooves) serve a dual purpose - the grooves provide a "channel" to help the heat escape, and they also help to de-glaze the pad surface, cleaning up the pads every time they're used. Some of the discs are made from higher-friction metal than normal discs, too, and the fact that they improve braking performance is well-documented.

Cross-drilled discs offer another route to heat dissipation, but one which can present some problems. Some of these discs can crack around the drilled holes after serious use. The trouble is that the heat "migrates" to the drilled holes (as was intended), but the heat build-up can be extreme, and the constant heating/cooling cycle can stress the metal to the point where it will crack. Discs which have been damaged in this way are extremely dangerous as they could break up completely at any time. Only fit discs of this type from established manufacturers offering a guarantee of quality, and check the discs regularly.

Performance discs also have a reputation for warping (nasty vibrations felt through the pedal). Now this may be so, but of course, the harder you use your brakes (and ones you've uprated may well get serious abuse), the greater the heat you'll generate. Cheap discs, or ones which have had a hard time over umpteen thousands of miles, probably will warp. So buy quality, and don't get too heroic on the brakes for too long.

Performance pads can be fitted to any brake discs, including the standard ones, but are of course designed to work best with heat-dissipating discs. Unless your Corsa's got a supercharged, turbocharged 2.0 litre 16-valve nutter of an engine under the bonnet, don't be tempted to go much further than "fast road" pads - anything more competition-orientated may take too long to come up to temperature on the road, and might leave you with less braking than before!

Lastly, fitting all the performance brake bits in the world is no use if your calipers have seized up. If, when you strip out your old pads, you find that one pad's worn more than the other, or that both pads have worn more on the left wheel than the right, your caliper pistons are sticking. Sometimes you can free them off by pushing them back into the caliper, but this could be a garage job to fix. If you drive around with sticking calipers, you'll eat pads and discs. Your choice.

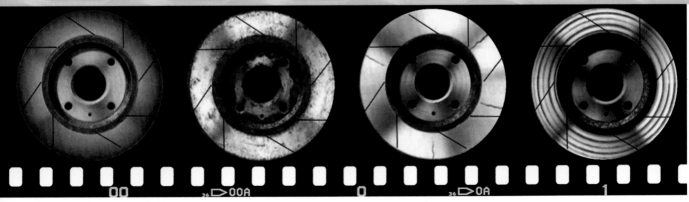

Brake
discs and pads

01 Loosen the wheel bolts, jack up the corner of the car you're working on, and take off the wheel. Make sure you've got an axle stand under a solid part of the car in case the jack gives out. Have a look in "Wheels & tyres" for more info on jacking up. First job is to prise off the pad retaining spring.

02 On the inside of the caliper, prise out the two plugs covering the caliper guide bolt heads. You now need a 7 mm Allen key to undo the two caliper guide bolts.

03 Lift away the caliper, complete with the inner brake pad . . .

Achtung!
Brake dust from old pads may contain asbestos. Wear a mask to avoid inhaling it. Dispose of old brake system components safely at your local waste recycling centre - don't just put them in the bin.

04 . . . which is clipped into the caliper piston, and easily un-clipped.

05 To get the new pads to fit, later on, you'll need to push the caliper piston back into the caliper. This will take some effort - here we are, using two sturdy screwdrivers, but water-pump pliers work well, too. If you push the pistons back too quickly (which is unlikely), there's a danger that the fluid seals in the master cylinder will flip round under the reversed hydraulic pressure, so take it steady.

06 Don't leave the caliper swinging by its hose - that's a good way to end up having to fit a new hose! Tuck it away on the anti-roll bar, or tie it up with a cable-tie.

07 By now, the outer pad may have fallen out on its own. But just in case it hasn't...

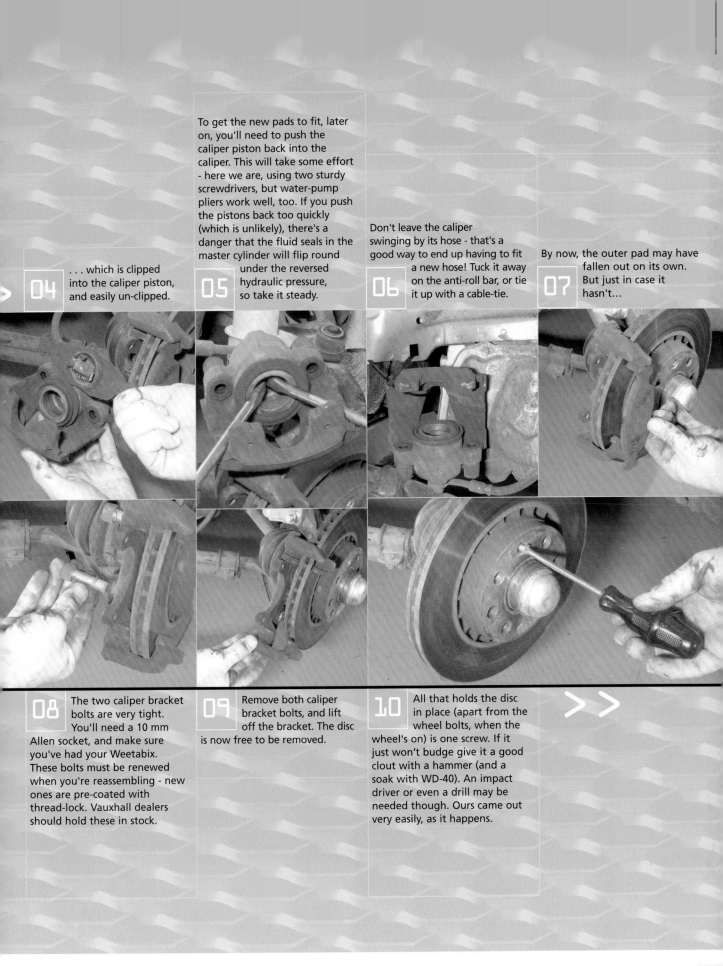

08 The two caliper bracket bolts are very tight. You'll need a 10 mm Allen socket, and make sure you've had your Weetabix. These bolts must be renewed when you're reassembling - new ones are pre-coated with thread-lock. Vauxhall dealers should hold these in stock.

09 Remove both caliper bracket bolts, and lift off the bracket. The disc is now free to be removed.

10 All that holds the disc in place (apart from the wheel bolts, when the wheel's on) is one screw. If it just won't budge give it a good clout with a hammer (and a soak with WD-40). An impact driver or even a drill may be needed though. Ours came out very easily, as it happens.

>>

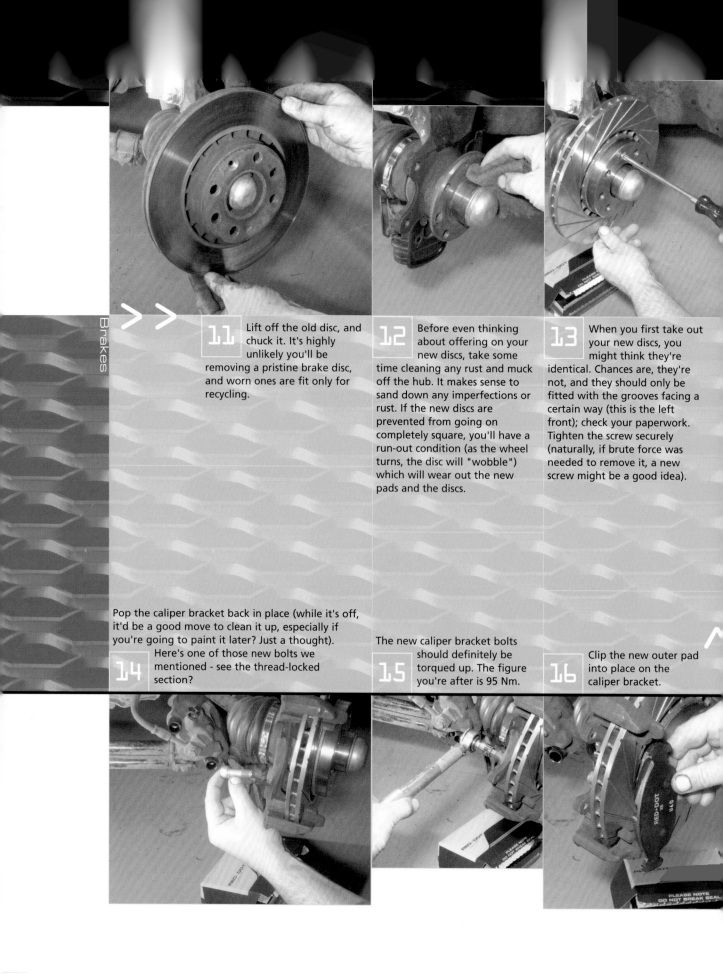

>>

11 Lift off the old disc, and chuck it. It's highly unlikely you'll be removing a pristine brake disc, and worn ones are fit only for recycling.

12 Before even thinking about offering on your new discs, take some time cleaning any rust and muck off the hub. It makes sense to sand down any imperfections or rust. If the new discs are prevented from going on completely square, you'll have a run-out condition (as the wheel turns, the disc will "wobble") which will wear out the new pads and the discs.

13 When you first take out your new discs, you might think they're identical. Chances are, they're not, and they should only be fitted with the grooves facing a certain way (this is the left front); check your paperwork. Tighten the screw securely (naturally, if brute force was needed to remove it, a new screw might be a good idea).

14 Pop the caliper bracket back in place (while it's off, it'd be a good move to clean it up, especially if you're going to paint it later? Just a thought). Here's one of those new bolts we mentioned - see the thread-locked section?

15 The new caliper bracket bolts should definitely be torqued up. The figure you're after is 95 Nm.

16 Clip the new outer pad into place on the caliper bracket.

17 Before clipping the inner pad into the caliper, it's worth smearing a little copper brake grease on the back of the pad, around the spring legs. Helps to prevent brake squeal.

18 Clip the inner pad into the caliper . . .

19 . . . then repeat the copper grease application on the outer pad . . .

Remember 1
It's a good idea to have your brake mods MOT-tested once you've fitted new discs and pads, and you might even be able to "blag" a free brake check at your local fast-fit centre if you're crafty! Brakes are a serious safety issue, and unless you're 100% confident that all is well, demo-ing your car's awesome new-found stopping ability could find you in the ditch…

Remember 2
New pads of any sort need careful bedding-in (over 100 miles of normal use) before they'll work properly - It's absolutely vital to follow the manufacturer's bedding in guidelines if you want the brakes to work as well as intended. If you build up the heat too soon they'll never work as well as they should.

20 . . . before sliding the caliper back over the disc. This is where you find out if you've pushed the caliper piston in far enough.

21 Fit the caliper guide bolts, and tighten them to the correct torque, too - this time, it's only 30 Nm.

22 The final act is to clip on the pad retaining spring. Easy in theory. The spring ends fit into the holes in the caliper, and the top and bottom lugs spring back round the "ears" on the caliper bracket.

One "downside" to fitted massive multi-spoked alloys is that people will be able to see your brakes! This being so, why not paint some of the brake components, possibly to match your chosen colour scheme (red is common, but isn't the only choice). Red brake calipers are often seen on touring cars, too. Corsas don't have rear discs, but painting the brake drums is acceptable under the circumstances. Don't buy fake rear discs, they don't fool anyone… For the less-sad among you, Vauxhall performance specialists will sell you a rear disc brake conversion kit.

Colour-coded calipers

Painting the calipers requires that they be clean - really clean. Accessory stores sell aerosol brake cleaner, which (apart from having a distinctive high-octane perfume) is just great for removing brake dust, and lots more besides! Some kits come complete with cleaner spray. Many of the kits advertise themselves on the strength of no dismantling being required, but we don't agree. Also, having successfully brush-painted our calipers, we would recommend it over spray paint.

Tricks n' tips
If you have trouble reassembling your brakes after painting, you probably got carried away and put on too much paint. Once it's fully dry, the excess paint can be trimmed off with a knife.

01 The best way to paint the calipers is to do some dismantling first. The kits say you don't have to, but you'll get a much better result from a few minutes' extra work. We removed the caliper, pads and mounting bracket, then took off the disc, and re-mounted the bracket and caliper on their own. Have a look earlier in this section for more info. Doing it our way means no risk of paint going on the pads or disc!

02 Get the wire brush out, and attack the rusty old caliper to get rid of all the loose muck. If the caliper's black with brake dust, try not to breathe any in. Squirt on your brake cleaner (our kit came with its own can), giving the caliper a good dose, and get wiping as soon as possible. Spraying alone will only loosen the muck, and a good scrub is the only answer. If you don't get it spotless, you'll get black streaks in the paint later.

03 Even though you may have removed everything except the caliper, there's still a bit of masking-up to do, like round the bleed nipples. How much masking you'll need depends on how big a brush you're using, and how steady your hand is!

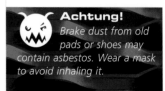

Achtung!
Brake dust from old pads or shoes may contain asbestos. Wear a mask to avoid inhaling it.

Our paint came in two tins - one paint, one hardener. Pour one into the other, stir, and you then have about four hours max before the paint sets hard in the tin. So if you're painting calipers and drums, it's best to do all the prep work, and be totally ready to start painting at all four

04 corners of the car, before you mix the paint.

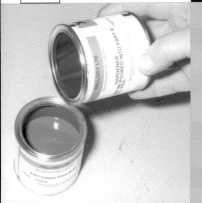

01 At least there's no dismantling with drums - get the rear end jacked up, wheels off (see "Wheels & tyres" if you need jacking info) and just get stuck in with the wire brush, sandpaper (to smooth the surface), then it's spray on the brake cleaner and wipe thoroughly.

Painting **drums**

Mask up the section of drum where the wheel bolts on - there's no point painting a bit which is covered by the wheel anyway, and it's not a good idea to get thick paint down the wheel bolt holes... Trim the mask up with a knife to get a neat edge. Also mask up the edge of the brake backplate (the bit that doesn't turn) - you'll hardly see the edge of it

02 when the wheel's on.

Painting the drums is much easier than the rather fiddly calipers. One piece of advice - for the drums, use a thicker, better-quality brush than the one they give you in the kit - you'll get a much smoother paint finish on the drums. Again, two coats of paint is a good idea. Another good idea is to let off the handbrake and turn the drum half a turn every so

03 often until the paint's dry.

05 Stick some card or paper under the brake, 'cos this paint's not easy to get off your driveway. And, er - get painting! Remember that you only have to paint the bits you'll see when the wheels are on. Once you start painting, it's a job knowing where not to paint! It's best to do more than one coat, we found. Follow the instructions with your kit on how long to leave between coats, but remember the time limit before the paint in the tin's useless. Wait 'til the paint's totally dry (like overnight, or longer) before reassembling.

Interiors

The Corsa's slinky curves extend to the dash design, which is great. But - the Corsa shows its GM/Opel German design origins by being very black inside. Apart from some seat fabrics which look like the end result of a bad night on the beer, the Corsa interior décor is dull with a capital D. But you need suffer no longer, because the interior really is one area where most of the goodies are pretty easy to fit, and provided you go for one particular theme (rather than a mixture), the end result can certainly help you forget you're in a base model, if indeed you are...

00

To be fairer to the Corsa, very few of today's standard interiors are anything to shout about, particularly when you compare them with the sort of look that can easily be achieved with the huge range of product that's out there. As with the exterior styling, though, remember that fashions can change very quickly - so don't be afraid to experiment with a look that you really like, because chances are, it'll be the next big thing anyway.

Removing stuff

Take it easy and break less

Many of the procedures we're going to show involve removing interior trim panels (either for colouring or to fit other stuff), and this can be tricky. It's far too easy to break plastic trim, especially once it's had a chance to go a bit brittle with age. Another "problem" with the Corsa is that the interior trim is pretty well-attached (and the designers have been very clever at hiding several vital screws), meaning that it can be a pig to get off. They also seem to love using Torx screws - invest in a set of Torx keys (like Allen keys), otherwise you'll come across a screw or two that won't come out using any other type of screwdriver. We'll try to avoid the immortal words "simply unclip the panel", and instead show you how properly, but inevitably at some stage, a piece of trim won't "simply" anything.

The important lesson here is not to lose your temper, as this has a highly-destructive effect on plastic components, and may result in a panel which no amount of carbon film or colour spray can put right, or make fit again. Superglue may help, but not every time. So - take it steady, prise carefully, and think logically about how and where a plastic panel would have to be attached. You'll encounter all sorts of trim clips (some more fragile than others) in your travels - when these break, as they usually do, know that many of them can be bought in ready packs from accessory shops, and that the rarer ones will be available from a Vauxhall dealer, probably off the shelf.

Door trim panel

You'll find plenty of excuses for removing your door trim panels - fitting speakers, re-trimming the panel, de-locking, even window tinting, so we'd better tell you how...

Open the window, by whatever means you have. Now, if you've got wind-up windows: prise the winder handle to open a gap between it and the circular disc behind. Work the edge of a piece of (clean) cloth/rag into the gap behind the handle, from underneath. Using a "sawing" action, work the cloth side to side, and also pull the ends of the cloth upwards. It may take some time, but what you're trying to do is snag the ends of the spring clip holding the handle in place - when you do, the sawing action should work the clip up and off, allowing the handle to be pulled from the splines. With patience, it does work - just watch for that spring clip flying off into the blue! There are tools for the job, but how often are you going to do this?

01

02 Prise off the trim panel from the inside of the door mirror.

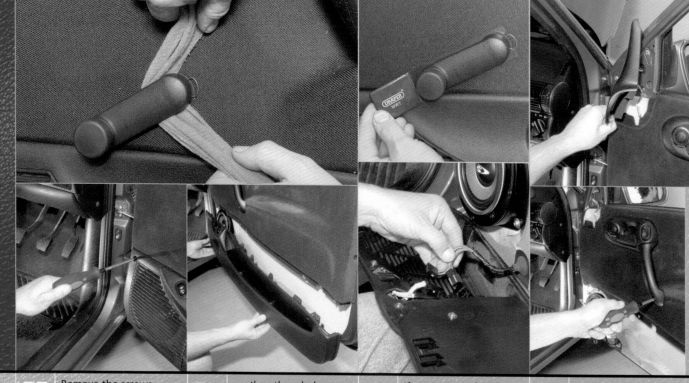

03 Remove the screws securing the door pocket - there's three along the top edge, and four below . . .

04 . . . then the whole pocket just comes away (and your shades/lighter/CDs go on the floor - so remove them first!).

05 If you've got electric windows, disconnect the wiring plugs from the window switches as the door pocket comes off.

06 The door pull handle is held on by a total of three screws - first take out the one you can see, at the bottom of the handle . . .

07 . . . now prise off the outer cover (disconnecting the tweeter wiring, if your ICE install's anything like ours!) . . .

08 . . . and remove the two screws.

09 The pull handle can now be removed - by this point, it might well have fallen off, of course.

10 The trim panel itself is now held by one more screw at the front . . .

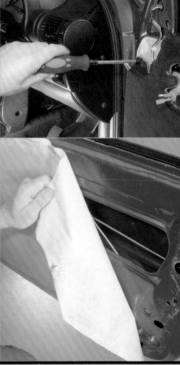

11 . . . and two screws at the rear.

12 Finally, prise the panel up at the top edge (next to the window channel) to release it, and lift it to clear the door lock button. Job done!

13 If you need access to the door inner workings (which you probably will), prise out the pegs which secure the two plastic mounts at the back edge of the door, and remove the mounts.

14 Take your time peeling off the weathersheet inside the door - it's there for a reason, to keep water out of the car. Peel it back slowly, and if you don't need to remove it completely, fold it back and stick it temporarily with some tape, to save wrecking it.

01 With the glovebox closed to start with, remove the two screws visible underneath it

Glovebox

One of the less attractive Corsa dash features is the glovebox - a hideous slab of black plastic, right in front of the passengers you'd like to impress. So - do we mod the whole panel, or just liven it up by doing the handle? Over to you...

Now open the glovebox and remove the three screws inside on the top edge (if you've got a

02 passenger airbag, there'll only be two screws).

03 Now the whole glovebox just slides out.

If you want to "enhance" the glovebox handle, those thoughtful chaps at Vauxhall just

04 clipped on a cover - unclipping is the work of a moment!

Dash vents

Left-hand end vent

The Corsa dash vents are actually quite stylish as they are, but there's no reason why you can't give "nature" a hand...

01 Remove the glovebox. Using a small screwdriver (and maybe a piece of card behind it, to prevent damage), prise down the vent grille past its normal lower stop - this takes some effort, but brute force is not advised!

02 The grille should click down just enough that you can see two screws inside the vent, one either side at the top. Once these screws have been loosened, there's a good chance they'll drop down behind the left-hand kick panel - fortunately, this comes off very easily! Also remove the bottom screw below the vent housing.

03 The vent housing is now free to come out, but you'll find it's held in place by being shoved into the vent ducting behind. As long as you can see the housing's otherwise free, this is one time when a bit of welly can be used.

Dash vents

Right-hand end vent

01 Vauxhall in their wisdom have combined the right-hand end vent housing with the main light switch assembly - just for fun. Pull out the main light switch, then press in the retaining clip from below, and pull off the switch knob.

02 Use a pair of thin-nosed pliers to squeeze the clips together, and withdraw the light switch from the panel.

03 Unclip and remove the fusebox cover . . .

04 . . . then remove the two screws behind it.

05 As with the left-hand vent, prise down the grille for access to the two screws inside. Try not to lose the screws!

06 Prise out the remaining switches (foglight, headlight aim) from the front.

07 Now for the fun part. The switch connector plugs have to be unclipped from the panel before it will come out. The main light switch connector can be released using a small screwdriver, from the front . . .

08 . . . but the others had to be unclipped from the back. To release the vent housing from the vent duct - give it a good tug!

01 First, pull off the knob from the recirc slider . . .

02 . . . and prise out the slider panel behind.

03 For research purposes, we took off the fan switch knob - then found you don't actually have to! For info, pull the switch out, press in the retaining clip from below, and take off the knob. The two other knobs just pull off.

Centre vents
and heater panel

04 As with the two end vents, prise down the two vent grilles (sensibly using some card to protect the dash) . . .

05 . . . for access to the two screws behind - that's one screw behind each vent.

06 With the top two screws removed, you can now take out the two lower screws, which are behind the recirc panel you removed earlier.

07 Now, with a firm but steady hand, you can pull out the heater panel - but only so far.

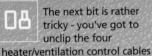

08 The next bit is rather tricky - you've got to unclip the four heater/ventilation control cables from the back of the panel. The cable ends are hooked over pegs on the heater control levers, and can be flicked off or unclipped with a small screwdriver. The first one's the hardest, as there's not much room to work . . .

09 . . . but as soon as one or two cables are off, you can pull the panel out further. Make sure you note which cable goes where! Here's the notes on our Corsa (yours might be different):

Driver's side "front" cable - Yellow
Driver's side "rear" cable - Grey
Passenger side cable - Black
Passenger side "horizontal" cable - Yellow

10 Even with the cables off, the panel's still held by the wiring plugs for various switches. Removing some of these is easy . . .

11 . . . but the plug for the hazard warning light switch is a pig to remove. Working through the front of the panel, release the tiny clips with a small screwdriver - the plug then slides out vertically.

12 If required, you can unclip the rear (black) section of the panel, by releasing the clips with your trusty small screwdriver.

13 After pulling off the remaining heater controls (if you haven't already) . . .

14 . . . you can separate the white plastic section from the main panel. Depending on the age of your Corsa, the white section may be held on by two small screws at the front, or by a retaining lug above the three controls.

15 The symbol panel for the three controls just lifts out (or falls out!).

149

Passenger "crash panel"

01 Take out the glovebox, and the left-hand end vent, as described earlier. Now remove the screw from the end of the panel . . .

02 . . . and the two screws from below.

03 Now the panel can be lifted out.

 Achtung!
If your Corsa has a passenger airbag, think very carefully before tampering with it. If you're removing it to either paint it or cover it with carbon-fibre film (or similar), this is not advisable - covering it will stop it working altogether. Removing the airbag is an involved procedure - details in the Haynes manual if you're keen.

Centre console

01 Prise off the cover panel at the front of the console . . .

02 . . . and remove the cross-head screw behind.

03 Unclip the gaiter (which has a plastic frame at the base) from the gear lever, and fold it upwards.

04 The console now slides to the rear, to disengage two pegs on the floor - the console can then be moved forwards and twisted around as necessary to remove it (feed the gaiter frame down through).

Mirror knobs
& window winders

01 As for window winders - okay, so not everyone's got them, but if you do, you can't be happy with how they look! Removal's a bit of a pain - either use the cloth method described in door trim panel removal earlier, or use a proper tool.

02 Our new winder handles - don't they look saucy?

03 They're quite easy to fit, too – with one small exception. They have to be completely dismantled before you start! All four screws and the centre cap have to come off, just to take out the centre mounting screw, which on the Corsa, you don't need – and which gets in the way of any attempt to fit the handle onto the old splines. Oh well.

04 When the handle's back together again (minus the centre-screw), they slip onto the splines, and there's a little Allen screw to pin 'em in place. Simple – and tasty enough to show up all that other black door furniture. So do something about it soon!

How about upgrading some of the door furniture? The old mirror knob just pulls off (sounds a bit rude). Most of the new knobs available slip into place, and have a grub screw for tightening up. Simple!

Other **options**

01 You might feel that all this ally stuff's a bit tacky – after all it has been done to death. That's how we felt, too, so we chose to remove a selection of bits from the door trim panel, and paint them instead. For more details on how to do this, see *"Get the cans out"* later on. Here's the primed-up bits getting rubbed down . . .

02 . . . and now top-coated and lacquered.

03 The final fitted result - discreet but tasty! Of course, there are other colours you could try…

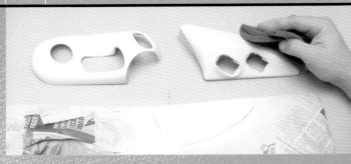

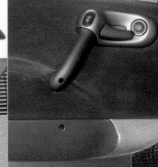

01 Remove the door trim panel as described earlier.

02 Check that your new buttons will actually fit through the hole in the door trim panel! Then hold it up to the old button, to get a rough idea how it'll look.

Door lock buttons

03 Do a "trial run" now. Attach the new button to the existing rod, using the screw clamp provided. Now test the operation of the lock button - will the screw clamp catch on the door frame? Where will the clamp need to be set, to avoid problems?

04 When you've sussed it out, mark where to cut off the old button . . .

05 . . . then get busy with the hacksaw.

06 Use the screw clamp to fit the new button to the sawn-off rod, and you're in business!

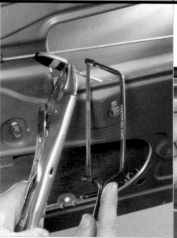

Flashing door pins

As you may have noticed, our door pins have wires and an LED. Time to feed them some electric! You need a live and an earth - or do you? We found an interesting solution - feed one LED wire an ignition live, and the other a permanent live. This doesn't blow the LED, as you might think, but when it gets two lives, it stops working - therefore, this way, when the ignition's on, the door pins don't flash. Do you want them going all the time you're driving? Thought not.

We then took the (grey) live wire from the door contact switch, which means the pins only flash when the doors are shut, and the ignition's off. Just what you want! Check that you've got the right wire by pulling the interior light fuse out of the fusebox, and test with a meter.

Running wiring into the doors is a pain on modern cars - they've all got massive multi-pin plugs you can see when the doors are open, but these are no help. You might eventually have to drill holes in the door edges to feed the new wires through (remember to seal the holes with silicone, if you try this). An alternative to drilling is to "re-assign" wires which you've stopped using - if a wire's redundant, you can decide what goes down it. For instance, our Corsa had a Vauxhall alarm, and the driver's door had a key-operated switch attached, with wires off it. When we disconnected the switch (in fitting our new alarm), we ended up with "spare" wires running through the door connector. Having checked them with a meter to make sure they weren't live, we traced the red and yellow wires inside the car, cut them off and soldered on our door-contact live and an ignition live from the fusebox.

If your Corsa has electric windows or mirrors, you could run a live off one of those, inside the door - but the LEDs will be on permanently if you don't try one of our dodges.

Door sill trims

You can get these in any colour you like, as long as it's chrome. One piece of advice, if you're planning major interior mods - fit the sill trims last. That way, there's less chance of scratching and scuffing 'em up during fitting the rest of the interior. Fitting isn't hard, but you will need a steady hand.

01 First, remove the plastic sill trim just inside the car (Torx screws), and peel up the rubber door seal.

02 Clean the sills with washing-up liquid (or, if they're realy filthy, with strong solvent). Dry them off thoroughly before going any further.

03 Do a trial fitting before peeling off the backing paper, so you know what to line the trim up with on the car. Our trims lined up at either end with the little notches already present in the sills - otherwise, mark where the ends of the trims will be with masking tape, as a guide. Also note how far onto the sills the trims will come - again, on our car, there was a handy line in the sill to follow.

04 Peel off the backing from the sticky pads, and hold your breath.

05 The sticky on the sticky pads is very, very sticky indeed. Make sure you've lined up the sill trim accurately before finally smacking it in place, because it won't be coming off again without a fight! Wipe over the tops of the trims, pressing down firmly to secure.

Anything but black?

The interior trim on the Corsa is at least curvy, and doesn't rattle much. And that's the best we can say about it. Fortunately, there's plenty you can do to personalise it, and there are three main routes to take:

Spray paint

Available in any colour you like, as long as it's… not black. This stuff actually dyes softer plastics and leather, and comes in a multi-stage treatment, to suit all plastic types - don't just buy the top coat, because it won't work! Special harder-wearing spray is required for use on steering wheels. Ordinary spray paint for bodywork might damage some plastics, and won't be elastic - good primer is essential. Make sure you also buy lots of masking tape.

As you're about to discover, we used "ordinary" spray paint very successfully on our Corsa, and there's no doubt it gives an excellent effect, matching totally with the car. But we're not kidding about prepping the panels for spraying - those silicone sprays for tarting-up plastic trim take a lot of work to get off. Give it plenty!

Adhesive or shrink-fit film

Available in various wild colours, carbon, ally, and, er… walnut (don't!). Probably best used on flatter surfaces, or at least those without complex curves, or you'll have to cut and join - spray is arguably better here.

Replacement panels

The easiest option, as the panels are supplied pre-cut, ready to fit. Of course, you're limited then to styling just the panels supplied. Not sure these have ever been spotted for a Corsa, but we continue to live in hope...

If you fancy something more posh, how about trimming your interior bits in leather? Very saucy. Available in various colours, and hardly any dearer than film, you also get that slight "ruffled" effect on tighter curves.

Get the cans out

For the Corsa interior, we found that the spray approach was the most successful - but that's just us, and for our chosen look. We tried (carbon-fibre-look) film for some things, otherwise complete colour coding would be a bit too much.

One thing to realise about painting is that it's a multi-stage process. With the Foliatec paint system, many people think they can get away by just buying the top coat, which then looks like a cheap option compared to film - wrong! Even the proper interior spray top coat won't stay on for long without the matching primer, and the finish won't be wear-resistant without the finishing sealer spray. So - buy the complete system! You'll also need a general-purpose degreaser, such as meths, perhaps. Just remember - the cloth shouldn't turn black when you're using your chosen solvent - if it does, you're damaging the finish! If you take out the black too far on a part that's not being sprayed all over, you'll have a nasty white-black finish to any non-painted surface...

Providing you're a dab hand with the masking tape, paint gives you the flexibility to be more creative. With our interior, we decided to try colour-matching the exterior of the car - our Corsa Sport came in Arden blue metallic, which ain't a bad colour for standard. Could we get ordinary car body paint to work on interior plastics? Only one way to find out...

Choice of paint's one thing, but what to paint? Well, not everything - for instance, we avoided high-wear areas like door handles. Just makes for an easier life. The clock "hood" and heater panel are obvious first choices, as is the curvy instrument surround. Having done the centre vents, it seemed sensible to carry on with the end vents, and we also took in the ashtray. There's no really useful "line" to mask to on the centre console, so we had the choice of either doing all of it or just a little highlighting.

Don't be afraid to experiment with a combination of styles - as long as you're confident you can blend it all together, anything goes! We didn't want to paint the "passenger crash panel" above the glovebox (too much blue), so we carbon-fibred it with film. We also carbon-fibred the glovebox handle, and a piece in the "tray" at the front of the console. Our chosen gear knob (chrome, because all the blue ones were the wrong shade) had a carbon-fibre panel, and our handbrake knob was almost all carbon fibre. This way, we managed to "tie together" the blue paint and fibre look, by keeping it going all round the cabin. Sometimes, by going for just one theme (like blue paint) you become a slave to it...

01 Clean up the surface to be sprayed, using a suitable degreaser - such as meths. You must use something strong, to get off any silicone-based products you may have used, as these are death to paint adhesion. If you're not going to paint the whole thing, don't degrease it all, or you might ruin the finish on the black bits.

02 Mask up the bits you don't want sprayed, as necessary. Make sure you protect all surfaces from overspray. Putting the topcoat on very "dusty" results in a lot of spray in the air. You can never do too much masking. Time taken masking will be repaid in time not spent re-doing the job.

03 After you've masked-up your chosen piece, it's worth giving it a final wipe over with solvent before applying any paint - in handling the piece to mask it, you'll have made it "dirty".

Painting trim

04 Apply a mist coat of primer - this is essential to help the paint "stick" to the plastic. Allow plenty of time for the primer to dry. If you're using ordinary spray as a topcoat (like we did), you'll need a special primer for plastics, which is readily available.

05 Now for the topcoat - this should be applied very "dusty", which means you spray from slightly further away than normal, and let the paint fall onto the job, rather than blast it on using the full force of the aerosol spray. Allow time for each one to dry (a few minutes) before banging some more on.

06 Once you're happy that there's even coverage, let the last top coat dry, then slap on the sealer coat (or lacquer, in our case). This final coat is intended to improve wear-resistance (not much good if your carefully-applied paint rubs off in a few weeks). You should only need a light coat to finish the job.

07 Let the paint go tacky (rather than fully dry) before peeling off the masking, and take care when you do - if the paint's too dry, you'll peel some of the paint off with the mask! If you're in any doubt, take your steadiest hand and sharpest knife to the edges of the masking tape before peeling.

Filming your Corsa

If you fancy creating a look that's a bit more special than plain paint colours, film is the answer - but be warned - it's not the easiest stuff in the world to use, and so isn't everyone's favourite. If you want a brushed-aluminium look, or fancy giving your Corsa the carbon-fibre treatment, there really is no alternative (apart from the lazy-man option of new panels, of course). For our Corsa, we chose to cover the passenger crash panel above the glovebox, and the glovebox handle (which helpfully has a detachable cover, so we detached it!).

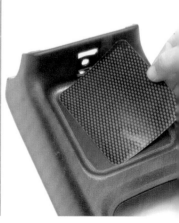

01 First clean and degrease- see the advice earlier in the section for painting.
On a heavily-grained finish, remember that the grain will show through thin film, and a deep grain means the film won't stick all over the surface. Not a good idea to go mad with the wet-and-dry (or Scotchbrite), to get rid of the grain - you'll destroy the surface totally.

02 Cut the film roughly to size, remembering to leave plenty of excess for trimming - it's also a good idea to have plenty to fold around the edges, because the film has a nasty habit of peeling off, otherwise.

03 Next, gently warm up both the panel, and the film itself.

04 Peel off the backing, being careful that the film stays as flat as possible. Also take care, when you pick the film up, that it doesn't stick to itself.

Applying film "crash" panel

05 Stick the film on straight - very important with any patterned finish. Start at one edge or corner, and work across, to keep the air bubbles and creases to a minimum. If you get a really bad crease, it's best to unpeel a bit and try again - the adhesive's very tacky, and there's no movement available.

06 Work out the worst of the air bubbles with a soft cloth - get the stuff to stick as best you can before trimming, or it'll all go horribly wrong. To be sure it's stuck (especially important on a grained surface), go over it firmly with the edge of your least-important piece of "plastic" - not a credit card.

07 Once the film's basically laid on, it's time for trimming - which is the tricky bit. We found it was much easier to trim up the tricky bits once the film had been warmed up using a hairdryer or heat gun, but don't overdo it! Make sure you've also got a very sharp knife - a blunt one will ripple the film, and may tear it.

08 To get the film to wrap neatly round a curved edge, make several slits almost up to the edge, then wrap each sliver of film around, and stick on firmly. If the film's heated as you do this, it wraps round and keeps its shape - meaning it shouldn't try and spring back, ruining all your hard work!

Glovebox handle

01
Removing the glovebox handle shouldn't tax anyone's skills too far - it just unclips.

02
Although it's not as important as it would be for spraying, it's still worth roughening the surface, to make sure the film's sticky sticks.

03
Just to prove that decent results are possible on smaller items with complex curves, we bring you - this! First, clean and roughen the surface, then cut the film roughly to size . . .

04 . . . stick it on straight, and get out any bubbles or creases.

05 Trim the edges - here, the corners are tricky, but by slitting the film, you can wrap the edges quite neatly. Warming the film from time to time helps.

06 Smooth around the edges with a soft cloth or rag, to make sure they're stuck.

Bum notes

There are limitations to using film, and the quality of the film itself has a lot to do with that. We had major problems doing any kind of job with one particular make of brushed-aluminium-look film - it was a nightmare to work with, and the edges had peeled the next day. Buying quality film will give you a long-lasting result to be proud of, with much less skill requirement and lots less swearing. But it still pays not to be too ambitious with it!

07 If you're worried the edges will lift, the instructions suggest painting on some nail varnish. Or you could use lacquer.

08 Clipping the finished handle back on. You could always paint the handle, and carbon-fibre the entire glovebox! Or…

Or - how about this?

Desperate to liven up our dull centre console, without spraying the whole thing, our mechanic got all creative suddenly. We first masked and sprayed an edge of blue to highlight the tray at the front of the centre console, then cut out a panel of carbon-fibre film to sit neatly inside. Haynes do arty mods!

01 To begin with remove the gearknob. It's not screwed on, and needs a good hard tug to remove it. Becareful not to pull too hard and damage the gear linkage.

02 If you're changing the gaiter as well as the knob, remove the centre console as described earlier. Unclip the gaiter, and lift it and the reverse gear selector collar off the gear lever. If you look carefully, you can see which way round the beige plastic bit at the base of the selector fits.

03 Depending on the design of your new gaiter, you might want to lift out this section of sound proofing matting from the gearchange mechanism - our gaiter was designed to clip over the white plastic "cage" underneath the matting.

04 And now - the time has come to be rid of that depressing old gaiter! Snip the cable-tie at the top . . .

Gear gaiter

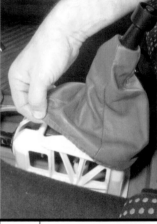

05 . . . and throw it! Don't be in a huge hurry to ditch the reverse gear selector, though - you'll be needing that! The original gaiter is stapled to a plastic "frame" - some replacement gaiters are meant to be fitted the same way, so un-staple your old gaiter now (watch your fingers!).

06 Turn your new gaiter inside-out, and fit the reverse gear selector into it, so that the selector operating collar (the bit you pull up on to select reverse) is through the gaiter. Tie your laces . . .

07 . . . then turn the gaiter the right way out.

08 Make sure you get the reverse selector the right way round (try working it, and you should get the idea), then fit the gaiter. Depending on which one you've got, either stretch it over the old plastic frame from the original gaiter, or fit it over the white plastic "cage".

Centre console mods

01 Because our gaiter wouldn't stretch over the original plastic frame, we found that, when the centre console was fitted back, you could see down the gap at the front of the console, past the new gaiter. In other words, we had too big a hole now, in the console. What we needed was something to fill the gap. We cut out a piece of card roughly to size, then attacked an old oil bottle with a Stanley knife, as it's black, plastic, and easy to cut to shape.

02 Trim the piece to size with scissors.

03 Now using a hot glue gun . . .

04 . . . the new size-reducing section of plastic is pinned in place.

05 You might not have the same "hole" grief we did - but you might still fancy a chrome gaiter surround. Fitting's pretty easy - hold the surround in place, and drill through. You'll need a pretty small drill bit though! Keep the drill vertical, or your screws will go in wonky.

06 Fit the screws, and the surround's sorted!

Gear knobs

01 Take your time when choosing your new knob - the Corsa has a lift-for-reverse gear lever, and not all the knobs out there are ideal to use with this. A good example is our first knob. The first step is to slip on the chrome collar . . .

02 . . . then choose a rubber sleeve that's a nice tight fit over the lever . . .

03 . . . and slip on the knob.

04 Final job is to fit and tighten up the grub screw on the collar. The height of this knob made it awkward to lift the reverse collar with one hand.

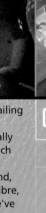

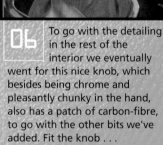

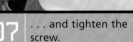

05 Our next knob was a blue anodised one. Fitting-wise, this is pretty easy! Fit the knob over the lever, turning it so the grub screw hole is at the front (where you won't see it), then fit and tighten the screw. Richbrook even supply a tiny shift pattern sticker, to finish it off. This knob works fine with the reverse gear collar.

06 To go with the detailing in the rest of the interior we eventually went for this nice knob, which besides being chrome and pleasantly chunky in the hand, also has a patch of carbon-fibre, to go with the other bits we've added. Fit the knob . . .

07 . . . and tighten the screw.

08 And here's one we made earlier!

01 Your sexy new gear knob and gaiter's making the sad black stick behind look even worse, so do something about it. First, pull the gaiter back off the rear of the knob, then tap the sleeve off from behind with a hammer and punch.

02 The gaiter is attached to a plastic frame, pushed through a hole in the carpet. Work the frame out of the carpet, and slide the gaiter off the handbrake lever. Note the slight lack of front seats - we're cheating!

03 First thing to check with the new sleeve is that it'll fit sensibly, and allow you to release the handbrake when it's fitted. This sleeve was too chunky! We used a nice chrome knob instead...

04 The old gaiter is stapled to a plastic frame - so we un-stapled it. To perform the same stapling trick requires a rather special stapler - this is an electric job, and very powerful it is, too. This sort of tool is dead easy to use, not expensive (about 20 quid) and should have plenty of uses for the car-modder. An ordinary mechanical stapler may not be man enough to staple through thick plastic.

Handbrake
sleeve & gaiters

05 The knob itself is attached to the handbrake lever by several grub screws.

06 Turn the gaiter inside-out, slip it over the lever, and use a cable-tie to attach it to the groove at the rear of the new knob.

07 Now carefully turn the gaiter the right way out. This takes a bit of time and patience - stay cool. Fit the gaiter into the carpet, and you're sorted.

08 You are now allowed to admire the finished result.

Coloured dials

01 If you haven't yet removed the steering wheel - don't! You don't really need to for this. Of course, if you're fitting a new wheel and a dial kit, it's a good plan to do both at once. First, remove three cross-head screws from the lower shroud.

02 Turn the wheel 90° one way, then prise out the trim cap and remove the screw behind. Turn the wheel back straight, then 90° the other way, and repeat the screw-removal process on the other side of the shrouds.

03 With a bit of persuasion, the lower shroud will now come down. Take out the rubber grommet which sits round the switch. You may need to pull the shroud outwards, to pass it over the ignition switch.

04 Now remove a total of three screws from the instrument panel surround - there's one each side at the bottom . . .

05 . . . and one more at the top . . .

06 . . . then, with a little bit of fiddling, the surround will come free, and lift out.

07 Now to remove the old clocks, and - who put that blue wheel there? Oh well. There's one screw either side at the bottom corners to remove . . .

Interiors

08 . . . then, if you're lucky, the whole panel comes out. If you're less lucky, the reason why the clocks won't come out is that you've got an old-fashioned speedo cable. Trace the thick cable under the bonnet down to the screw-on connection at the transmission, and unscrew it. This should give enough slack inside the car to pull the clocks out. The cable can then be unclipped from the back of the speedo itself, and the clocks removed.

09 The instrument main "glass" cover just slides off . . .

Tricks 'n' tips
Just make sure you get the right kit for your car, and don't start stripping anything until you're sure it's the right one - look carefully. Most dial kit makers want to know exactly what markings you have on your speedo and rev counter. If they don't ask, be worried - the kit they send could well be wrong for your car, and might not even fit.

10 . . . then the surround can be unclipped and removed.

11 Let's tackle those big dials first. Hold the rev counter needle up, and pull out the needle's stop peg with a pair of pliers.

12 Now remove the two tiny screws in the centre of the dial. Put 'em somewhere safe - there'll be plenty of other small, easily-lost items removed before you're finished!

13 Before you go vandalising your existing dials, now is good time to check that you've got the right kit for your set of clocks.

14 Now you have to slice up your old dials. The idea is to slit the thin plastic dial, so it'll come off without taking off the needle. Make as many cuts as you like, but don't bend the needle.

15 The smaller dials have needles which can safely be pulled off, and the dials just unclip and lift away.

16 Ever wondered how your clocks look, naked? Now you know.

Because your new dials have to have a bigger-than-normal hole in the centre (so they'll fit over the needles), the speedo and rev counter centres now have to be "covered up" with black tape, so the naked clocks don't show through. Lockwood provide a sheet of pre-cut black bits, and they recommend placing the **17** two halves using a small screwdriver. In with the right-hand half . . .

. . . and now the left-hand half. Try if you can to make them overlap just slightly - at any **18** rate, don't leave a gap, or you'll need a spot of black paint to cover up.

19 When you're ready, peel off the backing strips . . .

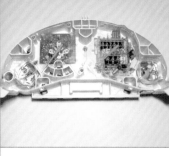

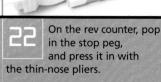
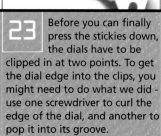
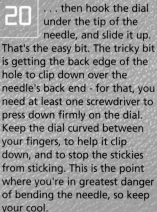
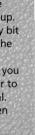

20 . . . then hook the dial under the tip of the needle, and slide it up. That's the easy bit. The tricky bit is getting the back edge of the hole to clip down over the needle's back end - for that, you need at least one screwdriver to press down firmly on the dial. Keep the dial curved between your fingers, to help it clip down, and to stop the stickies from sticking. This is the point where you're in greatest danger of bending the needle, so keep your cool.

21 Still keeping the dial curved, line up the screw holes and pop in the two tiny screws.

22 On the rev counter, pop in the stop peg, and press it in with the thin-nose pliers.

23 Before you can finally press the stickies down, the dials have to be clipped in at two points. To get the dial edge into the clips, you might need to do what we did - use one screwdriver to curl the edge of the dial, and another to pop it into its groove.

24 Press the dial down, and clean off any marks. Only three more to do!

25 With the speedo, the dial has to be fitted over the trip meter knob, which makes feeding in the needle end even trickier . . .

26 . . . but, as you can see, not impossible.

27 Work the dial into its two clips . . .

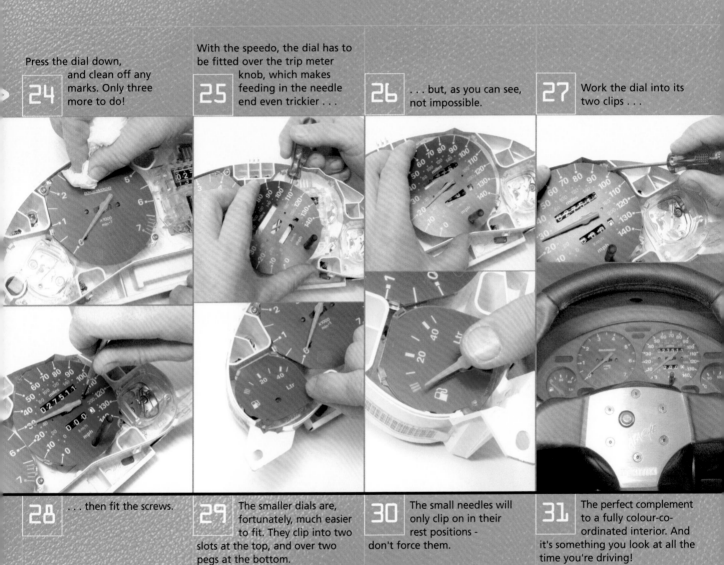

28 . . . then fit the screws.

29 The smaller dials are, fortunately, much easier to fit. They clip into two slots at the top, and over two pegs at the bottom.

30 The small needles will only clip on in their rest positions - don't force them.

31 The perfect complement to a fully colour-co-ordinated interior. And it's something you look at all the time you're driving!

Push button start

Like to have a racing-style starter button on your Corsa? Read on! A very cool piece of kit, and not too bad a job to wire up - the most difficult bit's probably mounting the button somewhere suitable (easy to get at, but still in full view so's you can impress your passengers!).

The idea of the racing starter button is that the ignition key is made redundant, beyond switching on the ignition circuit (it'd be a pretty negative security feature, if you could start the engine without the key at all).

This is one job where you'll be messing with big wires, carrying serious current - more than any other electrical job, don't try and rush it, and don't skimp on the insulating tape. Do it properly, as we're about to show you, and there's no worries. Otherwise, at best, you'll be stranded - at worst, it could be a fire.

01 First, DISCONNECT THE BATTERY. You may have ignored this advice before. You may not. Don't do so now.

02 Remove the column shrouds as described in the section on coloured dial kits, previously. Turn the ignition key to the first position, then insert a small screwdriver to release the lug . . .

03 . . . and separate the large wiring plug from the back of the ignition switch. There's a plastic cover to unclip too, to get access to the wires.

04 Using the Haynes manual wiring diagrams, identify the wire colours to do with the ignition switch. On our Corsa, there's a red/black wire for the starter solenoid (which you'll need), and two BIG black wires, either of which can be used to provide an ignition live supply to the new relay. So - again using the trusty small screwdriver, push out the red/black wire from the ignition switch wiring plug.

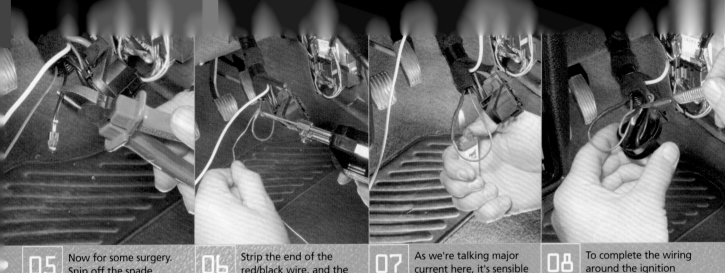

05 Now for some surgery. Snip off the spade connector from the red/black wire you just removed.

06 Strip the end of the red/black wire, and the solenoid wire from the new kit (in this case, blue). Then it's out with the soldering iron, and connect them up.

07 As we're talking major current here, it's sensible to insulate any new connections. We're using heat-shrink sleeving; be careful where you put that flame.

08 To complete the wiring around the ignition switch, strip a little insulation from one of the black wires we mentioned earlier, and connect on the ignition live supply to the relay. Soldering here isn't as easy - these wires are thick, and take ages to heat up. Ensure the connection is sound.

09 Clip the rear cover back on the ignition switch.

10 Then reconnect the switch plug to reassemble.

11 The kit's wiring included a relay (which you wire up) and fuse holder, and it's likely other kits will, too. In particular, the fuse should be mounted somewhere easy to get to, so the fuse can be replaced without dismantling half the dashboard! We tucked ours just under the bottom edge of the dash . . .

12 . . . secured by a screw, the hole for which we drilled earlier.

To complete the wiring for the push button, we need an earth (the live supply comes from the "other side" of the relay). On our Corsa, when we removed the heater control panel (which is our chosen location for the push button) we found two multi-plugs which didn't go anywhere. Brown is the normal colour for earth, so we tested the plug's brown wires, and - found an earth! So we snipped it at the plug . . .

. . . and connected to one side of our new push button starter switch. Once we'd also connected up our black wire from the relay, we decided to give it a quick test - just to make sure we'd got it all right before fitting it neatly to our chosen panel.

The trickiest bit with the remote starter button is figuring out where and how you're going to fit the button! We reckoned there were two sensible options on our Corsa - both of them in the heater control panel area (nice and central, for maximum visual impact). If you fancy taking the simpler option, here goes - first prise off the recirc slider knob from the lower heater panel . . .

13 To get to our fuse, all we'd have to do is take down the steering column lower shroud. Not too difficult a job.

14

15

16

17 . . . then prise off the lower panel itself. We thought drilling a hole on the right-hand side of this panel would be a good plan - see what you think.

18 Get out the drill and a nice piece of wood, and make a hole.

19 Slip in the switch . . .

20 . . . then turn the panel over, and secure the switch with the large nut provided.

That's option 1. Option 2, which gives a more "finished" look, is a fair bit more work - whether it's worth it is up to you. Remove the heater panel as described in "Removing stuff". Unclip the recirc panel as before. The switch can be mounted directly in the main heater panel, if you pack out the large square hole with a few big washers.

Mounting the switch that tiny bit further back causes problems when you try fitting the heater panel back together - the white plastic section won't let the switch sit in place. So - you'll need to trim it somewhat.

21 Back in the car, wire the switch up as before . . .

22 . . . then clip the panel back in place. Nice one!

23

24

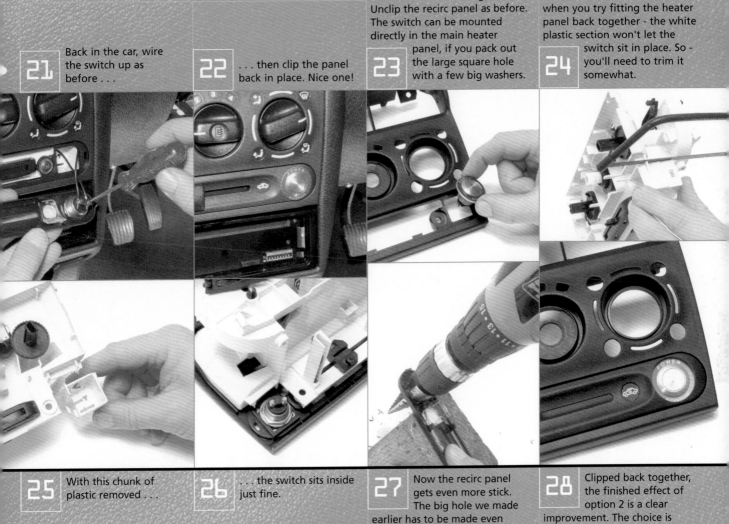

25 With this chunk of plastic removed . . .

26 . . . the switch sits inside just fine.

27 Now the recirc panel gets even more stick. The big hole we made earlier has to be made even bigger. The idea is that the switch is mounted in the heater panel itself, and the recirc panel clips back over it - looks more "fitted" to us. So that you can see all of the switch's red surround, though, the hole has to grow.

28 Clipped back together, the finished effect of option 2 is a clear improvement. The choice is yours!

Boring flooring?

Alright, so carpets have always been a dull colour because they have to not show the dirt - when was the last time you heard of a car with white carpets? What goes on the floor needn't be entirely dull, though, and can still be easy to clean, if you're worried.

Ripping out the old carpets is actually quite a major undertaking - first, the seats have to come out (you might be fitting new ones anyway), but the carpets and underfelt fit right up under the dashboard, and under all the sill trims and centre console, etc. Carpet acts as sound-deadening, and is a useful thing to hide wiring under, too, so don't be in too great a hurry to ditch it completely.

Chequerplate is tough but flexible, fairly easy to cut and shape to fit, has a cool mirror finish, and it matches perfectly with the racing theme so often seen in the modified world, and with the ally trim that's widely used too.

Tips 'n' tricks
If you're completely replacing the carpet and felt with, say, chequerplate throughout, do this at a late stage, after the ICE install and any other electrical work's been done - that way, all the wiring can be neatly hidden underneath it.

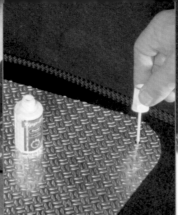

01 The easy option is to buy mats with chequerplate inserts. Another option is to buy separate chequerplates to fit to existing carpets, or to other mats.

02 Lay the plate into position on your mat, then take some Tipp-Ex, and dab a spot through the four holes in the plate.

03 Using a sharp implement, poke a hole through the mat where the spots were.

04 Bring the plate back in, and fit the first anodised "washer" and bolt through . . .

Chequerplate
heel mats

05 . . . so that the bolt pokes through the mat, and the large round "nut" can be screwed on the back.

06 Tighten the bolt with an Allen key. Repeat this so that all four corners of the plate are pinned on.

07 Our kit came with a load of stick-on velcro pads, which can be stuck to the underside of the round "nuts", and to the four corners of the mat itself.

08 And now - the finished result.

The halfway-house to a fully-plated interior is to make up your own tailored mats. Start by trimming up a piece of card to fit the curvy bits . . .

01

. . . then mark round onto some hardboard. The makers say not to fit their 'plate over carpets, because it'll flex too much and crack. For those of you who didn't know, most chequer is actually plastic look-alike, and it won't stand having your size 9s hoofing on it for long, so make up a solid-ish backing.

02

With the hardboard marked up, it's out with the jigsaw for some trimming, then try it in place. You only need a board for the flat part of the floor (where your feet go) - the 'plate can go behind the pedals unsupported.

03

Much try-and-trim later, you'll be ready to attack the silvery stuff. Mark it up . . .

04

Fully-tailored
chequer mats

  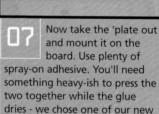 

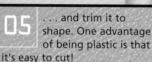

05 . . . and trim it to shape. One advantage of being plastic is that it's easy to cut!

06 When it comes to the tricky bits, lay it in and mark it roughly before cutting. Cut it too big to begin with, 'cos you can always trim more off.

07 Now take the 'plate out and mount it on the board. Use plenty of spray-on adhesive. You'll need something heavy-ish to press the two together while the glue dries - we chose one of our new rims, which did the job just fine!

08 Et voilà! The finished result. Okay, so you've spotted it's not a Corsa. But the effect's the same.

 Tricks 'n' tips
What about using one of your existing floor mats as a template? It's somewhere to start, anyway.

Under
neon light...

Everyone knows that interior neons are a cool way to spice up an ICE install, but there's no reason why you can't fit them somewhere other than in the boot. . .

01 There's not a great deal to this, really - decide where you want them, where you're going to get a live and an earth (and a switch, if necessary), then fit them. On our Corsa, the now-redundant electric mirror switch wiring provided the live and earth, after a quick check with the meter.

02 To plug in our mini-neons, we found we'd have to keep their cigar lighter plugs on, as they contain starters for the neons, so they wouldn't work if we just cut the plugs off for wiring up. Fortunately, we got hold of a cigar lighter socket "doubler" adapter, which we also "adapted" . . .

03 . . . soldering the wires from it onto our chosen ones in the Corsa door, giving us a socket to plug into.

04 We wanted our mini-neons to light up the door speaker cones (which have a reflective coating), so we stuck two of them in place behind the door grilles with black mastic . . .

05 . . . then we plugged in our cigar lighter plug and socket, and turned on the ignition.

06 We now have glow-in-the-dark door speakers. Sweet.

Bum notes
Interior neons are actually illegal, so driving with them on is a bad idea. The same is true of exterior neons. But there's nothing illegal about using them at shows and cruises.

Wheel cool

A new steering wheel is an essential first step to personalising your Corsa. It's a main point of contact between you and the car, it's sat right in front of you, and the stock ones are very dull.

Don't be tempted to fit too small a wheel if you've not got power steering. Corsa steering isn't heavy, but a tiny-rimmed steering wheel will make parking very difficult, especially with fat tyres.

One bit of good news is that, once you've shelled out for your wheel, it may be possible to fit it to your next car, too. When you buy a new wheel, you usually have to buy a boss (or mount) to go with it - the bosses are less pricey, so one wheel could be fitted to another completely different car, for minimum cost.

A trick feature worth investigating is the detachable wheel/boss. This feature comes in handy when you park up and would rather the car was still there when you come back.

A word about **airbags**

Many Corsas will have a driver's airbag fitted to the original wheel. So far, the market for replacement wheels with airbags is tiny, so fitting your tasty new wheel means losing a valuable safety feature.

But the problem with airbags doesn't end with simply disconnecting the damn thing, because all that'll happen then is your airbag warning light will be on permanently. Not only is this extremely irritating, it'll also be one of the reasons your newly-modded motor will fail the MOT (having the airbag itself isn't compulsory, but if the warning light's on, it's a fail - at least at the time this was written).

Two ways round this - either take out the clocks (see the section on fitting coloured dials) and remove the offending warning light bulb, or bridge the airbag connector plug pins with two lengths of wire attached to either side of a 5A fuse. Bridging the pins this way "fools" the test circuit (which fires up every time you switch on the ignition) into thinking the airbag's still there, and the warning light will go out as it should.

Airbags are expensive to replace (several £100s), and are classed as an explosive!!! There's any number of ways they can cause injuries or damage if you're not careful - check this lot out:

a Before removing the airbag, the battery MUST be disconnected. When the battery's off, don't start taking out the airbag for another 10 minutes or so. The airbag system stores an electrical charge - if you whip it out too quick, you might set it off, even with the battery disconnected.

b When the airbag's out, it must be stored the correct way up.

c The airbag is sensitive to impact - dropping it from sufficient height might set it off. Even if dropping it doesn't actually set it off, it probably won't work again, anyway. By the way, once an airbag's gone off, it's scrap. You can't stuff it back inside.

d If you intend to keep the airbag with a view to refitting it at some stage (like when you sell the car), store it in a cool place - but bear in mind that the storage area must be suitable, so that if the airbag went off by accident, it would not cause damage to anything or anyone. Sticking it under your bed might not be such a good idea.

e If you're not keeping the airbag, it must be disposed of correctly (don't put it out for the bin men!). Contact your local council for advice.

f Airbags must not be subjected to temperatures in excess of 90°C (194°F) - just remember that bit about airbags being an explosive - you don't store dynamite in a furnace, now do you?

Fitting a
wheel

Our Corsa had an airbag - skip the first few steps here if yours doesn't. Disconnect the battery, and wait at least 10 minutes. Move the column stalks fully up, out of the way. Insert a long T30 Torx key (or socket) into the holes behind the wheel, and remove the two airbag screws - they may be very tight!

01

Now that airbag "pad" can be lifted out of the wheel, and the yellow connector pulled off. Remove the airbag to a safe place. Get it indoors, in a cupboard, or maybe in the loft. Our workshop (like any decent garage) actually has a wall safe for storing airbags, to meet Health & Safety regs. That's how scary airbags are.

02

03 Next, unclip and disconnect the horn wiring plug.

04 The steering wheel nut is locked in place with a locktab washer - knock the tabs down flat with a small chisel (you can use a screwdriver, if you're careful!). The nut's not done up too tight. Take off the nut, and recover the locktab washer. Before you go much further, make sure that the steering wheel's straight - as confirmation, look to see that the front wheels are pointing straight-ahead.

05 And now - the bad news. You may very well need a puller to remove the wheel from its splines - it's incredibly tight on there. This might only be a feature of airbag-equipped cars, but - you have been warned. Before fitting the puller, refit the wheel nut by a couple of threads (to stop the wheel flying off). This is a special puller we're using, with legs which fit into the two holes in the wheel boss - an ordinary puller won't fit.

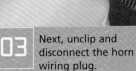

Tips 'n' tricks
A special puller may be needed to free the steering wheel from its splines. Buy or borrow a suitable puller before starting, or hope that you're luckier than we were!

06 Before the wheel will come off, on airbag cars, there are two screws to undo for the contact unit . . .

07 . . . then, as the wheel's removed, feed the wiring through it.

08 Follow the airbag yellow wiring down to the connector under the ignition switch, and disconnect it.

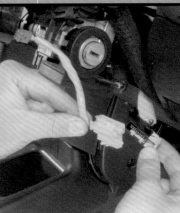

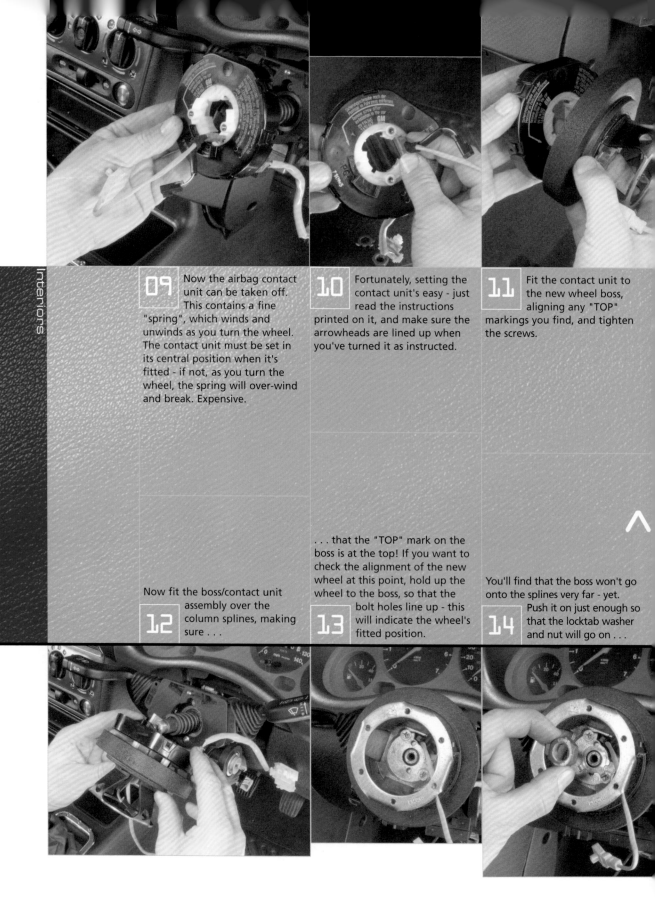

09 Now the airbag contact unit can be taken off. This contains a fine "spring", which winds and unwinds as you turn the wheel. The contact unit must be set in its central position when it's fitted - if not, as you turn the wheel, the spring will over-wind and break. Expensive.

10 Fortunately, setting the contact unit's easy - just read the instructions printed on it, and make sure the arrowheads are lined up when you've turned it as instructed.

11 Fit the contact unit to the new wheel boss, aligning any "TOP" markings you find, and tighten the screws.

Now fit the boss/contact unit assembly over the column splines, making sure . . .

12

. . . that the "TOP" mark on the boss is at the top! If you want to check the alignment of the new wheel at this point, hold up the wheel to the boss, so that the bolt holes line up - this will indicate the wheel's fitted position.

13

You'll find that the boss won't go onto the splines very far - yet. Push it on just enough so that the locktab washer and nut will go on . . .

14

15 . . . then tighten the nut securely. Tightening the nut pulls the boss further onto its splines, so do it up good 'n' tight - preferably, use a torque wrench (25 Nm). Remember - that boss ain't coming off without a fight, once the nut's tight, so make sure you've got it on straight!

16 When the nut's tight, use pliers to bend up the lockwasher tabs.

17 The wheel came with ready-made section of wiring to plug into the yellow airbag connector plug terminals - two lengths of wire, with a 5A fuse attached. Plug this fella in, and your airbag light will function as normal - even though the airbag itself is nowhere to be seen!

18 There is also an adaptor section of wiring for the horn button - attach one end to the existing horn wiring now.

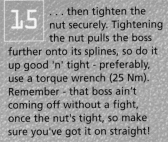

Line the wheel up with the bolt holes in the boss, then fit and tighten the Allen screws. Make darn sure these babies are tight (might be worth re-checking the tightness, after a few weeks). And there it is! One colour co-ordinated cockpit coming together quite nicely...

19 Fit the rubber boot over the boss, to hide any nasties . . .

20 . . . and - at last! Here's the wheel! Plug in the horn button to your new adaptor section first.

21

Pedalling your Corsa

01 The first step's easy - peel off the pedal rubbers. Our pedals were in two parts - backplates and top covers. Hold the plates up to the pedals, and decide where you'll be drilling through - see "Bum notes" if you've got problems.

02 The pedal spacing is pretty important, so, having worked out where our backplates would fit, we stuck the top covers and backplates on with Blu-tac, and checked the spacing! Also check that the side of the throttle pedal won't be dragging on the carpet.

A very nice race-equipment touch to your modded machine, pedal extensions really look the part when combined with full chequerplate mats - available in several styles and (anodised) colours...

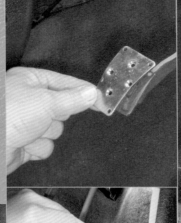

03 When you're ready, hold the first plate up to the pedal, and mark the pedal for drilling. You don't have to use all the bolt holes provided (and you probably won't be able to) - just use more than one, ok?

04 Drill that pedal! Either hold it up by hand, or place a scrap of wood behind it, so you don't end up with holes in the carpets. Don't drill more than one hole at once - it's better to fit the first bolt, then drill through the plate, to make sure it all lines up.

05 Fit the first nut and bolt, and tighten securely.

06 Ready for the top covers? Nuts, bolts, tighten, etc. Just remember to check every so often that the nuts haven't come loose.

Achtung!
Check your insurance company's position on pedal extensions. A while ago there was a big fuss after a couple of cars fitted with pedal extensions crashed, which resulted in pedal extensions being withdrawn from sale at a lot of places.

Bum notes

On plenty of pedal extension sets out there, the holes pre-drilled in the pedal extensions are in the wrong place. There's just no other way to say it. Using the intended mounting holes would mean drilling through the pedal and the pedal stem, which isn't possible. When you're buying a set of pedals, therefore, look at where the holes are drilled, and where the pedal stems are on your car. Otherwise, you'll either be making yourself a lot of work, or you'll be looking pretty stupid when you take the set back for a refund. Your choice.

Re-**trimming**

Okay, so you're definitely not happy with how the inside of your Corsa looks, but you're not sold on any of the off-the-shelf options for modding it, either. You know how you want it to look, though, so get creative!

There are any number of upholstery companies in Yellow Pages, and the back of the modified car mags, who will be able to create any look you want. If your idea of Corsa heaven is an interior swathed in black and purple leather, these guys can help.

Of course, if you're even slightly handy with things like glue and scissors, you might be able to use this one example we've got here as inspiration to get brave and DIY. Any upholsterers will still be a useful source for your materials.

Seats

This is really one for a pro upholstery outfit - it involves pulling your seats to bits. If you're determined to try trimming your seats on your own, our advice is to practise on a seat from the scrapyard first, 'til you've got the hang of it! Good luck, and we salute you!

The seats in our Corsa Sport were basically ok to sit in, but were a bit of a let-down to look at. The black patterned outer bolsters are ok, but the seat pattern was none too pleasant. As the rest of our interior's been colour-coded, we decided to go for light blue leather centre panels. Keeping the original seats also means we get to keep the standard seat belt tensioners (not very sexy, but might help to keep you from being splatted against the windscreen!).

If you're keeping the back seats, don't forget to give them the treatment too.

Door trim panels

What applies to seats can also be applied to your door cards. If you're gonna DIY, practise on something old first.

If you've had your seats trimmed, you'll obviously choose the same stuff for your doors - but here's a tip. Say you've gone for some nice bucket seats, in maybe a red-and-black pattern cloth. Would be nice to match your seats to the door panels here, too, wouldn't it? So how about doing what we did for another of our project cars, and contacting the seat manufacturer for a few square metres of the actual cloth they use to make the seats with? Should match then, shouldn't it? Hand material and cash to your upholstery experts, and wait. Or do it yourself.

Are you **sitting stylishly?**

Seats are the perfect complement to your lovingly-sorted Corsa. Besides the seat itself, remember to price up the subframe to adapt it to the mounting points in your car. Most people also choose the three- or four-point harnesses to go with it (looks a bit daft to fit a racing seat without it), but make sure the harness you buy is EC-approved, or an eagle-eyed MOT tester might make you take them out.

Decide whether you want reclining seats or non-recliners. With non-adjustable seats, how are your mates meant to get in the back? Through the tailgate? Or maybe there is no back seat... You can get subframes which tilt, so that non-reclining seats can move forward. Non-reclining racing seats should be tried for fit before you buy.

An alternative to expensive racing seats would be to have your existing seats re-upholstered in your chosen colours/fabrics, to match your interior theme. You might be surprised what's possible, and the result could be something truly unique. If you've got a basic model, try sourcing Sport or GSi seats from a breakers. A secondhand GSi interior bought there will be a lot cheaper than buying new goodies, and you know it'll fit easily (all Corsas are the same underneath) - but - it won't have that unique style. Specialist breakers may be able to supply something more original, such as a leather interior from a Cavalier GSi or a top-spec Calibra - might take some persuading to get it in, though!

01 As long as you don't have seat belt tensioners, whipping out the old front chairs is easy. How do you tell if you've got tensioners? Well, have you got an airbag? Tensioners and airbags usually go hand-in-hand. We'll deal with these first - then you can see how easy life is without them! First, remove the Torx screw at the front of the outer runner . . .

02 . . . then slide the seat forwards, and undo the Torx screw at the rear of the outer runner.

03 Now prise up the cover beside the seat - and there's the canister, which contains a strong spring, under tension. Remove the two Torx screws down inside, next to the canister . . .

04 . . . then carefully unclip and remove the trim panel from the side of the seat.

Front seat **removal**

05 Vauxhall thoughtfully provide a means of making the canister safe from going off - it's this funny little red plastic fork. Follow the instructions printed on the canister, and insert it fully in the slot provided. If the seats are put back in at any time, take the fork out, or the tensioners won't work in a smash.

06 Unscrew the large Torx bolt at the back of the outer runner, and the same bolt on the inner runner. You should now have one very loose seat.

07 The seats are just hooked in place at the front, so push them forward to disengage, and lift 'em out. If you're taking the rear seats out read on . . .

Rear seat removal

01 Start by prising off the little plastic cover at the front of the rear seat (one each side), and removing the screw underneath.

02 These hinges have to be unhooked from the floor brackets. Lift the seat upwards first, so the hinge clears the bracket, then use a screwdriver to press down on the bottom of the hinge, and stop it going back into the bracket. It's fiddly, but not hard. The cushion can now be ripped out!

03 Now it's into the boot, to deal with the seat backrest. Fold down the rear backrest(s), then remove the two screws each side securing the outer hinge covers.

04 Lift out the hinge cover each side, then remove the Torx bolt. If you've got a basic Corsa with a one-piece backrest, that's it.

05 On Corsas with a split-fold rear backrest, pop one half of the backrest upright, and remove the two Torx bolts from the inner hinge.

06 Repeat this for the other backrest, and both rear seats are history.

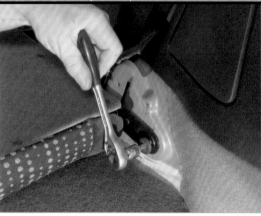

01 The first job (apart from working out which base is for left and right) is to fit the bases to the new seats.

02 The new chairs are now ready to fit - they hook over the front mounts in the floor, and (hopefully) the bolt holes in the new bases will line up with the two holes at the back.

Seat
fitting

The seat mounting bolt torque is only 20 Nm, but we thought we'd get it right by using a torque wrench anyway. **03**

04 And here's the new seat, complete with harnesses.

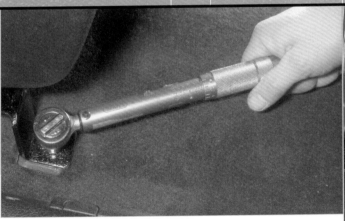

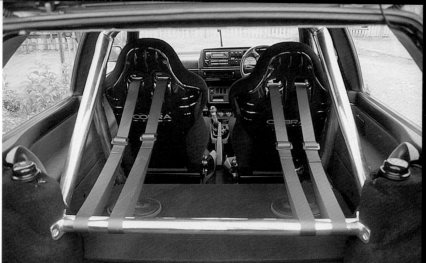

How strapped are you?

The only problem with harnesses is caused by where you have to mount them. Even with a three-point harness, you end up using one of the rear seat belt mounts, and it seriously reduces your ability to carry bodies in the back seats (webbing everywhere). The MOT crew say that, if you've got rear seats, you must have rear seat belts fitted, so you either "double-up" on your rear belt mounts (use the same mounts for your harnesses and rear belts) or you take the back seats out altogether. Removing the rear seats leaves the rear deck free for chequerplate, speakers, roll cages - whatever you like.

One thing you must never do is to try making up your own seat belt/harness mounting points. Vauxhall structural engineers spent plenty of time selecting mounting points and testing them for strength. Drilling your own holes and sticking bolts through is fine for mounting speakers and stuff, but you're heading for an interview with the Grim Reaper if you try it with seat belts. The forces in a big shunt are immense. We're not convinced either that the practice of slinging harnesses round a rear strut brace is kosher, from the safety angle - the strut braces could easily bend.

01 Before you can fit your new harnesses, the old belts have to at least be disturbed, if not ripped out completely. As we said earlier, you must use the existing seat belt mounts, for safety. The front belt is mounted to the floor, on a sliding rail. The rail front bolt is hiding behind a plastic cover . . .

02 . . . undo the bolt, then unhook the rail at the rear, and slide the seat belt off it.

03 Now the rear side trim panel has to come out, to get at the belt inertia reel. Remove the Torx screws securing the sill plastic trim panel at the front . . .

04 . . . and the trim panel at the rear. We'd previously removed our rear seat, to make fitting it easier.

Racing harnesses

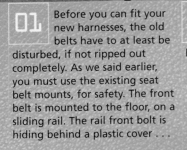

05 Peel off the rubber door seal along the front edge of the panel. Taking a flat-bladed tool, prise the panel off at the front edge, then work along the top edge, releasing the clip-on fasteners (and trying not to break any in the process).

06 Eventually, the panel can be worked free.

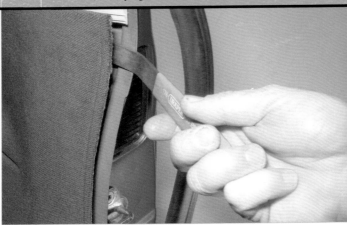

07 Before refitting the panel, the white clips at the top edge must be prised out from the side of the car, and slipped back into their positions on the trim panel - thumping the panel back on will only break them, if you don't.

08 Prise off the trim cap and unbolt the belt upper mounting.

09 With the trim panel out of the way, the belt can be unclipped from its guide . . .

10 . . . then the inertia reel can be unbolted and removed, and the whole belt taken out. Depending on the make and type of your new harnesses, you might need to re-use some of your original seat belt mounting bolts, so don't be in too big a hurry to skip the lot just yet.

11 The rear belts just unbolt from the floor mounts. We didn't feel it was vitally important to rip out the rear inertia reels, but if you must, they're behind the rear trim panels - removal's much the same as for the front reels.

12 Our belts came with quick-fit clip-on belt mounts, and these certainly simplify the fitting process. However, mounts like this do mean you can't tag on your old rear belts, if you're keeping them. The new "eye" mounts screw into the holes in the floor - one where the old sliding rail went, on the outside of the front seat, and one (or two, on a four-point harness) into the hole(s) where the rear belts went. Use an adjustable spanner to make sure they're done up tight.

13 The new harness has a quick-release catch which clips onto the eyes - dead simple!

14 The remaining mount is made on the inside of the new seat, where you'll find a hole intended for a belt mounting. The only snag here is that you may need to source your own nut to go with the eye bolt - one wasn't provided with our belt pack. Try to get a Nyloc nut with a plastic anti-loosening insert in it, for fairly obvious reasons!

Racing harnesses
- with rear seats

Fitting harneses while maintaining the standard belts isn't too tough either. All you need to consider is - are the standard bolts long enough to take both the old belts and the new straps, and still tighten up properly? Unbolt as before, then "assemble" all the bits onto the old bolt, and providing the old bolt's long enough, you can re-use it to pin the old and new stuff in together. Don't forget your torque wrench (35Nm).

Tricks 'n' tips
In case you're thinking of fitting a longer bolt, you'll soon find out that any old bolt won't do. Seat belt bolts usually have a different, finer-pitched thread than ordinary bolts. Don't force the wrong bolts in. Most car makers fit the same seat belt bolts, so either "source" some from a scrapyard, or go to a specialist nut 'n' bolt man.

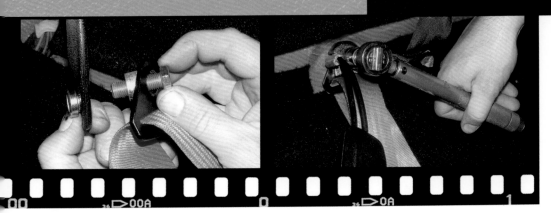

ICE

Head unit

Vauxhall's head units come with a separate display these days, meaning that although the body of the unit might be down in the middle of the console, the read-out is right at the top of the dash where it can be easily seen. Unfortunately, when you swap to almost all other head units, you have to go back to a display that's built into the fascia of the set itself.

The good news is that the increase in performance and quality is well worth you having to look a bit lower to see what track's playing. We went with a CD player for our install, and coupled to the rest of the gear we used, it sounded loads better. And we do mean LOADS.

Finally, when fitting anything like this to your car, read the instructions that come with the gear. We're giving you specific details about this car, rather than the stuff we're installing. If you are using another product brand or type, you need to know its individual requirements or you could end up doing some expensive damage.

01 Removing the Corsa's head unit isn't too tough, but you do need a small Allen key to get the blanking screws out of the removal holes. Once these were out of the way, we just used normal DIN removal keys to get the set out.

02 We removed the ashtray from under the head unit location, which not only made it easier to wriggle the sleeve free, but also allowed us to get to the very short Vauxhall wiring loom. When you're doing this, don't go heaving on the sleeve without first undoing the little bolt at the back of it. You'll need a small socket on an extension for this job.

03 The mounting cage was a simple fit into the existing hole, and we just used a specially-modified screwdriver to bend the retaining lugs over and secure it in place. The new unit was well supported in the dash once it was fitted and the ashtray was back in place.

04 The wiring loom didn't have the required ISO plugs fitted, so we soldered them onto the end of it. This gave us the necessary length to reach the car's loom, and made the install very tidy, too.

05 Matching up the wiring was easy because each cable was marked, so it was a case of cutting the terminals off the head unit loom, shortening the ISO adaptor wires, and then soldering them together.

06 Each joint was covered with heatshrink tubing for protection and neatness. A couple of cable ties finished the assembly off.

07 Once the new loom was plugged into the car, it was a simple job to connect the head unit to it, fit the aerial adaptor and signal leads, then slide the unit into the sleeve.

08 Once the trim ring was clicked into place, and the ashtray had been screwed back up, the job was done.

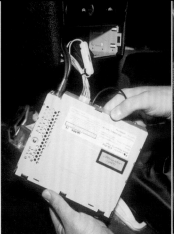

Amplifier

Every decent car stereo system needs separate amplification. Even if you've got a head unit that reckons it's kicking out loads of power, once you hook up an amplifier in its place, you'll be amazed at how much better an outboard power amp really is.

For the Corsa we used a four-channel unit, running the front speakers off two channels, and bridging up the other two to run the boxed sub woofer. We left the head unit to drive the back shelf speakers. They don't get that much use, so we thought it would cope with that.

Bearing in mind that the Corsa's boot isn't big, we decided to use a side-mounted rack that would keep the amp out of the way. Fitting it like this means that if the sub box ever gets removed for some reason, there's plenty of unused boot room for filling with goodies, and the fold-down seats can still be used when necessary. The vertical amp mount also meant that the controls were easily accessible for setting up.

01 Once we'd decided the amplifier was going to fit vertically on the passenger side of the boot, we began to make the amp rack by cutting a cardboard template to get the exact shape we needed.

02 When this template was about the right size, we drew round it . . .

03 . . . and cut the shape out in MDF.

Achtung! MDF dust is nasty stuff to breathe in. Wear a mask when you're cutting, drilling or sanding it.

This was checked and adjusted for fit until it was slightly small for the area we'd chosen. This was to allow for the carpet that we're going to trim it with later.

04

Having sized the amp board, the position of the amp mounting holes, the wiring holes and the quick-release Neutrik socket were marked . . .

05

. . . and then drilled out as required.

06

Doing this before trimming it makes the job much neater. Fitting the amp this way round keeps the wiring safe at the bottom of the boot, and leaves the controls at the top.

07

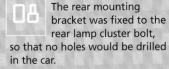

08 The rear mounting bracket was fixed to the rear lamp cluster bolt, so that no holes would be drilled in the car.

09 The earth cable was fitted under the rear seat bracket bolt, and again avoided drilling any holes in the Corsa's steelwork.

10 The amp wiring was brought through the corresponding holes on the board before the terminals were crimped in place and then covered with heatshrink for neatness and safety. The heatshrink also codes the wiring - red for positive, black for negative. Once the wires were ready, we screwed the amp into place and then connected the cables.

11 The finished boot shows the sub cabinet in place, the shelf connected to the Neutrik socket, and the amp neatly tucked out of the way. Tidy job.

Front speakers

Vauxhall have thought a bit more about the front speakers fitted to their Corsa, and they actually use a component set with a mid-range in the bottom of the door, and a tweeter much higher up by the door handle.

While the positioning isn't too bad, the drivers themselves could certainly use a hike in performance. We went for a set of components that would drop into the original locations - with a little work - and make the Corsa sing a lot better.

The only thing we cheated on was the wiring, which was hampered by the bloody great multi-plug that makes getting decent new wire in a job-and-a-half on its own. What we ended up doing was running new speaker wire from the amplifier up to the Corsa's existing speaker wires

where they would have joined the back of the head unit, and then soldering them together there.

Doing this wasn't totally ideal, but when you've tried for hours to get that door plug and socket out so that you can thread thicker speaker cable through it, you'll see we were right. If we were doing a competition installation we would have persevered, but this was the most straightforward way of doing it for this system. The crossover element is in the wire coming off the tweeter, so we could just hook the new speakers up to the old wire without any problems.

The Corsa's door panel was pretty straightforward to remove, but you need a bit of care to make sure you've got all the screws out before you try and heave the panel off.

01

The bottom section was held on by easily visible screws, but the top half was a bit more involved.

02

The tweeter mounting panel has to be unclipped from around the door pull handle to reveal the screws holding it in place.

03

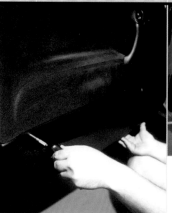

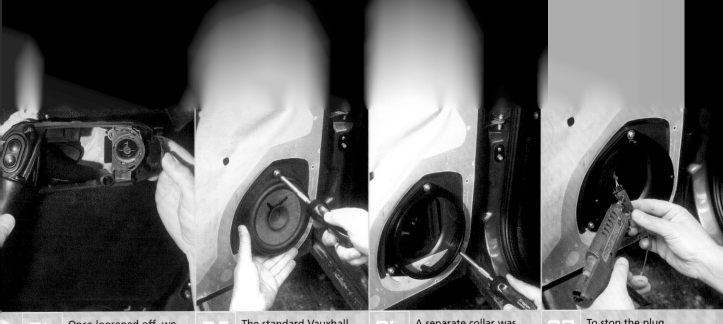

> **04** Once loosened off, we could remove the wiring to the window switch and the tweeter, and the door was ready for the next step.

05 The standard Vauxhall speaker was taken off the door, complete with its integral mounting collar.

06 A separate collar was fitted in its place, and the supplied wiring adapter was fitted to the original speaker plug to make it easy to join the new speaker in later.

07 To stop the plug rattling we stuck it to the inside of the collar with a dab of hot glue.

After pulling back the waterproofing membrane, the door skin was cleaned up with solvent cleaner to ensure the sound deadening **08** sheet would stick properly.

While this sheet doesn't need heating up like some other types, it needed plenty of rolling to get a good bond to the door skin. We even overlapped the speaker mounting to make it as dead as **09** possible.

10 With the sound deadening in place, the speaker was joined onto the adapter wire and then screwed into position.

11 As we mentioned earlier, the original wire was used because it's very difficult to get new wire into the Corsa door. This is because of the Vauxhall multipin-plug system that allows fast door removal. You can get decent speaker cable through this plug, but not without a lot of time and aggravation.

12 The original tweeter cover doesn't look too clever, so we decided to put the tweeter into the panel and show it off instead. This meant cutting the plastic grille slats out with small cutters . . .

13 . . . and then carefully opening out the hole with a small knife and some abrasive paper.

14 When the hole was big enough, the collar was fitted and then the tweeter was added.

15 The wire coming off the tweeter has the crossover element built into it, so we could connect it up to the standard Vauxhall cable without any problems.

Rear speakers

The Corsa's standard rear speakers are pitiful little units that have no place in a decent system that can really kick. Needless to say, we didn't use them, we got a shelf made from MDF, and stuck a decent pair of 6x9s in it instead.

There are a couple of things that you should be aware of when using an MDF shelf, and the main one is the weight. They weigh a ton when they've got speakers in, so make sure you've got yours well secured before you go hooning around. At least the Corsa stealth shelf doesn't have plastic hinge blocks that locate it, relying instead on wooden legs that go around the pins fitted in the car's side supports.

Also, the kit includes bits of string so that you can tie your shelf to your tailgate and lift it up when you open the hatch. Yeah right. Being so heavy, most hatch rams won't support the shelf in the upright position, so we left our bits of string off. You probably should too.

Achtung!
MDF dust is nasty stuff to breathe in. Wear a mask when you're cutting, drilling or sanding it.

01 We marked the speaker position on the underside of the shelf carefully to get both speakers in the same place.

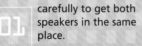

02 Using the speaker grille collar we drew in the position of the mounting screws...

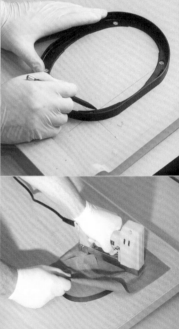

03 ... and then drilled the screw holes out to transfer that position to the top side. Then we flipped the shelf over and marked the oval hole with grille collar to give us the bit to cut out. A quick session with the jigsaw left us with the required holes, and then we sprayed the underneath of the shelf black.

04 With the shelf the right way up, a couple of pieces of speaker cloth were pulled tight and stapled across the speaker holes. This was done to stop the new carpet trim from sagging into the speaker in the future.

We stuck a little insulating tape over the staples to smooth them out before we started gluing the carpet and shelf together. We sized the carpet to make sure there was an adequate overlap under the shelf so that we could cut it off neatly. Then we stood the shelf on its edge on the upside-down carpet, ready for gluing. The glue was sprayed onto the shelf and the carpet, taking care to avoid the grille cloth that covered the speakers. Hardened glue could affect the way the speakers sound, so make sure you avoid spraying the sticky stuff onto them too. Once the glue had gone tacky, the shelf

05 was dropped forward onto the carpet and then flipped over to smooth out any wrinkles.

After masking up the shelf to give us some straight edges to work to, we glued the overlapping carpet and the shelf, and then finished off the trimming. The shape of the Corsa shelf's hinge area was particularly difficult to get neat because of the locating legs, but a sharp blade and a bit of

06 patience will get you an equally tidy result.

The 6x9s were screwed onto the shelf using the pilot holes we'd drilled earlier, and then the wiring was added to them. Be careful you don't slip off the screw and go through

07 the cone, though. We've seen it happen, and it's very depressing.

08 For the wiring hook-up we used push-on terminals for these speakers . . .

09 . . . and the cabling was tidied up using P clips to hold it at the front edge of the shelf. Then the quick-release Neutrik connector was fitted on the cable end so that it would plug into the socket fitted on the amp rack.

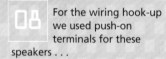

Fitting the Neutrik plug and socket was easy enough, but we did one on the bench so that you could get a better look at it.

Job one is to crimp the four supplied spade terminals to the wires that go to the amplifier, and put them onto the socket. The terminals in both bits of the Neutrik are marked so that you can keep the wiring correctly lined up.

The plug requires a bit more work, but is still easy. Unscrew the blue collar from the plug and it falls apart. Solder the four small ferrules onto your speaker wires, and then begin to assemble the plug.

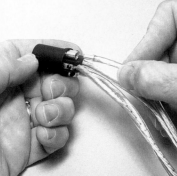

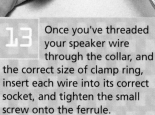

Once you've threaded your speaker wire through the collar, and the correct size of clamp ring, insert each wire into its correct socket, and tighten the small screw onto the ferrule.

After you've done them, you can push the bits together, and screw the blue collar down onto the plug body.

It should look like this when you've finished.

Sub woofer

To go with decent front speakers that give the sparkly mids and highs, we need a bit of bottom end. Something to give the music some grunt, and to worry the welded seams of our little Corsa. To do this we drafted in a sub woofer and a ready-made sub cabinet, screwed 'em together, and slapped 'em in the boot.

One thing we were careful about was screwing our sub cabinet in so that it didn't roll around. Not only can this be a real pain when the cabinet falls over and pulls the wire out of the terminal, but it can also be dangerous, particularly in a crash. The last thing you want when you're having an accident is half a ton of unhappy speaker and box coming hurtling into the cabin to remind you they weren't bolted down. It might sound unlikely, but it has happened before, and it has killed people. You've been warned!

01 The sub cabinet was first stuffed with wadding to smooth the speaker's performance. This wadding can be bought from local dress-makers who sell it for stuffing cuddly toys. That should be an interesting shopping experience for you - wandering into a fabric shop and asking for toy stuffing. Are we good to you, or what?

02 The wiring was already connected to the terminal cup that was fitted on the box, so the ends just needed stripping back and terminating with the correct fittings to join onto the sub woofer. The cable is coded with plus and minus symbols for easy connection. As long as you get the feed wire into the box the right way round, everything will be fine.

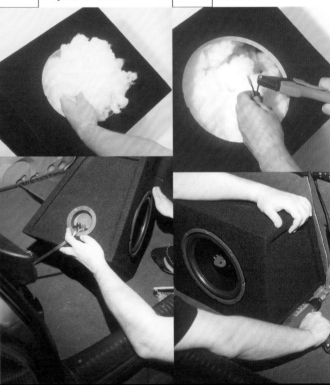

03 After carefully positioning the sub woofer to get the centre logo straight, the eight mounting holes were drilled with pilot holes, and then the screws were tightened steadily by hand to stop them getting stripped out. You can use a power screwdriver, but be careful not to go too tight and ruin the pilot hole you've just drilled or you'll have to put your speaker in at a funny angle once you've drilled some more holes.

04 The sub cable from the amplifier was clamped tightly under these screw terminals. Like the rest of the wiring, the cable was stripped back and then the ends protected with a short piece of heatshrink tube. This neatens the cable ends and makes it more difficult to short out the wiring. Just be sure to leave enough bare cable to connect to the terminal, eh?

05 Finally the box was screwed down to the boot floor panel with L brackets. This is a vital job since the box and speaker weigh so much that they can do damage to anything in the boot when you're driving about, let alone what they'd do if you had a major bump.

Wiring

Wiring up a car audio system is one of the most important jobs. If you don't do it correctly, you'll find yourself with all sorts of problems. Getting it right means decent music, no fire hazards, and no weird noises coming from the speakers. Getting it wrong can mean anything from hearing strange clicks and whirrs that aren't in the original mix, to your car going up in smoke. Don't laugh, it does happen.

When running amplifier power wire, you must use a fuse near the battery, and you must use a grommet to protect the wire where it goes through the bulkhead. You must also keep it as far as possible from any of the car's wiring to stop any aggro with airbags, seatbelt tensioners and things like that, particularly in a small car like the Corsa that's packed with these sorts of devices.

The signal cable from head unit to amplifier also needs to be kept away from the car's wiring, as well as the amplifier power cable, so it doesn't pick up any interference. Speaker wire is probably the least affected by this, but it's still a good idea to keep it away from the car's looms just in case. And, obviously, don't run cables over sharp edges that might cut into the wire once the carpet's been refitted or the seat gets moved. Do that to the power wire, you'll find out why you put the fuse next to the battery...

01 Adding the Corsa's amplifier power wiring to the battery wasn't a difficult job, especially as there was a spare bolt on the battery terminal just waiting to be used. We could even use the standard terminal cover when we'd finished.

02 Fitting the fuse holder meant drilling a hole on the front panel.

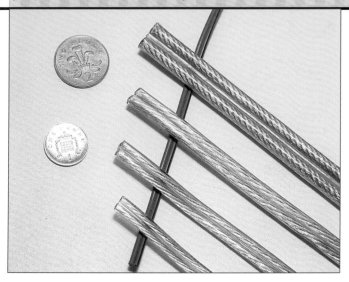

03 If you do any drilling of metalwork, don't forget to give the hole a blob of paint to stop rust getting a hold, and to let it dry properly.

04 After the paint had dried the fuseholder was screwed in place, and the wire was tidied up by cable-tying it to nearby Vauxhall looms. The cable went easily into the car through an existing grommet.

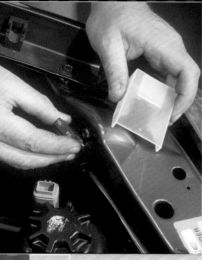

05 Only fit the fuse after the rest of the installation is finished. That way you don't get any nasty sparks or fires, ok?

06 To run the cables through to the amplifier safely, we had to strip the Corsa's interior out until there was just carpet left. This meant removing the sill trim rails and the covers that go over the seat mountings.

07 They are held in place with Torx screws, so you'll need the correct screwdriver tip to get them out.

08 This is one area to be very careful with. The seatbelt pre-tensioner is an explosive charge fitted to the seat, and this small plastic tag must be clipped in place before the seat is removed from the car.

09 The seat bolts are Torx fasteners as well, so make sure you've got something big enough to get them out before you get stuck in.

10 The seatbelts are easier to undo, but pay attention to the order of washers and spacers on the retaining bolt so that you can get them back together correctly.

11 To keep things neat, safe and interference-free, the wiring was laid out as far away from Vauxhall wiring as possible. Where they crossed we made sure it was at 90 degrees, and secured it with gaffa tape to make sure it didn't move.

12 We also used the ridges in the floor to give a little direction to the wire runs, and give some extra clearance when going over edges like the rear seat base.

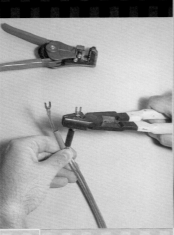
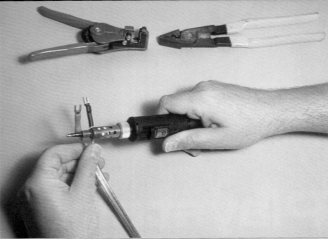

13 The terminals we used on the amplifier wiring were crimped on like this, starting with wire strippers to get rid of the wire's plastic insulation.

14 These special crimpers made squeezing the terminals onto the bare wire dead easy. Pliers like this are available at motor accessory shops and car audio stores, so try and get the right tool for the job.

15 To keep things looking neat and safe we used heatshrink tubing over the joints. We could have used a heatgun to shrink the tubing, but we had a gas-powered soldering iron so we used that instead. A quick blast of hot air from the exhaust was all that was needed to give the desired effect. Take care, though, not to touch any of the metal tip of the soldering iron to the heatshrink itself, otherwise it'll melt.

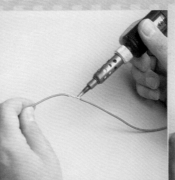

16 We had to cheat slightly with the Corsa's front speaker wiring because it ran through a multipin plug that stopped us running new speaker wire into the door. Instead, we joined the wire from the amplifier feed onto the front speaker wires at the head unit. We soldered this joint for the best connection, but if you've never soldered, you need to know how to do it.

17 When you need to join two wires, bare the ends back enough so that you can twist them together to give a strong join like these two here. If you're using heatshrink tube to protect the joint, don't forget to add it before you start soldering or you won't be able to get it on afterwards.

18 Once your iron is stinking hot, melt a dab of solder onto the tip and then place this against the joint area to heat it up. After a few seconds you can apply the solder wire to the iron tip and watch the solder flood through the joint. You need to end up with a smooth joint like this one, rather than two pieces of wire with a round blob of solder sitting on top of them. Keep the iron in place until the solder flows or you won't have a good connection.

19 To finish things off, a quick blast of hot air on the heat shrink makes a tidy joint that won't come apart in a hurry. If you haven't got heatshrink tube, insulation tape will do OK, just make sure it covers all the bare wire.

Playstation & screen

Bored of your CDs? Nothing on the radio? We have just the thing if you and a mate get bored, stuck in a 10-mile tailback on a bank holiday. Definitely a growing trend on the ICE scene, no top modded motor's complete these days without a games console, screen, DVD - where d'you stop? Just don't get caught playing it while you're moving, that's all.

Screen

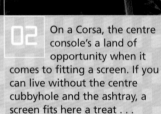

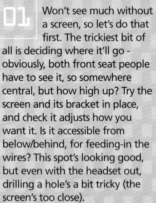

01 Won't see much without a screen, so let's do that first. The trickiest bit of all is deciding where it'll go - obviously, both front seat people have to see it, so somewhere central, but how high up? Try the screen and its bracket in place, and check it adjusts how you want it. Is it accessible from below/behind, for feeding-in the wires? This spot's looking good, but even with the headset out, drilling a hole's a bit tricky (the screen's too close).

02 On a Corsa, the centre console's a land of opportunity when it comes to fitting a screen. If you can live without the centre cubbyhole and the ashtray, a screen fits here a treat . . .

03 . . . the only bummer is, you can't just unclip the unwanted plastic bits from the console – a touch with the hacksaw's the only way.

04 Now the screen can be mounted on, and the video lead plugged together. This Centurion screen's a budget model, but still has built-in speakers and even a headphone socket. Looks good, but it's not working yet - let's finish the job.

05 Our screen came with an all-in-one lead containing the three-part video feed from the PS2 (or DVD), and also the power supply/earth. We'll connect up the PS2 later - for now, we want power to our screen. They give you a cigar lighter plug, but this looks a bit pants - let's do it properly. Prise apart the halves of your plug, and you get wires - chop the end off . . .

06 . . . strip the ends, and we have skinny red and black wires. The red's a live feed (you guessed it), which we're taking from the fusebox. The fusebox is a good spot to find an earth point for the black wire, too - or you can drill your own. The little green lights now tell us the screen's ready for input - let's give it some.

Playstation

01 To give power to your Playstation, you need an AC inverter - ours was about £50 from Comet. What this does is take your car's 12-volt DC electrics, and turns it into 240-volt AC, giving you a domestic three-pin socket in your car - how cool is that? As with our screen, our inverter came with a fag lighter socket, which we dismantled. This time, we took the live feed and earth from the same places as our amplifier (heavier leads).

02 Our inverter had to be in the boot, to be near the PS2 itself - but we didn't want to make a feature of it. We struggled a bit for some kind of mounting bracket, but we managed to make one from a huge Jubilee clip . . .

03 . . . and there he is, wired-up and looking sweet. The Playstation now has power - what else do we need?

04 There's a whole bunch of wires to run down the car, so this is a good excuse to remove a seat or two and lift the carpets (if you want to do a neat job, that is). Besides the two controllers, there's the video/audio outputs to our screen to connect. Luckily, they're so well colour-coded, there's no danger of messing this up.

05 Just to ensure nothing goes wrong when those carpets go back down, tape up each connection. This stops them coming apart, and also stops the connectors earthing-out on the car floor.

06 With power and video leads connected, and a screen that's ready to go, choose a suitable secure spot for the console, and it's plug . . .

07 . . . and play. Our first-ever Playstation install, and it goes like a dream. Total cost, including screen, inverter and PS2 (with free game) - about £400. Now that's what we call a bargain - true in-car entertainment, and maximum respect.

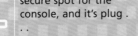

12 Engines

Faster, faster!

So now your car talks the talk, but does it walk the walk, as in walking away from everything at the next set of lights... Not everyone's into mega-performance, which is why the bolt-on goodies like induction kits and big-bore exhausts are big business. Serious engine tuning costs, and not just in the initial expense - it goes without saying your insurance company will throw a wobbly at a gas-flowed head, and might refuse cover entirely on a 2.0 litre 16-valve conversion.

The induction kit and sports exhaust are undoubtedly good fun things to fit, and they improve the airflow through the engine, helping it to "breathe" better. This improved breathing helps when you go for the accelerator initially, so improving the response you feel, while the rear box sounds nice and fruity, so everyone's happy. But unless you spend a ton of money, seriously modifying or even replacing your standard engine, you will not gain much extra "real" power. You simply won't get huge power from simple mods. Most insurers don't increase premiums for a performance rear box or induction kit. Why? Because they don't make enough difference!

The "bolt-on" goodies work better as part of a radical tuning package (new head, cam(s), four-branch manifold, etc) - and setting-up the engine properly after fitting these parts makes a huge difference. If you're halfway serious about increasing the go of your Corsa, talk to an engine tuner with access to a rolling road, to prove what's been done has actually made a useful gain.

Fitting all the performance goodies in the world will be pretty pointless if the engine's already knackered, but it might not be as bad as you think. One of the best ways to start on the performance road is simply to ensure that the car's serviced properly - new spark plugs, HT leads, distributor cap and rotor arm (where fitted), an oil and filter change, and (where possible) a check of the ignition timing are a good basis to begin from. Correct any obvious faults, such as hoses or wiring plugs hanging off, and look for any obviously-damaged or leaking components, too.

Breathe
with me...

One of the simplest items to fit, the replacement air filter element has been around for years, and has only recently been overtaken in popularity by the induction kit.

Replacement **element**

This a replacement element which fits inside the standard air filter box, and it's therefore a very discreet way of tweaking your engine - no-one can tell it's fitted, looking under the bonnet.

01 A replacement air filter is dead easy to fit - release the clips securing the air cleaner top cover . . .

02 . . . then lift the cover enough to lift out the old element. Take care not to strain the wiring from the airflow meter as the air cleaner cover is lifted up.

03 Before you fit the new element, if you can, clean out the inside of the filter housing. Use a damp cloth, and make sure that none of the dust and muck goes into the engine.

04 Some performance filters have to be oiled before fitting - follow the instructions provided; don't ignore this part, or the filter won't be effective. Fit the new element the right way up - it may have a "TOP" or arrow marking, or may only fit one way. If the filter won't fit, check whether you actually have the right one - don't force it in, and don't cut it to fit, as either of these will result in gaps, which would allow unfiltered air to get in. Refit the air cleaner cover, and secure with the clips.

Achtung!
Don't simply take out the air filter completely - this is a really dumb idea. The fuel system's air intake sucks in air, and also dust, dirt and leaves from the front of the car - it's also designed to suck in oil fumes from the engine itself (through the "breather" connection). Without a filter, all this muck would end up in the sensitive parts of the fuel injection system, and will quickly make the car undriveable. Worse, if any of it makes it into the engine, this will lead to engine wear. Cheaper performance filters can be of very suspect quality - if your new filter disintegrates completely inside six months, it'll do wonders for the airflow, but it'll also be letting in all sorts of rubbish!

Induction kit

These allow even more air into the system than a replacement filter, and are a very popular fitment. The fuel system must be set up professionally after fitting to get the maximum from the mod.

With an induction kit, the standard air filter housing and ducting are junked, and the new filter bolts directly to the airflow meter, using a special adapter plate supplied with the kit. Some kits also feature special air inlet ducting (hoses) to feed the new filter with the coldest possible air from the front of the car - cold air is denser, and improves engine power. Feeding the filter with cold air is in theory good for maximum performance with a hot engine or in hot weather, but in colder conditions with a cold engine, driveability and fuel economy might suffer.

As a final bonus the induction kit, which operates without all the normal ducting provided as standard, gives the engine a real throaty roar when you go for the loud pedal.

01 Remove the large screw at the front of the engine bay which secures the air inlet duct, and take it away. You may choose to refit this later, as it can work together with the new bits to provide cool air to the filter.

06 The kit contains an adapter sleeve for mounting the induction cone. First job with this is to bolt on the little curved mounting bracket with the nut and bolt provided.

07 Now slip the sleeve into the inlet duct, making sure the mounting bracket lines up with the rubber mounting on the inner wing.

08 Arrange the large "panel" washers either side of the old air cleaner box's rubber mounting, then slip the mounting nut and bolt through and tighten it up.

09 Tighten the Jubilee clip you fitted earlier, then slip on the induction cone . . .

02 Release the large hose clip (it wasn't a Jubilee clip on our car, and had to be prised apart) which secures the inlet trunking behind the air cleaner lid . . .

03 . . . then prise off the clips at the side of the lid and take off the lid, together with the old air filter element.

04 The base of the air cleaner is just clipped in, on rubber mounts - one at the lower front, and two upper pegs at the rear. Away with that foul plastic bucket!

05 The first step in fitting the new kit is to slip on a Jubilee clip over the inlet duct you've got left. Don't tighten it yet - we're only fitting it now so it doesn't get forgotten later.

10 . . . and tighten its Jubilee clip, too. Hey - now we're gettin' there!

11 The last job is to mount your cold-air inlet duct. We fed ours down to a point just behind our meshed front bumper, and secured it to a convenient hole in the inner wing, using a cable-tie.

12 As we said at the start, you could even recycle the old air inlet duct, if you cable-tie it to the front panel.

Replacement engine

If the engine really is past it, or you'd like a simpler route to better performance, why not consider an engine change? The trick is, of course, to make absolutely sure the "new" engine's better than the old one - some so-called "reconditioned" engines have actually been known to be worse!

An engine change can easily be done in a day (with the right equipment). If your car's done a huge mileage, dropping in a newer lower-mileage motor will make a big difference. As long as the new engine's the same size as the old one, it won't affect the insurance - all you do is tell the DVLA about the change, and they'll update the car's registration document with the new engine number.

One advantage of owning a Corsa is that there's the whole Vauxhall engine family to choose from - one of the more popular "advanced" mods is to pull out a 2.0 litre engine (perhaps from a cheap old 8-valve Cavalier) and slot it in under the bonnet. It's not quite that easy of course, or everyone would be doing it. Then there's the 150 bhp 2.0 16-valve motor from the Astra GTE/GSi, or Cavalier/Calibra - turn that Corsa into a beast. Some have even gone for the 2.5 V6 conversion!

Fitting a larger engine is an easy enough upgrade for a talented DIY-er, but the insurers must still be told, and it's likely they'll insist on a full engineer's report (these aren't that expensive - look in the Yellow Pages, under "Garage Services" or "Vehicle Inspection").

No quicker but it looks nice

Even a boggo Corsa's engine bay can be made to look better , with just a few simple mods.
First up - try cleaning the engine. If it's covered in grot get busy with the degreaser (Gunk's a good bet), then get the hosepipe out. You can take it down to the local jetwash if you like, but remember your mobile - if you get carried away with the high-power spray, you might find the car won't start afterwards!

Get the polish to all the painted surfaces you reasonably can, and don't be afraid to unbolt a few of the simpler items to gain better access. We're assuming you've already fitted your induction kit, but if not, these do away with a load of ugly black plastic airbox and trunking, in favour of nice-looking product. Take off the rocker cover (or engine cover), and paint it to match your chosen scheme

(heat-resistant paint is a must, really, such as brake caliper paint), set off with a few chrome goodies. A strut brace is a nice underbonnet feature, especially when chromed. Braided hose covers (or coloured hose sets), ally battery covers and bottles, mirror panels - all give the underbonnet a touch of glamour.

Coloured dizzy cap?

If you're changing the cap, remove the old one (usually held on by two spring clips, but some have screws).

Turn the old and new caps over, and look underneath for notches in the rim, which locate in the distributor - turn the caps so that they are sitting exactly the same way. One by one, transfer the HT leads from the old cap to exactly the same position on the new one, then fit the new cap and secure with the spring clips or screws.

HT leads must be fitted in the right order - muck it up, and you'll have a Corsa which won't start. The trick here is to work step-by-step - never pull all the leads off at once, unless you've marked them first.

When you've done all the plug leads, fit the new "king" lead to the ignition coil (later coil-pack models will only have four HT leads to worry about). Trace the lead from the connection in the centre of the cap up to the coil. In all cases, if the old leads are held in by clips or cable-ties, make sure the new leads are also tied up or clipped in tight (but without stretching them).

Achtung!
If you're braiding coolant hoses, feel them first to make sure they're cold. Have a bowl ready to catch the coolant in (antifreeze is poisonous despite its sweet smell, and will make a mess of your paintwork if you douse the engine bay and front wings with it!). Also, don't forget to top-up the coolant level before heading out in your newly-braided-up machine.
If you're planning to braid your fuel lines, disconnect the hoses very carefully - have some rags wrapped around the pipes, so you don't spray high-pressure fuel everywhere.

OPEL
e1*96/27*0053*03
WOL0SBF08W4126610
1430   KG
2430   KG
1-0790   KG
2-0700   KG

Braided
hoses

Turning your engine bay into something resembling that of a racing machine should only be done when the engine's completely cold to start with - like first thing in the morning. The smell of burning flesh is never pleasant, especially when it's yours! Depending on which hoses you decide to treat, you could be removing ones containing hot coolant or fuel, so be careful.

First step is to remove your chosen hose. If supplies of braiding are limited, go for the hoses at the top of the engine first, then the ones underneath you can't see won't matter so much. Vauxhall tend to use spring-type clips, best released using pliers, but you might find Jubilee clips. If the hose is stuck, be careful how you free it, or you could snap the plastic pipe stub underneath. This sort of thing can really ruin your day.

01

Unroll your braiding, then expand it to the right size using a suitable blunt object. Like a broom handle.

02

Once the braiding's roughly the right size, you can slip your pipe in.

03

Trim off the excess, then smooth out the braiding round the bends, as it tends to gather up and look nasty otherwise.

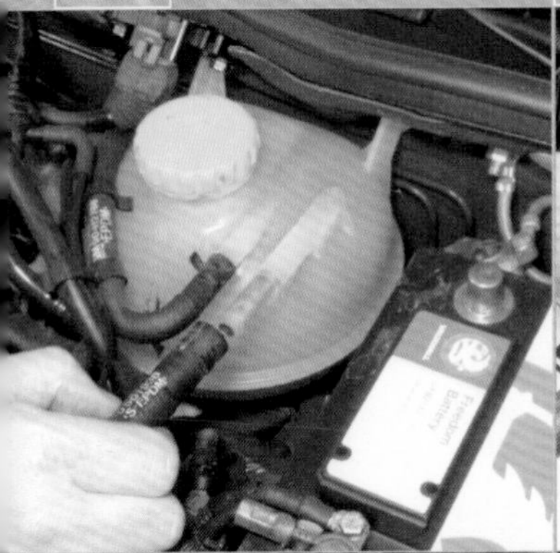

04

Slide a new Jubilee clip into an end fitting, then fit one end of the pipe in place. The hose clip is supposed to slide right up inside the end fitting, so it clamps the hose, the end of the braiding, and the end fitting (even when tight, the end fittings are still sometimes loose, though).

05

When you're sure the hose is fully onto its fitting, tighten the hose clip securely.

06

Fit the other hose clip and end fitting, then fit the other end of the hose and tighten the clip in place. It's pretty difficult to be sure the hose clip's in the right place on the stub - make sure it is otherwise you'll have a leak! If any of the end fittings rattle, you can put a stop to it by packing the fittings with silicone (preferably black).

07

ECU "chipping"

UNICHIP

DASTEK

piggyback computers

Tel:+ 27 12 347 1747
Fax:+ 27 12 347 1747
e mail:
dastek @ icon.co.za

WARNING
DO NOT
SWITCH OFF

Engines

All Corsas have fuel injection, controlled by an engine management system with a "computer" at its heart, known as the ECU, or Electronic Control Unit. The ECU contains several computer chips, at least one of which has programmed onto it the preferred fuel/air mixture and ignition advance setting for any given engine speed or load - this information is known as a computer "map", and the system refers to it constantly while the car's being driven.

Obviously, with the current trend towards fuel economy and reducing harmful exhaust emissions, the values in this "map" are set, well, conservatively. With a little tweaking - like richening-up the mixture, say - the engine can be made to produce more power, be more responsive, or both.

Companies like Superchips offer replacement chips which feature a computer map where driveability and performance are given priority over outright economy (although some companies claim that, under certain conditions, even fuel economy can be better with their products). It's best to combine a chip with other enhancements, and to have the whole lot set up at the same time. By the time you've fitted an induction kit, four-branch manifold, big-bore pipe, and maybe even a fast-road cam, adding a chip is the icing on the cake - chipping an already-modified motor will liberate even more horses, or at least combine it with majorly-improved response. Vauxhall tuning specialists are best placed to advise you on the most effective tuning mods.

Another feature programmed into the standard ECU is a rev limiter, which cuts the ignition (or fuel) progressively when the pre-set rev limit is reached. Most replacement chips have the rev limiter reset higher, or removed altogether. Not always a good thing - if the engine's not maintained properly (low oil level, cambelt changes neglected), removing the rev limiter and running beyond the red line would be a quick way to kill it.

Now the bad news

Chipping is often thought of as an easy, "no-tell" route to increased performance and driveability - after all, the ECU is well-buried inside the car, not on show under the bonnet, so who's gonna know?

Needless to say, the insurance companies have been wise to this trick for a long time. Many insurers hate covering chipped cars, so make sure you ring them before you splash out on one.

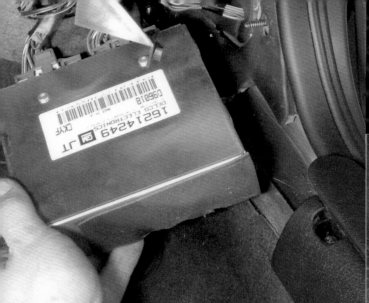

Gaining access to the ECU

01 On all Corsas, the ECU is tucked inside the car, next to the driver's right foot. The footwell trim panel has to come off first - loosen and remove the Torx screws which hold the sill trim to it.

02 There's another screw at the top of the panel, right in the corner, then there's this slotted clip which you turn using a screwdriver.

03 When the panel's ready to come off, work it round the bonnet release lever - the big silver box inside is the fella you're after.

04 Depending on which model you've got, you may find a plastic frame around the ECU, with various sections of wiring harness attached. The frame's held in place by a plastic nut in front and behind the ECU. The frame only needs to be released and swung aside to get at the ECU.

05 The ECU is retained by a large clip at the rear . . .

06 . . . when this is released, the whole unit comes free, for access to the wiring plugs. Make sure that the ignition is turned off (take the key out) before you disconnect any ECU wiring, or you'll wreck it. Some ECU wiring plugs are held in place by locking clips or covers - useful, to stop them coming loose while you're going along!

Exhausts

It's gotta be done, hasn't it? Your rusty old exhaust lacks the girth to impress the girls, and doesn't so much growl as miaow. Don't be a wimp and fit an exhaust trim - they'll fool nobody who really knows, and they certainly won't add to your aural pleasure (oo-er). Sort yourself out a decent back box upgrade, and even a timid 1.0 litre Corsa can begin to cut it at the cruise.

What a back box won't do on its own is increase engine power - although it'll certainly sound like it has, provided you choose the right one, and fit it properly. Check when you're buying that it can be fitted to a standard system - you'll probably need something called a reducing sleeve for a decent fit, which is a section of pipe designed to bridge the difference between your small-diameter pipe and the larger-diameter silencer. Try to measure your standard pipe as accurately as possible, or you'll have major problems trying to get a decent seal between the old and new bits - don't assume that exhaust paste will sort everything out, because it won't.

Fashion has even entered the aftermarket exhaust scene, with different rear pipe designs going in and out of style. Everyone's done the upswept twin-pipe "DTM" style pipes, while currently the trend seems to be "the bigger the better". Particularly with the upswept pipes, your rear bodywork may need protecting from the heat of the exhaust gases, and a trendy add-on is the heat-reflective ally panel - this is also available in several designs, with the riveted look (similar to the ally filler cap) gaining most approval. Some people, though, reckon these panels are just tacky, and serve no useful purpose whatsoever!

If you've got a capacity-challenged Corsa, you might need to lightly modify even your standard rear bodywork to allow for a bigger rear pipe, and you almost certainly will if you get a bodykit done.

You will begin to see some useful power gains if you go for the complete performance exhaust system, rather than just the back box. Like the factory-fit system, the sports silencer again will only work at its best if combined with the front pipe and manifold it was designed for! Performance four-branch manifolds alone can give very useful power gains for some Corsas. Watch what you buy, though - cheap exhaust manifolds which crack for a pastime are not unknown, and many aftermarket systems need careful fitting and fettling before you'll stop them resonating or banging away underneath. A sports rear box alone shouldn't attract an increased insurance premium, but a full system probably will.

One other point to consider, if your Corsa's been slammed to the floor - will your big new sports system be leaving behind a trail of sparks as it scrapes along the deck? Shouldn't do, if it's been properly fitted, but will the local multi-storey be out-of-bounds for your Corsa from now on?

Fitting a **back box**

01 First we've got to lose some rusty bits. It's best to remove the nearside rear wheel for this, but it's not absolutely essential. Loosen the rear wheel bolts, then jack up the whole back end of the car, and take off the wheel. Have a look in "Wheels & tyres" for more info on jacking up. The back box splits just over the rear "axle". First, loosen off the clamp nuts (hopefully, not too rusty - WD-40 works wonders).

02 Our box was suspended at the rear, on two rubbers. One unusual twist is that, behind each rubber, there's a spring clip to prevent the rubber slipping off. Use a screwdriver to prise the clip off sideways . . .

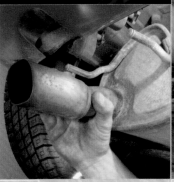

03 . . . then persuade the rubber off the peg. These can be a real pain to get free, sometimes - use your largest screwdriver as a lever (some of that WD-40 might help, too).

04 Now all you've got to do is separate the pipes - ie split the box from the rest of the system. We won't try and pretend it's easy - large hammers, chisels and plenty of swearing are usually compulsory for this. Soak the joint in some more of that wonderful aerosol spray, and give it a few taps with a hammer (denting the pipes won't help them separate, but might relieve the frustration). Usually, twisting the pipes relative to each other is the most successful way to separate them. Good luck!

05 Before you go offering up your new silencer, clean up the joint area on the front pipe, then smear on some exhaust assembly paste. Put some inside the end of the new silencer too, if you like, but don't use too much, or lumps of it will break off and partly block your new free-flowing system - not good!

06 Slide on your new box, complete with a new clamp. We found that a normal exhaust clamp was hitting the rear axle, and so had to resort to a band-type clamp (which looked a lot like a Jubilee clip). Position the box by twisting it on the front pipe until it's clear of all suspension bits, then tighten the clamp securely.

07 When refitting the rear rubber mounts, a little washing-up liquid helps them slide on (yes, really). Don't forget those little spring clips which hold the rubbers on, at the back.

08 That's what I call a phat oval - nice one!

Know your enemy - this is what your cat looks like inside. Is it any wonder they restrict gas flow?

Fitting a
de-cat pipe

All Corsas have a catalytic converter (or "cat"), which acts like a restrictor in the exhaust, inhibiting the gas flow and sapping some engine power (maybe 5 to 10%). You can buy replacement sections which do away with the cat (a "de-cat pipe"), and these certainly have a useful effect.

Sadly, by taking off or disabling the cat, your car won't be able to pass the emissions test at MOT time, so you'll have to "re-convert" the car every 12 months. This probably means that the car is illegal on the road with a de-cat pipe fitted - you'd have no defence for this, if questions were asked at the roadside, and potentially no insurance if the unthinkable happens. Sorry, but we have to say it...

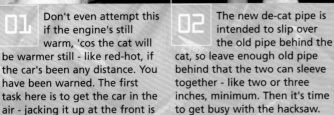

01 Don't even attempt this if the engine's still warm, 'cos the cat will be warmer still - like red-hot, if the car's been any distance. You have been warned. The first task here is to get the car in the air - jacking it up at the front is enough (see "Wheels & tyres" for jacking info). Offer the de-cat pipe up to the existing cat, and eye the pipe up for cutting (yes, vandalism is compulsory).

02 The new de-cat pipe is intended to slip over the old pipe behind the cat, so leave enough old pipe behind that the two can sleeve together - like two or three inches, minimum. Then it's time to get busy with the hacksaw.

03 At the front joint to the cat, there's two nuts and bolts to undo. Make sure you take note of how all the bits fit together, and that you get all the washers, springs, etc - you will need all of 'em later. Take the old cat away. I know you don't want to hear this, but at some point in the future, the cat might have to go back on (like at MOT time). So don't just drop it on the floor, or otherwise abuse the poor thing, or it'll never work again.

04 Clean up the rear pipe, and the joint at the front, before offering in the de-cat pipe. You might want to put a smear of exhaust paste on the sleeved joint you'll be making at the back. Oh, and slip on the new clamp before you fit the de-cat pipe (don't tighten the clamp nuts yet, though).

05 At the front joint, use the new sealing ring provided when you reassemble all the bits. If the old nuts are rusted-up or rounded-off, it makes sense to fit new ones - and if the old cat's going to go back on sometime, a smear of copper brake grease on all threads would make sense.

06 When the front joint's secure, tighten up the rear clamp nuts.

07 And there it is - one de-catted Corsa, with (in theory) a measurable and feel-able gain in horses. Strictly-speaking, completely and utterly illegal to use on the road, as it won't pass an MOT in this condition. But you don't want to hear that. Just remember we told you, that's all.

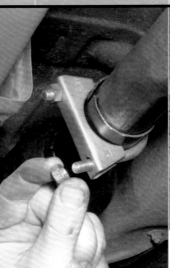

Safety and tools

Safety

We all know that working on your car can be dangerous - and we're not talking about the danger of losing your street cred by fitting naff alloys or furry dice! Okay, so you'd be hard-pushed to injure yourself fitting some cool floor mats or a tax disc holder, but tackle more-serious mods, and you could be treading dangerous ground. Let's be honest - we have to put this safety section in to cover ourselves, but now it's in, it would be nice if you read it…

Burning/scalding

The only way you'll really burn yourself is if your car's just been running - avoid this, and you won't get burned. Easy, eh? Otherwise, you risk burns from any hot parts of the engine (and especially the exhaust - if you've got one, the cat runs very hot), or from spilling hot coolant if you undo the radiator hoses or filler cap, as you might when you're braiding hoses.

Fire

Sadly, there's several ways your car could catch fire, when you think about it. You've got a big tank full of fuel (and other flammable liquids about, like brake fluid), together with electrics - some of which run to very high voltages. If you smoke too, this could be even worse for your health than you thought.

a Liquid fuel is flammable. Fuel vapour can explode - don't smoke, or create any kind of spark, if there's fuel vapour (fuel smell) about.

b Letting fuel spill onto a hot engine is dangerous, but brake fluid spills go up even more readily. Respect is due with brake fluid, which also attacks paintwork and plastics - wash off with water.

c Fires can also be started by careless modding involving the electrical system. It's possible to overload (and overheat) existing wiring by tapping off too many times for new live feeds. Not insulating bare wires or connections can lead to short-circuits, and the sparks or overheated wiring which results can start a fire. Always investigate any newly-wired-in kit which stops working, or which keeps blowing fuses - those wires could already be smouldering…

Crushing

Having your car land on top of you is no laughing matter, and it's a nasty accident waiting to happen if you risk using dodgy old jacks, bricks, and other means of lifting/supporting your car. Please don't.

Your standard vehicle jack is for emergency roadside use only - a proper trolley jack and a set of axle stands won't break the overdraft, and might save broken bones. Don't buy a cheap trolley jack, and don't expect a well-used secondhand one to be perfect, either - when the hydraulic seals start to fail, a trolley jack will drop very fast; this is why you should always have decent stands in place under the car as well.

Steering, suspension & brakes

Screwing up any one of these on your car, through badly-fitted mods, could land you and others in hospital or worse. Nuff said? It's always worth getting a mate, or a friendly garage, to check over what you've just fitted (or even what you've just had fitted, in some cases - not all "pro" fitters are perfect!). Pay attention to tightening vital nuts and bolts properly - buy or borrow a torque wrench.

To be absolutely sure, take your newly-modded machine to a friendly MOT tester (if there is such a thing) - this man's your ultimate authority on safety, after all. Even if he's normally a pain once a year, he could save your life. Think it over.

Even properly-fitted mods can radically alter the car's handling - and not always for the better. Take a few days getting used to how the car feels before showing off.

Wheels

Don't take liberties fitting wheels. Make sure the wheels have the right stud/bolt hole pattern for your car, and that the wheel nuts/bolts are doing their job. Bolts which are too long might catch on your brakes (especially rear drums) - too short, and, well, the wheels are just waiting to fall off. Not nice. Also pay attention to the bolt heads or wheel nuts - some are supposed to have large tapered washers fitted, to locate properly in the wheel. If the nuts/bolts "pull through" the wheel when tightened, the wheel's gonna fall off, isn't it?

Asbestos

Only likely to be a major worry when working on, or near, your brakes. That black dust that gets all over your alloys comes from your brake pads, and it may contain asbestos. Breathing in asbestos dust can lead to a disease called asbestosis (inflammation of the lungs - very nasty indeed), so try not to inhale brake dust when you're changing your pads or discs.

Airbags

Unless you run into something at high speed, the only time an airbag will enter your life is when you change your steering wheel for something more sexy, and have to disable the airbag in the process. Pay attention to all the precautionary advice given in our text, and you'll have no problems.

One more thing - don't tap into the airbag wiring to run any extra electrical kit. Any mods to the airbag circuit could set it off unexpectedly.

Exhaust gases

Even on cars with cats, exhaust fumes are still potentially lethal. Don't work in an unventilated garage with the engine running. When fitting new exhaust bits, be sure that there's no gas leakage from the joints. When modifying in the tailgate area, note that exhaust gas can get sucked into the car through badly-fitting tailgate seals/joints (or even through your rear arches, if they've been trimmed so much there's holes into the car).

Tools

In writing this book, we've assumed you already have a selection of basic tools - screwdrivers, socket set, spanners, hammer, sharp knife, power drill. Any unusual extra tools you might need are mentioned in the relevant text. Torx and Allen screws are often found on trim panels, so a set of keys of each type is a wise purchase.

From a safety angle, always buy the best tools you can afford - or if you must use cheap ones, remember that they can break under stress or unusual usage (and we've all got the busted screwdrivers to prove it!).

DO Wear goggles when using power tools.

DO Keep loose clothing/long hair away from moving engine parts.

DO Take off watches and jewellery when working on electrics.

DO Keep the work area tidy - stops accidents and losing parts.

DON'T Rush a job, or take stupid short-cuts.

DON'T Use the wrong tools for the job, or ones which don't fit.

DON'T Let kids or pets play around your car when you're working.

DON'T Work entirely alone under a car that's been jacked up.

Legal modding?
No such thing!!

The harsh & painful truth

The minute you start down the road to a modified motor, you stand a good chance of being in trouble with the Man. It seems like there's almost nothing worthwhile you can do to your car, without breaking some sort of law. So the answer's not to do it at all, then? Well, no, but let's keep it real.

There's this bunch of vehicle-related regulations called Construction & Use. It's a huge set of books, used by the car manufacturers and the Department of Transport among others, and it sets out in black and white all the legal issues that could land you in trouble. It's the ultimate authority for modifying, in theory. But few people (and even fewer policemen) know all of it inside-out, and it's forever being updated and revised, so it's not often enforced to the letter at the roadside - just in court. Despite the existence of C & U, in trying to put together any guide to the law and modifying, it quickly becomes clear that almost everything's a "grey area", with no-one prepared to go on record and say what is okay to modify and what's not. Well, brilliant. So if there's no fixed rules (in the real world), how are you meant to live by them? In the circumstances, all we can promise to do is help to make sense of nonsense...

Avoiding roadside interviews

Why do some people get pulled all the time, and others hardly ever? It's often all about attitude. We'd all like to be free to drive around "in yer face", windows down, system full up, loud exhaust bellowing, sparks striking, tyres squealing - but - nothing is a bigger "come-on" to the boys in blue than "irresponsible" driving like this. Rest assured, if your motor's anywhere near fully sorted, the coppers will find something they can nick you for, when they pull you over - it's a dead cert. Trying not to wind them up too much before this happens (and certainly not once you're stopped) will make for an easier life. There's showing off, and then there's taking the pee. Save it for the next cruise.

The worst thing from your point of view is that, once you've been stopped, it's down to that particular copper's judgement as to whether your car's illegal. If he/she's having a bad day anyway, smart-mouthing-off isn't gonna help your case at all. If you can persuade him/her that you're at least taking on board what's being said, you might be let off with a warning. If it goes further, you'll be reported for an offence - while this doesn't mean you'll end up being prosecuted for it, it ain't good. Some defects (like worn tyres) will result in a so-called "seven-day wonder", which usually means you have to fix whatever's deemed wrong, maybe get the car inspected, and present yourself with the proof at a police station, inside seven days, or face prosecution.

If you can manage to drive reasonably sensibly when the law's about, and can ideally show that you've tried to keep your car legal when you get questioned, you stand a much better chance of enjoying your relationship with your modded beast. This guide is intended to help you steer clear of the more obvious things you could get pulled for. By reading it, you might even be able to have an informed, well-mannered discussion about things legal with the next officer of the law you meet at the side of the road. As in: "Oh really, officer? I was not aware of that. Thank you for pointing it out." Just don't argue with them, that's all...

Documents

The first thing you'll be asked to produce. If you're driving around without tax, MOT or insurance, we might as well stop now, as you won't be doing much more driving of anything after just one pull.

Okay, so you don't normally carry all your car-related documents with you - for safety, you've got them stashed carefully at home, haven't you? But carrying photocopies of your licence, MOT and insurance certificate is a good idea. While they're not legally-binding absolute proof, producing these in a roadside check might mean you don't have to produce the real things at a copshop later in the week. Shows a certain responsibility, and confidence in your own legality on the road, too. In some parts of the country, it's even said to be a good idea to carry copies of any receipts for your stereo gear - if there's any suspicion about it being stolen (surely not), some coppers have been known to confiscate it (or the car it's in) on the spot!

Number plates

One of the simplest mods, and one of the easiest to spot (and prove) if you're a copper. Nowadays, any changes made to the standard approved character font (such as italics or fancy type), spacing, or size of the plate constitutes an offence. Remember too that if you've moved the rear plate from its original spot (like from the tailgate recess, during smoothing) it still has to be properly lit at night. You're unlikely to even buy an illegal plate now, as the companies making them are also liable for prosecution if you get stopped. It's all just something else to blame on speed cameras - plates have to be easy for them to shoot, and modding yours suggests you're trying to escape a speeding conviction (well, who isn't?).

Getting pulled for an illegal plate is for suckers - you're making it too easy for them. While this offence only entails a small fine and confiscation of the plates, you're drawing unwelcome police attention to the rest of your car. Not smart. At all.

Sunstrips and tints

The sunstrip is now an essential item for any modded motor, but telling Mr Plod you had to fit one is no defence if you've gone a bit too far. The sunstrip should not be so low down the screen that it interferes with your ability to see out. Is this obvious? Apparently not. As a guide, if the strip's so low your wiper(s) touch it, it's too low. Don't try fitting short wiper blades to get round this - the police aren't as stupid as that, and you could get done for wipers that don't clear a sufficient area of the screen. Push it so far, and no further!

Window tinting is a trickier area. It seems you can have up to a 25% tint on a windscreen, and up to 30% on all other glass - but how do you measure this? Er. And what do you do if your glass is tinted to start with? Er, probably nothing. Of course you can buy window film in various "darknesses", from not-very-dark to "ambulance-black", but being able to buy it does not make it legal for road use (most companies cover themselves by saying "for show use only"). Go for just a light smoke on the side and rear glass, and you'd have to be unlucky to get done for it. If you must fit really dark tints, you're safest doing the rear side windows only.

Some forces now have a light meter to test light transmission through glass at the roadside - fail this, and it's a big on-the-spot fine.

Single wiper conversion

Not usually a problem, and certainly not worth a pull on its own, but combine a big sunstrip with a short wiper blade, and you're just asking for trouble. Insufficient view of the road ahead. There's also the question of whether it's legal to have the arm parking vertically, in the centre of the screen, as it obscures your vision. Probably not legal, then - even if it looks cool. Unfortunately, the Man doesn't do cool.

Lights

Lights of all kinds have to be one of the single biggest problem areas in modifying, and the police are depressingly well-informed. Most people make light mods a priority, whether it's Morette conversions for headlights or Lexus-style rear clusters. If they fit alright, and work, what's the problem?

First off, don't bother with any lights which aren't fully UK-legal - it's just too much hassle. Being "E-marked" only makes them legal in Europe, and most of our Euro-chums drive on the right. One of our project cars ended up with left-hand-drive rear clusters, and as a result, had no rear reflectors and a rear foglight on the wrong side (should be on the right). Getting stopped for not having rear reflectors would be a bit harsh, but why risk it, even to save a few quid?

Once you've had any headlight mods done (other than light brows) always have the beam alignment checked - it's part of the MOT, after all. The same applies to any front fogs or spots you've fitted (the various points of law involved here are too many to mention - light colour, height, spacing, operation with main/dipped headlights - ask at an MOT centre before fitting, and have them checked out after fitting).

If Plod's really having a bad day, he might even question the legality of your new blue headlight bulbs - are they too powerful? Keeping the bulb packaging in the glovebox might be a neat solution here (60/55W max).

Many modders favour spraying rear light clusters to make them look trick, as opposed to replacing them - but there's trouble in store here, too. One of the greyest of grey areas is - how much light tinting is too much? The much-talked-about but not-often-seen "common sense" comes into play here. Making your lights so dim that they're reduced to a feeble red/orange glow is pretty dim itself. If you're spraying, only use proper light-tinting spray, and not too many coats of that. Colour-coding lights with ordinary spray paint is best left to a pro sprayer or bodyshop (it can be done by mixing lots of lacquer with not much paint, for instance). Tinted lights are actually more of a problem in daylight than at night, so check yours while the sun's out.

Lastly, two words about neons. Oh, dear. It seems that neons of all kinds have now been deemed illegal for road use (and that's

interior ones as well as exteriors, which have pretty much always been a no-no). If you fit neons inside, make sure you rig in a switch so you can easily turn them off when the law arrives - or don't drive around with them on (save it for when you're parked up). Distracts other road users, apparently.

ICE

Jungle massive, or massive public nuisance? The two sides of the ICE argument in a nutshell. If you've been around the modding scene for any length of time, you'll already know stories of people who've been done for playing car stereos too loud. Seems some local authorities now have by-laws concerning "music audible from outside a vehicle", and hefty fines if you're caught. Even where this isn't the case, and assuming a dB meter isn't on hand to prove the offence of "excessive noise", the police can still prosecute for "disturbing the peace" - on the basis of one officer's judgement of the noise level. If a case is proved, you could lose your gear. Whoops. Seems we're back to "do it - but don't over-do it" again. If you really want to demo your system, pick somewhere a bit less public (like a quiet trading estate, after dark) or go for safety in numbers (at a cruise).

Big alloys/tyres

One of the first things to go on any lad's car, sexy alloys are right at the heart of car modifying. So what'll interest the law?

Well, the first thing every copper's going to wonder is - are the wheels nicked? He'd need a good reason to accuse you, but this is another instance where having copies of receipts might prove useful.

Otherwise, the wheels mustn't rub on, or stick out from, the arches - either of these will prove to be a problem if you get stopped. And you don't need to drive a modded motor to get done for having bald tyres…

Lowered suspension

Of course you have to lower your car, to have any hope of street cred. But did you know it's actually an offence to cause damage to the road surface, if your car's so low (or your mates so lardy) that it grounds out? Apparently so! Never mind what damage it might be doing to your exhaust, or the brake/fuel lines under the car - you can actually get done for risking damage to the road. Well, great. What's the answer? Once you've lowered the car, load it up with your biggest mates, and test it over roads you normally use - or else find a route into town that avoids all speed bumps. If you've got coilovers, you'll have an easier time tuning out the scraping noises.

Remember that your new big-bore exhaust or backbox must be hung up well enough that it doesn't hit the deck, even if you

haven't absolutely slammed your car on the floor. At night, leaving a trail of sparks behind is a bit of a giveaway…

Exhausts

One of the easiest-to-fit performance upgrades, and another essential item if you want to be taken seriously on the street. Unless your chosen pipe/system is just too damn loud, you'd be very unlucky to get stopped for it, but if you will draw attention this way, you could be kicking yourself later.

For instance - have you in fact fitted a home-made straight-through pipe, to a car which used to have a "cat"? By drawing Plod's attention with that extra-loud system, he could then ask you to get the car's emissions tested - worse, you could get pulled for a "random" roadside emissions check. Fail this (and you surely will), and you could be right in the brown stuff. Even if you re-convert the car back to stock for the MOT, you'll be illegal on the road (and therefore without insurance) whenever your loud pipe's on. Still sound like fun, or would you be happier with just a back box?

It's also worth mentioning that your tailpipe mustn't stick out beyond the very back of the car, or in any other way which might be dangerous to pedestrians. Come on - you were a ped once!

Bodykits

The popular bodykits for the UK market have all passed the relevant tests, and are fully-approved for use on the specific vehicles they're intended for. As long as you haven't messed up fitting a standard kit, you should be fine, legally-speaking. The trouble starts when you do your own little mods and tweaks, such as bodging on that huge whale-tail spoiler or front air dam/splitter - it can be argued in some cases that these aren't appropriate on safety grounds, and you can get prosecuted. If any bodywork is fitted so it obscured your lights, or so badly attached that a strong breeze might blow it off, you can see their point. At least there's no such thing as Style Police. Not yet, anyway.

Seats and harnesses

Have to meet the UK safety standards, and must be securely bolted in. That's about it. It should be possible to fasten and release any seat belt or harness with one hand. Given that seat belts are pretty important safety features, it's understandable then that the police don't like to see flimsy alloy rear strut braces used as seat harness mounting points. Any other signs of bodging will also spell trouble. It's unlikely they'd bother with a full safety inspection at the roadside, but they could insist on a full MOT test/engineer's report inside 7 days. It's your life.

While we're on the subject of crash safety, the police also don't like to see sub boxes and amps just lying on the carpet, where the back seat used to be - if it's not anchored down, where are these items gonna end up, in a big shunt? Embedded in you, possibly?

Other mods

We'll never cover everything else here, and the law's always changing anyway, so we're fighting a losing battle in a book like this, but here goes with some other legalistic points we've noted on the way:

a It's illegal to remove side repeaters from front wings, even to create the ultimate smoothed/flushed motor. Sorry.

b All except the most prehistoric cars must have at least one rear foglight. If there's only one, it must be fitted on the right. We've never heard of anyone getting stopped for it, but you must also have a pair of rear reflectors. If your rear clusters ain't got 'em, can you get trendy ones? Er, no.

c Fuel filler caps have to be fitted so there's no danger of fuel spillage, or of excess fumes leaking from the top of the filler neck. This means using an appropriate petrol-resistant sealer (should be supplied in the kit). Oh, and not bodging the job in general seems a good idea. Unlikely to attract a pull, though.

d Front doors have to retain a manual means of opening from outside, even if they've been de-locked for remote locking. This means you can't take off the front door handles, usually. It seems that rear door handles can be removed if you like.

e Tailgates have to have some means of opening, even if it's only from inside, once the lock/handle's been removed. We think it's another safety thing - means of escape in a crash, and all that.

f You have to have at least one exterior mirror, and it must be capable of being adjusted somehow.

g If you fit new fog and spotlights, they actually have to work. No-one fits new lights just for show (or do they?), but if they stop working later when a fuse blows, relay packs up, or the wiring connectors rust up, you'd better fix 'em or remove 'em.

h Pedal extensions must have rubbers fitted on the brake and clutch pedals, and must be spaced sufficiently so there's no chance of hitting two pedals at once. This last bit sounds obvious, but lots of extension sets out there are so hard to fit that achieving this can be rather difficult. Don't get caught out.

i On cars with airbags, if you fit a sports wheel and disconnect the airbag in the process, the airbag warning light will be on permanently. Apart from being annoying, this is also illegal.

j Pace-car strobe lights (or any other flashing lights, apart from indicators) are illegal for road use. Of course.

k Anything else we didn't think of - is probably illegal too. Sorry.

Any questions? Try the MOT Helpline (0845 6005977). Yes, really.

Thanks to Andrew Dare of the Vehicle Inspectorate, Exeter, for his help in steering us through this minefield!

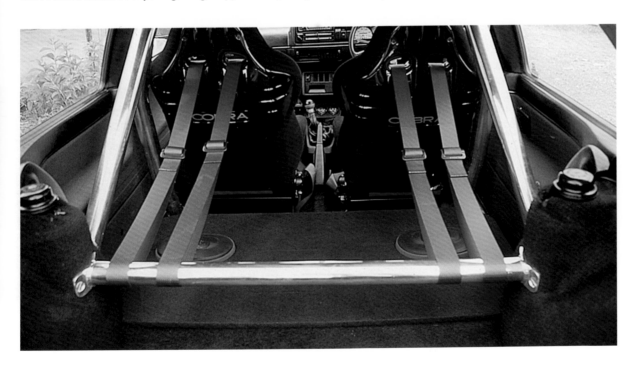

Thanks to:

We gratefully acknowledge all the help and advice offered from the following suppliers, without whom, etc, etc. Many of those credited below went way beyond the call of duty to help us produce this book - you know who you are. Cheers, guys! Roll the credits...

Alpine
01908 611556

Audioscape
01473 327510

Auto Acoustics
01932 849211

Autoleads
01420 476767

**Brown & Geeson
Distribution Ltd** (Momo)
01268 764411

Corbeau Seats Ltd
01424 854499

CT Autoparts
08000 283 284

Demon Tweeks
01978 664466

Eurostyling (Folia Tec)
01908 324950

Halfords
08457 626 625

K & N Filters
01925 636950

Kustomorphose (France)
(00 33) 02 37 34 77 15

LA & RW Piper (upholsterers)
01963 441431

Larkspeed
08707 440101

Mille Miglia (UK) Ltd
01626 832222

On Line Autosport
01543 252010

Performance Parts Direct
01252 517272

**Performance
Products Ltd**
01244 321300

Personal Identity
01462 811866

Pioneer GB Ltd
01753 789700

R & A Design
01472 811711

RAID
01664 823792

Red Dot Racing Ltd
020 8888 2354

Richbrook
0208 543 7111

Ripspeed at Halfords
0845 609 1259

S.A.D. Motorsport (Ed)
(body styling)
01935 432352

Savage, Trillogy
01280 822865

Sony
01932 816532

SPAX
01869 244771

Toyo Tyres
01933 411144

**A special
thankyou to:**
Brodie Baxter
Kim Baxter
Andy Butler (ICE words)
Zoë Harrison (ICE pics)
Jon Hill (cover shots)
Ellen and Alan Larkin
Stewart Smith

Project Manager	Louise McIntyre
Designer	Simon Larkin
Page Build	Paul Skuse at Azur
Workshop	Paul Buckland
Pete Trott
Editor	Dan White
Consultant	Bryn Musselwhite
Editorial Assistant	Carole Turk
Production Controll	Kevin Heals

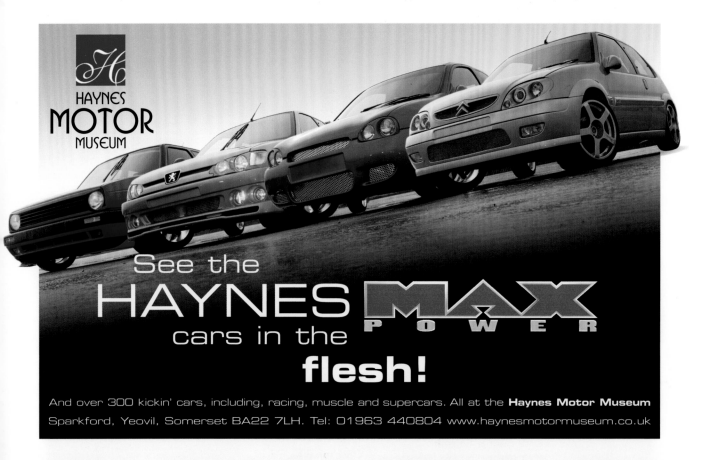

Haynes Car Manuals

* = Classic Reprints

Haynes Manuals

Haynes Car Service and Repair Manuals are available from car accessory retailers.
For further information or to find your nearest stockist, call
01963 442030 or visit
www.haynes.co.uk